Rhea County, Tennessee, Tombstone Inscriptions

Transcribed by:
The Works Progress Administration
1938

Janaway Publishing, Inc.
2007

> *Notice*
>
> This book has been reproduced from carbon-copies of the original transcriptions of court records by the Works Progress Administration (WPA) in 1930s. In many instances, the resulting text is light, the documents are physically flawed, and foxing (or discoloration) occurs. The pages of this reprint have been digitally enhanced and, where possible, the flaws and markings eliminated in order to provide clarity of content and a pleasant reading experience.

Rhea County, Tennessee, Tombstone Inscriptions

Originally transcribed by:
The Works Progress Administration (WPA)
1938

Reprinted by:

Janaway Publishing, Inc.
732 Kelsey Ct.
Santa Maria, CA 93454
(805) 925-1038
www.JanawayGenealogy.com

2007, 2012

ISBN-10: 1596411414
ISBN-13: 9781596411418

Made in the United States of America

PREFACE

The transcript from which this book was printed was an onion skin carbon copy of the original document typed over 60 years ago by the Works Progress Administration (WPA). The print quality varied throughout the work---this would seem to be due to the wear on the carbon paper. We have made an effort to make all the print as legible as possible. This is a second generation copy of the original, and there will be a few places where the writing cannot be made out.

The Publisher

TENNESSEE

RECORDS OF RHEA COUNTY
TOMBSTONE INSCRIPTIONS

HISTORICAL RECORDS PROJECT
OFFICIAL PROJECT NO. 465-44-3-115

COPIED UNDER WORKS PROGRESS ADMINISTRATION

MRS. JOHN TROTWOOD MOORE
STATE LIBRARIAN & ARCHIVIST, SPONSOR

ELIZABETH D. COPPEDGE
STATE DIRECTOR OF WOMEN'S & PROFESSIONAL PROJECTS

PENELOPE JOHNSON ALLEN
STATE SUPERVISOR

CAROLINE SMALL KELSO
SUPERVISOR

GEORGE GANNAWAY
FLOYD POOLE
COPYISTS

ALMA NICHOLS
TYPIST

MAY 13, 1938

RHEA COUNTY

CEMETERIES
INDEX

A

	PAGE
ABEL'S PRIVATE CEMETERY	1, 4 incls.
ADKIN'S CEMETERY	5
ANDERSON CEMETERY	6
AUGDEN CEMETERY	7, 10 incls.

B

BANKSTON FAMILY CEMETERY	11
BEARD (HENRY) FAMILY GRAVEYARD	12
BELL FAMILY CEMETERY	13
BOLEN FAMILY CEMETERY	14
BRADY COMMUNITY GRAVEYARD	15
BRADY COMMUNITY GRAVEYARD NO. 2	16
BRADY (TOM) GRAVEYARD	17
BRADY FARM GRAVEYARD	18
BRAMLETT (BILL) GRAVEYARD	19
BREEDING GRAVEYARD	20
BREWER GRAVEYARD	21
BROWN CEMETERY	22, 23
BURCHARD CEMETERY	24
BUTTRAM CEMETERY	25, 51 incls.

C

CITY CEMETERY	52, 56 incls.
COOK (DR.) PRIVATE GRAVEYARD	57
COLLEGE HILL CEMETERY	58, 66 incls.
CONCORD CEMETERY	67, 69 incls.
CORVIN FAMILY CEMETERY	70
COVE CEMETERY (CRAN MOORE'S)	71, 72
CRAWFORD CEMETERY	73
CUMMINGS COMMUNITY GRAVEYARD	74, 75

D

DANIELS FAMILY CEMETERY	76
DAVIS FAMILY CEMETERY	77
DEVANEY GRAVEYARD	78
DEVAULT CEMETERY	79-80
DYER CEMETERY	81

E

EARLY FAMILY CEMETERY	82
EDWARDS' GRAVEYARD	83
EVEN'S CEMETERY	84-85

Rhea County, Tennessee, Tombstone Inscriptions

CEMETERIES INDEX

E

	PAGE
EWING COMMUNITY GRAVEYARD	86
EWING GRAVEYARD	87, 90 incls.

F

FAIRVIEW CEMETERY	91, 94 incls.
FARLEY CEMETERY	95
FERGUSON CEMETERY	96
FOUST GRAVEYARD	97, 98
FRENCH CEMETERY	99, 111 incls.
FRIENDSHIP GRAVEYARD	112, 116 incls.

G

GARGAN CEMETERY	117
GARRISON CEMETERY	118, 119
GASS FAMILY GRAVEYARD	120
GASS (COLORED) GRAVEYARD	121
GIBSON GRAVEYARD	122, 123
GILES FAMILY GRAVEYARD	124
GILBREATH CEMETERY	125
GILLESPIE GRAVEYARD	126
GILLIAM GRAVEYARD	127, 128
GRAVETT FAMILY GRAVEYARD	129

H

HALL FAMILY CEMETERY	130
HERSE CEMETERY	131
HICKEY COMMUNITY GRAVEYARD (COLORED)	132
HICKMOTT FAMILY CEMETERY	133
HIGH POINT CHURCH GRAVEYARD	134
HILTON CEMETERY	135
HINDES GRAVEYARD	136
HOLLAND AND GODBY GRAVEYARD	137
HOLLOWAY (JOHN) FAMILY GRAVEYARD	138
HOWERTON CEMETERY	139
HUGHES CEMETERY	140
HURST GRAVEYARD	141

I

INGLE GRAVEYARD	142
IRLAND CEMETERY	143

J

JARGAS CEMETERY	144

CEMETERIES
INDEX

J
	PAGE
JENKINS CEMETERY	145
JOHNSON CEMETERY	146
JONES CEMETERY	147

K
KERLEY CEMETERY	148
KIRKLAND COMMUNITY GRAVEYARD	149, 150
KIUKIA CEMETERY	151, 153 incls.

L
LAWSON FAMILY CEMETERY	154
LEUTY GRAVEYARD	155, 161 incls.
LOCKE CEMETERY	162, 163
LONE MOUNTAIN CEMETERY	164, 177 incls.
LONG COMMUNITY GRAVEYARD	178, 179
LOWE COMMUNITY GRAVEYARD	180, 182 incls.

M
MACEDONIA CHURCH CEMETERY	183
MARLER FAMILY CEMETERY	184
MAR'S HILL GRAVEYARD	185
MARSH FAMILY GRAVEYARD	186
MARTIN FAMILY GRAVEYARD	187
MCCALEB GRAVEYARD	188
MCCLENDON COMMUNITY GRAVEYARD	189
MILLER COMMUNITY GRAVEYARD	190, 191
MONROE FAMILY GRAVEYARD	192
MONTGOMERY CEMETERY	193, 198 incls.
MOORE CEMETERY	199
MORPHY CEMETERY	200
MT. SULPHUR GRAVEYARD	201, 202
MT. TABOR GRAVEYARD	203
MYNATT CEMETERY	204, 205

N
NEW PORT GRAVEYARD	206, 208 incls.
NORMAN FAMILY GRAVEYARD	209

O
OAKMAN CEMETERY	210
PAINE FAMILY CEMETERY	211
PARKER FAMILY GRAVEYARD	212

Rhea County, Tennessee, Tombstone Inscriptions

CEMETERIES
INDEX

P — AGE

PATRICK FAMILY CEMETERY	213
PENDLETON GRAVEYARD	214
PETERSBURG GRAVEYARD	215
PIERCE CEMETERY	216, 221 incls.
PORTER CEMETERY	222
PORTER GRAVEYARD	223
PORTER (JAMES) FAMILY GRAVEYARD	224
PRICHET (GEN.) FAMILY GRAVEYARD	225

R

RECTOR GRAVEYARD	226
REED FAMILY GRAVEYARD	227
ROBERTS AND HARRIS GRAVEYARD	228
ROBINSON FAMILY GRAVEYARD	229
ROBISON CEMETERY	230
RODDY GRAVEYARD	231
RODDY FAMILY GRAVEYARD	232
ROGERS CEMETERY	233, 235 incls.
ROSE FAMILY CEMETERY	236
ROSS FAMILY GRAVEYARD - RODDY SCHOOL HOUSE	237
RUSSELL FAMILY CEMETERY	238

S

SALEM CEMETERY	239, 240
SANDELL FAMILY CEMETERY	241
SANFORD FAMILY CEMETERY	242
SCHOOLFIELD FAMILY GRAVEYARD	243
SHADWICK CEMETERY	244
SHAVER CEMETERY	245, 247 incls.
SMITH CROSS ROADS CEMETERY	248
SMITH (ADD) COMMUNITY GRAVEYARD	249, 250
SMITH AND WILKEY GRAVEYARD	251, 254 incls.
SMYRNA CEMETERY	255, 258 incls.
SNEED FAMILY CEMETERY	259
SOUTHERLAND CEMETERY	260
SPENCE CEMETERY	261, 266 incls.
SPENCE FAMILY CEMETERY	267
SPIVEY CEMETERY	268, 269
SPRING CITY CEMETERY	270, 287 incls.
STEBBINS OR PRESBYTERIAN CEMETERY	288, 290 incls.
STEVINS CEMETERY	291
STEWART CEMETERY	292
STUCK FAMILY CEMETERY	293
SULLIVAN HILL GRAVEYARD	294
SWAFFORD CEMETERY	295, 296

CEMETERIES
INDEX

T
	PAGE
TALLENT (BILL) GRAVEYARD	297
TEASLEY FAMILY GRAVEYARD	298
TELIC GRAVEYARD	299
THOMISON FAMILY GRAVEYARD	300
THOMPSON GRAVEYARD	301
TODD FAMILY GRAVEYARD	302
TRAVIS CEMETERY	303

U
UCHEE (COLORED) GRAVEYARD	304

V
VAUGHN CEMETERY	305
VAUGHN FAMILY GRAVEYARD	306

W
WALKER CEMETERY	307, 310 incls.
WASSOM GRAVEYARD	311
WATERHOUSE FAMILY CEMETERY	312, 313
WATERHOUSE COMMUNITY GRAVEYARD	314, 316 incls.
WEBB CEMETERY	317, 318
WILKS AND THOMPSON (COLORED) GRAVEYARD	319
WOLF CREEK CEMETERY	320, 323 incls.

Y
YOTHER CEMETERY	324

FAMILY GRAVEYARDS UNKNOWN	325, 334 incls.

RHEA COUNTY

TOMBSTONE INSCRIPTIONS
ABEL'S (PRIVATE) CEMETERY

Located about 1½ miles south of Dayton; about ¼ mile off the main State Highway No. 41, and on the right hand side of road traveling south. This property was formerly owned by John Abels, and is known as the "Abel Farm." It is now rented by Elmer and Carl Kelly, and same resides thereon. Located in 4th. District of Rhea County, and in suburb, Abel Town.

Frank Abel
(?)

Frank
Son of
C. W. & Tillie Abel
Apr. 4, 1898
July 30, 1898

Tillie
Wife of
C. W. Abel
Apr. 17, 1870
July 27, 1898

Hettie Grace
Dau. of
F. H. & M. M. Abel
Jan. 3, 1885
Sept. 23, 1885

L. L. Coulter
Died Mar. 20, 1936
Aged 80 yrs.

Arvazine
Wife of
L. L. Coulter
Feb. 5, 1857
Sept. 30, 1889

Ula Coulter
Aug. 11, 1889
Sept. 18, 1889

O. C. Coulter
Dec. 15, 1887
Dec. 16, 1887

S. H. Fleming
April 26, 1835
Sept. 3, 1868

Mother - Myra J. Hodges
Jan. 5, 1840
July 24, 1916

Father - Daniel Hodges
Nov. 29, 1825
Apr. 8, 1897

D. T. Abel
Aug. 22, 1852
Mar. 23, 1886

Jimmie Fleming (Son of
June 30, 1863   S. H. & M. J.
Oct. 27, 1863   Fleming.)

Florence Edna Abel
Wife of
William K. Tipton
1889 - 1926 - Mother

Catharine M.
Dau. of
Claude & Effie Abel
Sept. 7, 1913
Jan. 17, 1915

M. A. Abel
Dau. of
J. J. & L. M. Abel
July 8, 1842
April 25, 1848

L. M.
Wife of
J. J. Abel
May 29, 1812
July 14, 1851

ABEL'S (PRIVATE) CEMETERY
(Continued)

Erected in memory of
Our Husband and Father
J. J. Abel
Mar. 10, 1815
Feb. 10, 1902

E. A.
Wife of
J. J. Abel
Oct. 1, 1826
Jan. 9, 1910

Thomas B. Abel
Son of
J. J. & E. A. Abel
June 24, 1861
April 11, 1864

Ellen M. Abel
Dau. of
J. J. & E. A. Abel
Feb. 29, 1864
Jan. 8, 1865

Mother - Mary A.
Wife of
R. P. Abel
Feb. 13, 1822
Aug. 29, 1889

R. P. Abel
Mar. 25, 1818
Jan. 1, 1864
At New Albany, Ind.
and buried there

Father & Mother
Margaret Abel
1776
Nov. 2, 1861

Cain Abel
1766
July 3, 1850

Sister
Mary R. Abel
April 19, 1813
June 17, 1888

Lou D.
Wife of
John Abel
Sept. 7, 1890
Aged 31 yrs. & 2 D's
"God in his wisdom has recalled
the precious boon His love had
given and though the body
slumbers here, the soul is safe
in Heaven."

John Abel
May 22, 1855
Apr. 5, 1910

R. K. Jr.
Nov. 8, 1921
Dec. 5, 1930
"Sonny Abel."

John C.
Son of
R. K. & Grace Abel
Born & died Jan. 9, 1918

Mary J.
Dau. of
C. W. & E. E. Abel
July 2, 1850
Aug. 18, 1852

James M.
Son of
C. W. & E. E. Abel
Feb. 3, 1863
Feb. 17, 1878

Ester E. Abel
Mar. 15, 1826
Dec. 9, 1911

C. W. Abel
Nov. 17, 1819
Jan. 8, 1889

R. E. Abel
Nov. 8, 1866
June 24, 1891

Rhea County, Tennessee, Tombstone Inscriptions

ABEL'S (PRIVATE) CEMETERY
(Continued)

In memory of
Father & Mother,
M. M. Abel
Sept. 5, 1822
May 18, 1875

J. R. Abel
Sept. 20, 1816
Dec. 20, 1900

Mary A.
Dau. of
J. R. & M. M. Abel
Aug. 11, 1850
Oct. 10, 1854

William L.
Son of
J. R. & M. M. Abel
Sept. 5, 1853
Sept. 22, 1854

M. J. Martin
Daughter of
J. R. & M. M. Abel
Apr. 12, 1852
Aug. 26, 1888

Harry
Son of
Alex & Eddeth Abel
Jan. 26, 1914
Feb. 22, 1922

Sarah F. Sharp
Dau. of
J. P. & Louisa Abel
Aug. 14, 1873
Jan. 22, 1902
Erected by Father.

Tennie Morgan
Wife of
W. M. Pass
Aug. 23, 1854
July 16, 1891

Dora
Dau. of
J. E. & M. E. Abel
Dec. 13, 1899 - Apr. 27, 1900
"Darling gone to rest."

J. T. Abel
Dec. 9, 1875
Dec. 20, 1895

Alta
Wife of
C. A. Sharp
Mar. 11, 1875
Sept. 4, 1894

Eliza
Wife of
J. P. Abel
May 18, 1851
Aug. 22, 1882

Richard Thomas
Native of Ireland

Roy Ray
Son of
M. R. & J. A. Abel
Nov. 12, 1879
Feb. 4, 1881

Julia
Wife of
M. W. Abel
Apr. 2, 1856
May 22, 1936

M. W. Abel
Feb. 23, 1855
July 16, 1886

Frank Coy
Son of
M. R. & J. A. Abel
Jan. 26, 1882
July 28, 1886

J. J. Manass
Dec. 20, 1895
Age 36 y's. 7 m's. 4 D's.
"May he rest in peace."

Lannie
Son of
J. B. & Orlena Walker
Aug. 27, 1874
Dec. 20, 1895

ABEL'S (PRIVATE) CEMETERY
(Continued)

Sarah F.
Dau. of
J. B. & Orlena Walker
Aug. 27, 1864
Dec. 31, 1891
"How soon fades
the tender flower."

Orlena Wife of
J. B. Walker
May 4, 1841
Oct. 10, 1886

David Greer
Co. H - 4th. Mich. Cav.

Gracie P. Smith
Jan. 5, 1903
Aug. 21, 1904
"Our darling."

RHEA COUNTY

TOMBSTONE INSCRIPTIONS
ADKINS' CEMETERY

The Adkins' Cemetery is twelve miles northeast of Dayton. Follow Highway No. 30. Go to Washington which is seven miles northeast of Dayton. Leave Highway and take the road east going five miles. The land belongs to Hickson. There are thirty three unmarked graves.

T. J. Adkins July 1850 Dec. 13, 1902	Donea Adkins Mar. 1845 Aug. 5, 1904 "Gone to a better land."

1

RHEA COUNTY

TOMBSTONE INSCRIPTIONS
ANDERSON CEMETERY

The Anderson Cemetery is twelve and a half miles northwest of Dayton. Follow Highway No. 30 from Dayton going six miles. Leave Highway and take the road north going six and one half miles to Anderson Cemetery. At the time the Cemetery started the land belonged to the Andersons. There are twelve unmarked graves.

C. E. Anderson
Apr. 13, 1870
Feb. 12, 1904

Ap Anderson
Oct. 13, 1863
Mar. 2, 1902
"Gone but not forgotten."

Andy Nichols

RHEA COUNTY

TOMBSTONE INSCRIPTIONS
AUGDEN CEMETERY

The Augden Cemetery is ten miles west of Dayton. Follow Highway No. 30 from Dayton going to the top of the mountain which is five miles from Dayton. Leave the Highway and take the gravel road southwest. The Augden Cemetery is on the side of the road. There is a School and Church House just in front of the Cemetery. The land belongs to John Evens, but was once called the Snow farm. There are eighty eight unmarked graves in the Augden Cemetery.

W. D. Rigsby
Mar. 31, 1859
Apr. 2, 1913
(Dayton Lodge No. 2)

Holy Bible, thy will
be done.
Jennis Mansfield
Mar. 15, 1817
Feb. 13, 1901

Infant of
R. A. and E. R. Able
July 14, 1909
July 22, 1909
"Budded on earth
to bloom in Heaven."

Bernice Pickett
Josephine C. Lee
Mar. 3, 1851
Nov. 6, 1927

Ira Lee
Oct. 27, 1896
Aged 58 yrs. 6 mos. 2 dys.
"At rest."

Jordan, James N.
June 3, 1937
Aged 75 yrs. 4 mos. 16 dys.

Sarah M. Hutchins
Jan. 11, 1828
Nov. 19, 1907

Elizabeth Reed
March 26, 1899
Aged 89 yrs.

Edd F. Sykes
1878 - 1930

His wife -
Edna B. Sykes
1879 - 1900

L. S. Sykes
July 25, 1841
Oct. 28, 1902
"Blessed are the dead
which die in the Lord."

Miss Cathrine B. Anderson
Mar. 29, 1934
Age 7 yrs.

Rev. James H. Snow
Oct. 30, 1857
Jan. 7, 1933

Betty Moseley
Wife of
Rev. James H. Snow
Dec. 14, 1851

Altheat
Dau. of
H. T. and S. G. Keeney
Apr. 22, 1895
Dec. 4, 1896

Effie N Pickard
Dau. of Frank & Ella Pickard
July 8, 1881
Sept. 19, 1886
"God be with you
'till we meet again."

Rhea County, Tennessee, Tombstone Inscriptions

AUGDEN CEMETERY
(Continued)

Grace M.
Dau. of
Frank and Ella Pickard
Jan. 5, 1893
Apr. 13, 1897
"Plucked from earth
to bloom in Heaven."

Francis Marion Pickard
July 8, 1852
Oct. 28, 1901
"I must work the work
of him that bought me,
while it is day the night
cometh when no man can
work."
John 9 : 4

Byron V. Morgan
Nov. 5, 1893
Sept. 15, 1926
B. of L. F. & E

Jessie Mildred
Dau. of
Henegar and Ida Morgan
Jan. 17, 1891
May 7, 1898
Age 7 yrs, 3 mos. 20 dys.

Snow -
Infant
Feb. 8, 1894
Feb. 9, 1894

Infant -
Born & died
July 4, 1892
(Children of W. L. & M. E
Snow.)

Wolfe -
Dearest Father, he has
left us, and our loss we
deeply feel, but 'Tis God
who has bereft us, He can
all our sorrows heal."

R. Wolfe
Jan. 2, 1825
Apr. 13, 1903

Vesta Wolfe
July 17, 1876
Aug. 17, 1920
"Gone but not forgotten."

D. L. Ritchey
Apr. 18, 1933
Aged 82 yrs. 2 mos. 28 dys.

Sarepta Ritchey
Feb. 18, 1847
Dec. 11, 1904
"Gone Home."

Our darling infant -
Child of
H. and V. Wolfe
Born Nov. 27, 1899

Laura E. Smith
Sept. 10, 1875
Mar. 28, 1909
"Here lies she, who in this
life was a kind mother,
a true wife, she was by many
virtues blest and hilly among
the best."

Dr. J. F. Wilson
Born in Highland County, Ohio
July 10, 1821
Died Graysville, Tenn.
Oct. 11, 1903
Served in the war between the
north and south, 1861.
First Lieut., Co. G -
144 th. I. N. D. Inf. Royal

Robert B. Stewart
Mar. 10, 1832
Apr. 3, 1898

Rhea County, Tennessee, Tombstone Inscriptions

AUGDEN CEMETERY
(Continued)

Edith E. Rigsby
Wife of
Wed W. Rigsby
Sept. 5, 1885
June 10, 1910
"'Tis but the casket lies here the gem that filled it sparkles yet."

Chas. E. Mowry
Oct. 29, 1834

Nancy E. Mowry
Wife of
Chas E. Mowry
Nov. 15, 1840
Sept. 29, 1903

Minnie
Dau. of
C. E. and N. E. Mowry
May 21, 1871
Sept. 25, 1886

Our mother –
Polly, wife of
Augustus Mowry
Nov. 23, 1794
Nov. 18, 1886

Charles F. Ward
Feb. 23, 1854
July 9, 1894
"At rest."

Bertha A. Wright
June 20, 1893
May 16, 1910
"Weep not for me."

Frederic P. Smith
April, 1863
Jan. 1927
"At rest."

Nettie Pleasant Tolle
Dec. 19, 1885
Apr. 28, 1908
"At rest."

Philip Samuel Tolle
Sept. 2, 1880
Feb. 8, 1906
"At rest."

Mother –
Anna S. Gillett
Oct. 18, 1857

Father –
Andrew D. Gillett
Nov. 13, 1848
Jan. 8, 1929

Cecil Davis
Mar. 18, 1905
Oct. 31, 1909
"Gone Home."

Robert Pitts
Nov. 6, 1870
July 20, 1926
"At rest."

Oatious R.
Son of
R. and N. A. Pitts
Feb. 28, 1901
Oct. 9, 1918

Noah Myers
1849 –
Sept. 29, 1909

Mrs. S. E. Myers
Dec. 26, 1934
Aged 83 years.

John James Tolle
June 29, 1845
March 6, 1907
"Blessed are the dead who die in the Lord"

Henry Gilbert
Jan. 29, 1887

Sarah C. Humphrey
Wife of
Morris Humphrey
July 23, 1836 – Sept. 9, 1904

4
AUGDEN CEMETERY
(Continued)

Capt. Morris Humphrey
Apr. 20, 1834
Feb. 14, 1902

MILLER

Husband and wife -

John S. Miller
Apr. 13, 1809
June 8, 1887

Sophronia C.
Oct. 6, 1809
Dec. 31, 1895

Daisy Humphrey
June 10, 1877
May 31, 1911
"None knew her
but to love her,
none named her
but to praise her."

Infant of
Mr. and Mrs. J. D. Olinger
Nov. 18, 1904
Nov. 19, 1904
"Gone to a better land."

Our darling -
Mildred Marie Sparks
Dau. of
C. A. and D. M. Sparks
Born and died
May 10, 1921
Baby -

B. F. Harwood
Sept. 2, 1842
June 26, 1911
"Only sleeping."

J. Z. Tack Harwood
Sept. 29, 1879
Aug. 24, 1931

Leroy Hudson
Feb. 14, 1897
Nov. 18, 1918
Pioneer Inf.
"Gone but not forgotten."

Thelma - Our darling
Dau. of
J. D. and N. R. Pickett
Feb. 22, 1922
Dec. 20, 1922

Nick Marler
Jan. 25, 1887
Nov. 14, 1927

Emmerratter Olinger
May 14, 1925
July 15, 1926

George Mack
Age 52
and two children
Gladys, age 14
Hellen, age 8

C. L. B. L. Stuart

RHEA COUNTY

TOMBSTONE INSCRIPTIONS
BANKSTON FAMILY CEMETERY

The Bankston family Cemetery is two miles southeast of Dayton. Follow the Henry Ferry Road from Dayton. Keep the main road to the Bankston farm. The Cemetery is out in a field from the main road. There are six unmarked graves in this Cemetery.

    A. J. Bankston
    Co. A - 1st. G. A. Inf.

RHEA COUNTY

TOMBSTONE INSCRIPTIONS
BEARD (HENRY) FAMILY GRAVEYARD

District No. 2. Go from Dayton north on the Dixie Highway 13 miles to the Dr. Miller farm, one mile north of Penvine, then ½ mile east of Dr. Miller's farm on the old Henry Beard farm. Here, located on a little hill, are three graves.

BEARD

Father -	Mother -
J. H. Beard	Pocahontus
May 18, 1843	Wife of
	J. H. Beard
	Apr. 2, 1847
	Mar. 5, 1931

Son or daughter - Grave unmarked.

RHEA COUNTY

TOMBSTONE INSCRIPTIONS
BELL FAMILY CEMETERY

The Bell family Cemetery is four miles southeast of Dayton. From South Dayton follow the Armstrong Ferry Road going to the Ferry. The Cemetery is about one mile up the river from the Ferry on the old Mary Bell farm. The land now belongs to N. E. McCabe. There are four unmarked graves.

C. R. Bell 1883 - 1886	L. T. Bell Age 80
G. W. Bell 1831 - 1863	S. P. Bell 1802 - 1885
Mary Bell Jan. 13, 1827 Feb. 13, 1908 Age 81 yrs. 1 mo. "Peace and good will to all."	S. J. Bell 1828 - 1883 J. Donam Age 65 yrs.

RHEA COUNTY

TOMBSTONE INSCRIPTIONS
BOLEN FAMILY CEMETERY

The Bolen family Cemetery is three miles and three quarters east of Dayton. Take Highway # 30 from Dayton leaving the Highway at the Camp Ground Hill one mile from Dayton. Follow the S. S. road which leads by the Salem Church where the Cemetery is near by. The land belongs to Allens. There are seven unmarked graves.

Bolen

T. M. Bolen
June 10, 1822
Aug. 28, 1890
Age 68 yrs. 2 mos. & 18 days.

RHEA COUNTY

TOMBSTONE INSCRIPTIONS
BRADY COMMUNITY GRAVEYARD

Go 17 miles north of Dayton on the Dixie Highway, take left hand on old road from Odom crossing at C. S. Railroad, then one mile, north on old Brady farm, now called Milburn White farm which is one mile south of Spring City. This graveyard has been abandoned for several years. Many graves, possibly fifty, are unmarked, and many stones are broken down.

Amanda
Wife of
W. P. Broyles
Dec. 25, 1852
Dec. 19, 1900

Concrete form,
two graves not
dated or named.

Farley Brady
Mar. 7, 1795
Nov. 9, 1889
"Sleep on Father,
take thy rest,
God called thee,
He knoweth best."
(He was a pious
and popular old
gentleman. Was
a large land owner.)

John K.
Infant son of
Isaac and Caroline Brown
Dec. 30, 1878
3 yrs. 5 mos. 27 dys.

In memory of
Sarah, wife of
Farley Brady
Feb. 17, 1815
Feb. 6, 1858
43 yrs.
"Affections truth we raise,
'Tis all we can do 'Till
death shall our earthlydays
our friendship to renew."
(Has been dead for about 100 yrs.)

Rosana Roddy
Sept. 2, 1781
Sept. 15, 1840

RHEA COUNTY

TOMBSTONE INSCRIPTIONS
BRADY COMMUNITY GRAVEYARD

This is part two of the Brady Community graveyard, and is located in District No. 2, about 1 mile south of Spring City on the old Stage road. To reach this graveyard, take the Lon Foust Highway 18 miles to Spring City. This is only a small part of the Farley Brady graveyard. It is so entangled with vines and undergrowth that it is almost impossible to reach all of it. There is one tall stone with name and dates worn off. Two infant children of J. H. and Jane Thompson, with the inscription, "Children, we will see you in Heaven."

1

RHEA COUNTY

BRADY FARM GRAVEYARD
TOMBSTONE INSCRIPTIONS

The name of this graveyard is unknown and it is located in District No. 1. It is very old and abandoned. There are probably about twenty graves with no names or dates. It is located in a beautiful grove about one half acre on the Butter farm, formerly known as the Brady farm. It extends down to the very bank of the river.

RHEA COUNTY

TOMBSTONE INSCRIPTIONS
BRADY (TOM) GRAVEYARD

From Dayton, go north on the Dixie Highway 18 miles to Spring City, turn east on the Rhea Springs Road, then go 3 miles past the Rhea Springs water mill, turn off the State Highway on the river road, going 3 miles to Tom Brady farm. This seems to be a very ma very old graveyard. There are five graves with large limestone slabs covered over. A few rough stones. No names or dates are given. About ½ acre of land and about fifty graves.

1

RHEA COUNTY

TOMBSTONE INSCRIPTIONS
BILL BRAMLETT FAMILY GRAVEYARD

The Bill Bramlett family graveyard is located 1 mile south of the John Holloway graveyard. Bill Bramlett and five others are buried here. Mr. Bramlett died May 13, 1923. No other dates are given. This is also on the Dividing ridge. Take the State Highway about 15 miles north of Dayton, turn east about two miles. Here you will find the above mentioned graveyard. It is also on the old Holloway farm.

RHEA COUNTY

TOMBSTONE INSCRIPTIONS
BREEDING GRAVEYARD

Dist. No. 1. A very old graveyard set with Cedars. Go out the Dixie Highway 18 miles to Spring City, go east 2½ miles to Rhea Springs, go east of Rhea Springs 1 mile to Toe string road, turn north on Toe String road and go 2 miles to the Perry Jolly farm. West of the road upon a little cedar covered hill, you will find the above named graveyard.

PAUL

A. D. Paul
Jan. 8, 1779
Dec. 12, 1864
65 yrs.

Cynthia Paul
Nov. 5, 1802
Apr. 17, 1854
Age 51 yrs. 5 mos. 12 da.

Wm. J. Breeding
July 8, 1832
Age 21 yrs.

Byram Breeding
Feb. 23, 1832
Age 60 yrs.

Jane Breeding
Born 1772
May 23, 1844
Age 72 yrs.

Margaret Thompson
Jan. - 1843
Age 71 yrs.

Sarah Ann
Daughter of
John B. & Sarah Ann Breeding
40 yrs.
Dec. 18, 1882
Feb. 25, 1922
"Her life was an open book."

John B. Breeding
May 28, 1833
Dec. 7, 1903
Age 70 yrs. 6 mos. 9 da.

Sarah A.
Wife of
J. B. Breeding
Jan 22, 1841
Aug. 12, 1883
42 yrs.

Stiphen Breeding
Aug. 28, 1810
Oct. 27, 1883

Margaret J. Breeding
Nov. 14, 1882

Thomas Breeding
Feb. 28, 1804
Jan. 18, 1877
73 yrs.

Mary Breeding
Jan. 10, 1812
May 25, 1862
50 yrs.

Nancy E. Breeding
Nov. 10, 1852
Nov. 29, 1858
6 yrs.

Nancy Wyrick
(No dates.)

Probably 45 unmarked graves.
Graveyard in fairly good condition!

RHEA COUNTY

TOMBSTONE INSCRIPTIONS
BREWER GRAVEYARD

District No. 1. Leaving Dayton, take the Lon Foust Highway 18 miles to Spring City, then take the Grand View road or Highway No. 68 going to Grand View which is about six miles from Spring City. At Grand View, turn east on the mail route, going by Mt. Sulphur three miles north of Grand View, then continue the same route 3 miles further across the Whites Creek Bridge. There nearby is this Cemetery.

Laura
Daughter of
B. B. and S. J. Loden
Oct. 3, 1889
Jan. 24, 1890
"Only sleeping."

Frederick Smith
Cross and hand clasp
engraved.)
Mar. 13, 1883
Nov. 19, 1904
"I will arise and
go to my Father."

In sacred Memory of
Alexander Smith
Oct. 8, 1885
July 25, 1898
"Gone, but not forgotten."

Mary A. Smith
Mar. 1846
Apr. 4, 1932
"Asleep in Jesus."
(Holy Bible engraved.)
"Come ye Blessed."

B. F. Smith
Apr. 9, 1829
Apr. 5, 1897
68 yrs.
Dead 40 yrs.
"I have fought a good
fight."

In memory of
Martha Smith
Apr. 20, 1880
Apr. 25, 1880
5 dys.
"Gone, but not forgotten."

In sacred memory of
Litten Hase
Aug. 9, 1820
Apr. 13, 1896
76 yrs.
"Gone, but not forgotten."

Robert Miller
Aug. 24, 1852
May 1, 1888
"Gone, but not forgotten."

Nancy F. Clifton
Aug. 20, 1853
Sept. 25, 1888
35 yrs.

Children
R. E., N. F., Flora, George,
Bert, Thomas.

There are 45 graves, unmarked.

RHEA COUNTY

TOMBSTONE INSCRIPTIONS
BROWN CEMETERY

The Brown Cemetery is five miles northeast of Dayton. Leave Dayton on Highway # 27 going three miles north. Leave the Highway taking the Shades Valley road east. It is two miles from the main Highway to the Brown's Cemetery. The land belongs to Foust and Frailey. There are seventy three unmarked graves.

Riley S. Brown
Mar. 23, 1867
Sept. 28, 1888
Age 21 yrs. 5 mos. 5 days.

D. J. Brown
Oct. 6, 1824
Oct. 5, 1895

J. L. Brown
Jan. 22, 1826
June 12, 1900

Father –
J. H. Brown
Oct. 9, 1854
Oct. 20, 1913

Joseph Travis
Dec. 15, 1799
March 17, 1877

Levina Travis
Oct. 24, 1802
Departed this life
Feb. 24, 1889

Lucinda Travis
Oct. 15, 1839
Feb. 15, 1900

Laura Belle Travis
May 26, 1873
Dec. 3, 1891

B. B. Travis
Co. H – 3 Tenn. Cav.

Oran A. Sneed
Son of
W. H. & Beulah Sneed
1919 –

Robt. N. Crow
Oct. 26, 1891
Aged about 74 yrs.

Elizabeth
Wife of
Robt. N. Crow
Sept. 16, 1808
Nov. 10, 1891

Sarah Elizabeth Woodie
June 29, 1894
June 3, 1905

Squire Blevins
Feb. 6, 1815
March 14, 1889

Our Mother –
Mary
Wife of
Squire Blevins
June 10, 1824
Apr. 17, 1891
"At rest."

Sarah Woody
Oct. 20, 1845
July 4, 1899
"At rest."

Hugh Woody
May 22, 1841
Dec. 29, 1905
"At rest."

BROWN CEMETERY

Mary Rudd
Wife of
C. T. Rudd
May 15, 1871
June 9, 1922
"Gone but not forgotten."

Hannah Walker
June 13, 1841
July 21, 1911

Baby Hannah -
Jan. 24, 1887
Jan. 27, 1887

Lulu Walker
1897 - 1898

Roy Walker
1906 - 1906

George Walker
1908 - 1908

Hannah Walker
1910 - 1910

J. N. Smith
Aged 76 yrs. 3 mos. 7 days.

M. R. Smith
May 9, 1800
May 25, 1913

T. N. Smith
"Asleep in Jesus."

Fraley -

Mary Etter Fraley
Sept. 10, 1888
Dec. 21, 1915

Haver Fraley
July 6, 1889

Dallas Cox
Died 2 - 20 - 1937

Wilkey

Margaret Wilkey
Died 1 - 18 - 1937

RHEA COUNTY

TOMBSTONE INSCRIPTIONS
BURCHARD CEMETERY

The Burchard Cemetery is two and one half miles east of Dayton. Take Highway #30 from Dayton going to the Camp Ground Hill which is one mile east of Dayton. Leave the Highway at the Camp Ground Hill, taking the S. S. road. Keep the left road for one and a half miles. The Cemetery is located on the Burchard farm which now belongs to Lester Pearcy. There are nineteen unmarked graves in this Cemetery.

Father
Alfred B. Kelly
Mar. 21, 1882
June 12, 1928
"God took, He will
restore, He doeth
all things well."

Samie Dalis Kelly
Feb. 27, 1911
Dec. 15, 1918
"Christ loved him
and took him home."

I. R. Kelly
Nov. 11, 1873
July 18, 1908
"Asleep in Jesus."

W. A. Kelly
Mar. 6, 1834
Dec. 9, 1904
"Asleep in Jesus."

Walter E. Shaver
Son of
Samuel & Mary C. Shaver
Sept. 2, 1885
July 20, 1912
"Hope."

Thomas F. Shaver
Son of
Samuel L. & Mary Shaver
June 3, 1874
Mar. 31, 1902

Cornelius Shaver
June 5, 1807
June 10, 1874

Jane H. Shaver
Dec. 22, 1812
May 5, 1873

Mary Ella Shaver
Daughter of
J. U. & E. J. Shaver
Sept. 27, 1874
Dec. 15, 1876
"Sleep on dear child
and take thy rest in
Jesus arms forever blest."

Jane
Duaghter of
J. U. & E. J. Shaver
Jan. 23, 1861
Feb. 20, 1879
"Her happy soul
has winged its way
to one pure bright
eternal day."

Rhea County, Tennessee, Tombstone Inscriptions

RHEA COUNTY

TOMBSTONE INSCRIPTIONS
BUTTRAM CEMETERY

Located 2½ miles north of Dayton on left hand side of road traveling north, in suburb, Walnut Grove. Near Walnut Grove Union Church and school combined. Well kept and not many graves without tombstones. Located in 3rd. District of Rhea County.

Wallace Gaines Tallent
June 10, 1908
April 1, 1932

Crecia E.
Wife of
C. H. Stanfill
1877 - 1932

Hugh L. Peavyhouse
Aug. 16, 1936
Aged 32 years, 5 months, 23 days.

Jimmy Newell
1920 - 1928

B. Franklin Moore
1869 - 1929

Infant of
Mr. & Mrs. Frank Moore
Born & died Feb. 25, 1901

Anderson Jackson Gross
Aug. 26, 1851
June 30, 1933

Harriet M. Gross
Oct. 15, 1853
Aug. 2, 1929

Paul Gross Jones
March 5, 1908
May 31, 1926

Annie V.
Daughter of
Mr. & Mrs. N. T. Walker
July 4, 1911
Apr. 10, 1928

Keylon, Lillie May
Wife of
M. J. Keylon
Oct. 19, 1879
Sept. 26, 1933
"Asleepn in Jesus. Peaceful rest whose waking is supremely blest."

J. D. Pritchet
March 10, 1927
Aged 65 yrs.

Mamie L.
Wife of
O. W. Davis
Oct. 16, 1904
Mar. 11, 1936

James Bankston
June 26, 1916
June 26, 1916
"Our loved one."

Minnie
Wife of
J. H. Mulkey
Apr. 29, 1890
Mar. 5, 1936
"Our beloved sister & wife. Gone to rest."

Delora
Wife of
Geo. Wilson
May 24, 1910
May 4, 1936

Minnie
Wife of
J. N. Yates
Sept. 12, 1861
May 4, 1932

Rhea County, Tennessee, Tombstone Inscriptions

BUTTRAM CEMETERY
(Continued)

Robert W. Poague
9 - 7 - 1906
12 - 25 - 1935

Victor B. Poague
11 - 7 - 1898
6 - 24 - 1906

Emmitt O. Arnold
Feb. 25, 1896
Nov. 12, 1934

Jackie
Son of
Claude & Thelma
1925 - 1932

"At rest."
Charlie E. Snider
Aug. 30, 1890
Jan. 14, 1935 - Father

Mrs. Polly Ann Smith
January 8, 1934
Aged 74 years.

Wm. Richard Attridge
1865 - 1934

M. J. Hefner
1893 - 1934

Marvin Hefner
February 6, 1936
18 years

William Tennor
February 29, 1936
Aged 34 yrs.

Laura Kiker Abel
Oct. 15, 1875
Oct. 3, 1935

Erma Louise Hendricks
Sept. 12, 1932
Feb. 11, 1934

Emma E.
Wife of
J. A. Coleman
Dec. 24, 1891
Sept. 9, 1928 - Mother

John Gibbs Allen
1866 - 1927

Mrs. Johanna Ploughaus
Mar. 28, 1878
Mar. 4, 1934 - Mother

Clarence R. Sneed
Sept. 13, 1904
Jan. 7, 1926
"Dearest brother, thou hast
left us, here, thy loss we
deeply feel, but 'tis God that
hath bereft us, He can all our
sorrows heal."

Malven Rockholt
1897 - 1928

W. H. Rockholt
1869 - 1932

Mus'n - W. H. Redgeley
Co. F - 77 Ohio Inf.

Thelma Thomas
1908 - 1915

John A. Bryant
Sep. 20, 1838
Sep. 19, 1903

Nick A. McCabe
September 14, 1936
Aged 67 years, 8 months, 16 days

Ethel
Dau. of
N. A. & M. E. McCabe
July 19, 1901
Oct. 11, 1902

BUTTRAM CEMETERY
(Continued)

Willie F. McCabe
Feb. 11, 1905
Aug. 3, 1906
"Darling, we will miss thee."

Harry Alexander
Son of
N. A. & M. E. McCabe
Mar 25, 1907
Feb. 1, 1908

James Thomas
Son of
N. A. & M. E. McCabe
Aug. 13, 1913
Feb. 18, 1915

William H. Poe
Jan. 23, 1844
Apr. 12, 1906
"Father, we miss thee."

Mary E.
Wife of
W. H. Poe
June 19, 1846
Feb. 16, 1922
"At Rest."

Rachel
Wife of
W. L. Shideler
May 11, 1836
July 31, 1915
"We will meet again."

Ellen Mize
Wife of
J. R. Wyatt
Nov. 4, 1863
June 14, 1915
"She is not dead,
but sleeping."

Ruth Dickey
Oct. 20, 1912
Age 9 mos.

Infant son of
O. B. & M. A. Roberts
Born & died
Dec. 21, 1924

Arvin
Dau. of
J. W. & M. A. Pogue
Apr. 3, 1916
Mar. 8, 1917

Infant son of
J. W. & Mary Pogue
Born & died Mch. 2, 1909

Mary
Wife of
J. W. Pogue
May 3, 1880
Mch. 17, 1909

Nannie C. Hensley
Mar. 6, 1864
June 20, 1914

Basket, J. E.
Co. C - 1st. Tenn. Inf.

Mother - Frances C. Baskett
Apr. 3, 1843
Jan. 17, 1917

Father - John E. Baskett
June 10, 1842
July 11, 1892

BOYD

E. H. Boyd
1845 - 1920 - Father

Mary C. Boyd
1847 - 1930 - Mother

Eula K. Boyd
1880 - 1933 - Sister

Rhea County, Tennessee, Tombstone Inscriptions

BUTTRAM CEMETERY
(Continued)

Joe Leslie Kelly
1916 - 1918 - Baby

Grace G. Norton
1873 - 1933

Jennie Alice
Wife of
J. A. Walker
Oct. 10, 1893
Dec. 1, 1914
"The angels of God
have taken with a message,
Oh do not fear - Today
she's with Jesus for all
eternity's years.   J. A. W.

Willie Head
Feb. 11, 1898
Mar. 14, 1919

Jennings
Son of
J. H. & Frankie McKenzie
Mar. 4, 1926
July 8, 1928

Katharine
Dau. of
W. W. & Katie Miller
Nov. 30, 1913
Aug. 11, 1914

Guy
Son of
W. W. & Katie Miller
Dec. 30, 1915
Feb. 11, 1916

MILLER

John T. Miller
Aug. 15, 1838
May 9, 1911

Aimee Miller
1882 - 1918

Roscoe Miller
1872 - 1920

Father - Martin C. Weaver
1853 - 1920

Mother - His wife,
Alice J.
1854 - 1929

Helen Elizabeth Chauncey
Feb. 8, 1915
July 10, 1915
"Gone to be an Angle."

MORGAN
Delia P. Morgan
1879 - 1936

Sallie Morgan
Sep. 13, 1876
Sep. 26, 1925

Infant of
J. C. & S. M. Morgan
(?)

Infant of
J. C. & S. M. Morgan
(?)

Anna K.
Wife of
F. H. Dixon
Dec. 4, 1874
Jan. 9, 1909

Ora F.
Dau. of
W. B. & Ada Kelly
Oct. 22, 1885
June 16, 1886
"Sleep sweet Babe"

Amanda P. Morgan
Oct. 18, 1852
Mar. 18, 1919
"Here lies Mother."

Pearl Irene
Dau. of
W. H. Morgan
Nov. 7 - 1898 - Feb. 12, 1919
"She was too good, too gentle
and fair, to dwell in this cold
world of care."

Rhea County, Tennessee, Tombstone Inscriptions

BUTTRAM CEMETERY
(Continued)

John P. Morgan
Jan. 26, 1871
Nov. 26, 1923

Robert L. Allen
June 15, 1848
April 14, 1933

His wife
Vesta K. Allen
June 19, 1856
Oct. 30, 1934

James R. Crawford
May 27, 1834
Dec. 3, 1910

Mary C. Crawford
Sept. 21, 1843
Sept. 12, 1920

Mary A. Crawford
Aug. 17, 1842
Sept. 5, 1909

Elizabeth C. Gillespie
March 22, 1854
March 16, 1889

Thomas J. Gillespie
April 10, 1844
May 11, 1912

Tillie
Wife of
H. H. Taylor
1871 - 1908

H. H. Taylor
1865 - 1924

J. Hudson
Son of
S. G. & B. G. Stout
Oct. 11, 1907
Aug. 30, 1908

Carl
Son of S. G. & B. G. Stout
Jan. 23, 1915
Feb. 1, 1915

Mary Hutcheson
Mother of
W. H. Rodgers
1835 - 1912

Infant son of
Leland & Inez Rodgers
1924

W. H. Rodgers
1860 - 1924

Leland N. Rodgers
1890 - 1931

BLEVINS

W. F. Blevins
1835 - 1925 - Father

Mary E. Blevins
1842 - 1910 - Mother

Braxton B. Blevins
1876 - 1929

Katie A.
Wife of
Joe Gravett
July 21, 1882
May 20, 1903

Joseph H. Leonard
Son of
J. & K. A. Gravett
Feb. 22, 1908
June 8, 1908

L. C.
Wife of
S. D. Bridgeman
Dec. 29, 1857
Jan. 17, 1909

Woodmen of the World Memorial -
John J. Kelly
June 29, 1876
Feb. 12, 1931

Rhea County, Tennessee, Tombstone Inscriptions

BUTTRAM CEMETERY
(Continued)

T. J. Brewer
Born Manchester, Tenn
Feb. 8, 1859
Died Dayton, Tenn.
Jan. 22, 1909

Nannie
Wife of
T. J. Brewer
Born McMinnville, Tenn
Aug. 24, 1861
Died Dayton, Tenn.
Feb. 8, 1900
Aged 38 yrs. 5 mo. 14 da.

Mildred
Dau. of
W. E. & P. J. Brewer
Aug. 3, 1911
Feb. 27, 1930

Martha Brewer
Mother of
T. J. B.
Born in Manchester, Tenn.
Feb. 21, 1822
Died in Dayton, Tenn.
Aug. 17, 1895
Age 73 yrs. 5 mos. 26 d's.

Dayton Gross
Son of
T. J. & Nannie Brewer
Apr. 30, 1888
July 19, 1889
"Our darling."

"Gone Home."
Carrie, Dau. of
J. D. & T. E. Patton
Mar. 28, 1895
Sept. 3, 1909
"Let our Father's will be done.
She shines in endless day."

Louisa J. Knight
Wife of
F. A. Fisher
July 29, 1843
Sept. 20, 1921

Francis A. Fisher
Co. M - 9th. U. S. Vol. Cav.
Dec. 7, 1843
Oct. 14, 1913

S. W. McDonald
Apr. 7, 1858
July 27, 1923

Eulalia A. Bennett
Wife of
S. W. McDonald
Dec. 27, 1868
Dec. 12, 1915

SHERMAN

Walter A. Sherman
3 - 4 - 1882
7 - 3 - 1925

Robert M. Sherman
1 - 31 - 1854
7 - 14 - 1912

Rosa D. Sherman
7 - 10 - 1859
4 - 28 - 1912

Eliza E.
Wife of
T. P. Collins
June 30, 1864
July 7, 1909

BAILEY

William C. Bailey
May 21, 1861
Apr. 25, 1929

Anna Lee Bailey
Apr. 15, 1898
Oct. 13, 1916

Roland Bailey
May 30, 1910
May 17, 1911

Rhea County, Tennessee, Tombstone Inscriptions

BUTTRAM CEMETERY
(Continued)

Mrs. Anna Bailey Smith
Wife of
W. M. Smith of Medford, Ore.
Feb. 16, 1858
Aug. 17, 1915
"She lived the life of a
christian for more than
40 years and all these years
she knew in whom she believed."

John Roddy
Feb. 17, 1854
Mar. 7, 1923

Sarah Bailey Roddy
Dec. 9, 1856
Apr. 29, 1922

Wylie R. Howard
1854 - 1914

Clinton
Son of
Mr. & Mrs. J. G. Ballard
Jan. 20, 1887
July 3, 1915

Infant daughter of
Marvin & Lelia Williamson
Sept. 16, 1916

Tillman G.
Son of
Marvin & Lelia Williamson
1912 - 1914

Edwin E. Williamson
1907 - 1935

Mary Lou
Wife of
J. N. Ewing
Dec. 11, 1870
June 26, 1911

E. B. Ewing
Apr. 24, 1866
Apr. 21, 1931

Julia
Wife of
E. B. Ewing
May 31, 1872
March 8, 1925

Josephine Frazier
Jan. 16, 1850
Feb. 17, 1918

Samuel Frazier
April 15, 1848
June 16, 1926

J. N. Jones
Apr. 22, 1881
July 16, 1916

Myrtle Campbell Godsey
July 19, 1888
Nov. 29, 1918

W. C. Godsey
Sept. 20, 1844
Oct. 28, 1924

His wife,
Mary J. Godsey
July 26, 1854
May 13, 1926

Frederick Wayne Darwin
May 13, 1916
Mar. 29, 1923

J. N. Yates
June 18, 1854
Feb. 11, 1916

S. Ann Hixson
Sept. 26, 1869
May 26, 1914

W. C. Hixson
Feb. 13, 1862
Apr. 18, 1922

J. F. Dosson
Apr. 22, 1839
Dec. 30, 1914

BUTTRAM CEMETERY
(Continued)

Woodmen of the World Memorial
Thomas A. Darwin
Feb. 3, 1872
Aug. 14, 1917

Jack B. Darwin
Aug. 27, 1913
June 23, 1915

Lillie W. Gillespie
1853 - 1929

Robert N. Gillespie
1846 - 1929

George Tucker Cunnyngham
1880 - 1924

Edith Helton
Jan. 7, 1918
May 5, 1918
"Our Darling."

Alex Dickson
June 14, 1852
Oct. 15, 1917

Rachel N. Shankle
Feb. 11, 1841
Aug. 1, 1917
"A tender Mother
& a faithful friend."

Anna Lee
Dau. of
D. R. & M. L. Bolen
Sept. 1, 1902
Sept. 10, 1919

D. R. Bolen
June 30, 1865
Nov. 7, 1914
"In Heaven."

Ruth
Dau. of
Robert & Vera Purser
Feb. 10, 1914
Feb. 22, 1914

W. B. Benson
June 4, 1844
Aug. 19, 1913

Ed. Benson
Died Dec. 9, 1934

Sidney L. Ellis
Nov. 8, 1857
May 5, 1914

Martha Jane
Wife of
John Wyatt
May 10, 1840
Jan. 6, 1915

Bulah
Dau. of
H. G. & H. S. Hamby
Oct. 12, 1904
Mar. 17, 1917

J. Luther Bolen
Oct. 18, 1876
Feb. 6, 1922

Emma Jean
Wife of
Gus S. Whaley
1902 - 1928

Infant son of
O. W. & B. M. McKenzie
Apr. 20, 1923

William S. Love
Feb. 2, 1892
Nov. 29, 1931

M. E. Hatfield
Wife of
B. A. Dodd
July 2, 1868
Feb. 5, 1924

Margie Dodd
Mar. 10, 1902
Aug. 23, 1915

Rhea County, Tennessee, Tombstone Inscriptions

BUTTRAM CEMETERY
(Continued)

Sewell
Son of
M. L. & G. J. Slawson
Nov. 4, 1916
May 25, 1919
"Weep not Papa & Mama
for me, for I am waiting
in glory for thee."

John M. Hall
Co. 1 - 38th. Ohio Inf.
U. S. A.
May 31, 1832
Sept. 15, 1911

T. M. Carter
Sept. 3, 1828
July 11, 1914

Hazel Ruth Marler
Nov. 24, 1916
Jan. -- ?

Murvin King
June 27, 1917
Age 13 months

Mauda
Dau. of
H. B. & Ollie Smith
Mar. 17, 1917
Apr. 21, 1919
"Darling, we miss thee."

J. R. Woody
Apr. 10, 1925
Apr. 19, 1925

Walter
Son of
W. R. & Ressie Woody
Nov. 2, 1921
July 31, 1927
"Sleep on sweet babe and take
thy rest. God called thee home.
He thought it best."

William R. Woody
Feb. 1, 1893
Nov. 5, 1927

William R. Woody
Feb. 1, 1893
Nov. 5, 1927

Harold J. Woody
Sep. 21, 1922
Oct. 1, 1922

Ruth Woody
Dec. 7, 1920
May 20, 1922

In memory of our Mother
Louisa C. Davis
Nov. 14, 1842
Nov. 28, 1912
"She hath done what she could."

R. M. Davis
June 12, 1843
July 7, 1909

Nellie J. Heiskell
Apr. 8, 1843
May 12, 1913
"Gone to a better land."

Henegar
Son of
W. T. & Clara Yates
Apr. 28, 1917
Sept. 18, 1917
"A little time on earth he spent,
"till God for him, his angels sent.
Budded on earth to bloom in Heaven."

C. G. Lewis
Aug. 14, 1894
Jan. 14, 1922
Capt. 56th. Inf. U. S. A.

Clyde Leonard Marler
May 19, 1920
Feb. 14, 1921

Mother - Mrs. P. M. England
Oct. 27, 1835
May 30, 1922

Father - P. M. England
Dec. 11, 1833
Jan. 25, 1912

Rhea County, Tennessee, Tombstone Inscriptions

BUTTRAM CEMETERY
(Continued)

Marie McClendon Semmes
Nov. 8, 1889
July 4, 1911

Ada Cook
Wife of
R. P. Abel
Nov. 1869
Aug. 1921

Eunice Parham
Wife of
Brown W. Abel
Jan. 1897
Oct. 1930

Brown W. Abel
Son of
R. P. & Ada Abel
1894 - 1934

Marion
Wife of
E. T. Morgan
June 16, 1870
Jan. 6, 1909

E. T. Morgan
1857 - 1923

Mildred Hill
July 6, 1911
Oct. 7, 1911

S. J. Brandon
Feb. 23, 1838
Oct. 20, 1911

Clifford G. Stansbury
June 25, 1897
Nov. 21, 1920

Arvie
Wife of
Lee Kelly
Jan. 11, 1891
Aug. 19, 1927

Chas. Rice Robinson
Sept. 5, 1851
May 22, 1929

Ella Ann Colville
Wife of
C. R. Robinson
Sept. 14, 1856
Jan. 8, 1924

Eula May
Dau. of
C. R. & Ella A. Robinson
Apr. 6, 1878
Mar. 20, 1882

Sarah Virginia Thomison
Sept. 10, 1848
Jan. 19, 1929

Katie Aikersone
Wife of
J. D. Cate
1872 - 1932

Infant of
W. F. & B. L. Buttram
Born & died
Sept. 1, 1921

Infant of
W. F. & B. L. Buttram
Sept. 1, 1921
Sept. 8, 1921

Doyle F. Reed
July 11, 1936
27 years

J. W. Ingle
1866 - 1926

P. L. Foust
Jan. 2, 1857
Nov. 15, 1928

Laura Lee Sanborn
11 - 15 - 1877
1 - 31 - 1936

Rhea County, Tennessee, Tombstone Inscriptions

11

BUTTRAM CEMETERY
(Continued)

Martha Eliza Sanborn
1869 - 1930

James P. England
1862 - 1933 -Father

Lula M. England
1867 - 1928 - Mother

Henegar Morgan
Oct. 10, 1858
Feb. 5, 1926

Charles Edward Broyles
1861 - 1930

Nancy J.
Wife of
J. W. Wyatt
1859 - 1933

Abbey A. Fisher
1889 - 1928
117 Inft. 81
Div. World War

Robert Laurence Quilliam
Jan. 11, 1936
Aged 1 day

N. D. Reed
1847 - 1927

Margaret T.
Wife of
N. D. Reed
1858 - 1932

Whitney Gillespie
Son of
S. P. & P. M. Swafford
Mar. 5, 1920
May 26, 1921

Mrs. J. M. Darwin
Aged 59 years
Feb. 2, 1936

W. Thurman
Son of
W. G. & Annie Taylor
May 7, 1903
June 4, 1921

Della
Wife of
J. W. Vance
July 19, 1855
May 9, 1933

J. W. Vance
Mar. 26, 1852
Feb. 24, 1922

Aubrey C. Wilson
Indiana - PVT - 1 CL
381 Amb. Co. 96 Div.
June 9, 1935

Frances Jewell
1898 - 1933

S. E. Jewell
Died July 1, 1936
Aged 64 years, 7 months, 25 days.

George W. Harrison
1882 - 1929

Mattie Harrison
July 18, 1898
Oct. 10, 1931

Kelly R. Smith
Aug. 25, 1915
Mar. 16, 1929

John S. Foust
Jan. 21, 1868
Aug. 5, 1930

James T. Crawford
1869 - 1935

Father - J. William Harrison
Dec. 11, 1881
Aug. 10, 1931

Rhea County, Tennessee, Tombstone Inscriptions

BUTTRAM CEMETERY
(Continued)

B. F. McDonald
1882 - 1926

Fletcher Welch
1902 - 1931

T. O. Brooks
Jan. 29, 1862
Apr. 29, 1936

H. L. Brooks
Oct. 27, 1895
Nov. 29, 1935

Mother - Mary Ann Brown
(Richey)
Jan. 2, 1850
Apr. 26, 1930

D. B. Brady
Mar. 17, 1862
May 19, 1931

Eva Gean
Dau. of
K. M. & M. R. Shipley
Dec. 13, 1927
Feb. 1, 1928

Louise
Dau. of
James U. & Viola Thornburg
Oct. 23, 1919
Dec. 26, 1920

James U. Thornburg
May 3, 1936
Aged 46 years, 11 months, 17 days

Clyde
Son of
A. F. & C. E. Knight
Nov. 2, 1919
Aug. 22, 1920

Woodmen of the World Memorial
William A. Thornburg
Jan. 15, 1864
Oct. 8, 1919

Robert Wise
June 16, 1893
Oct. 29, 1919

Sidney
Son of
W. A. & L. R. Knight
Nov. 28, 1916
Oct. 3, 1919

M. G. McDonald
June 22, 1839
April 3, 1922

Virginia T. Miller
Mar. 20, 1868
Oct. 28, 1924

C. F. McDonald, Jr.
July 18, 1916
May 21, 1919

Father - T. B. Wier
Apr. 30, 1856
Aug. 16, 1919

Martha Matilda Conner Weir
Nov. 27, 1935
Aged 73 years, 7 months, 29 days.

James Wilkey
Nov. 21, 1898
Oct. 29, 1918
"His words were kindness,
his deeds were love.
His spirit humble, he rests above."

Bertha Wilkey
Jan. 21, 1909
Nov. 24, 1918
"She was the sunshine of our home."

Joan
Dau. of
J. F. & M. M. Burka
Born & died Aug. 31, 1926

Eva Ann Cunnyngham
1858 - 1932

Rhea County, Tennessee, Tombstone Inscriptions

BUTTRAM CEMETERY
(Continued)

Larry
Son of
L. E. & P. M. Cunnyngham
1915 - 1916

Sallie A. Morgan
Feb. 15, 1864
Oct. 9, 1930

Katy Brady
May 11, 1907
Nov. 10, 1916

Catherine E.
Dau. of
F. B. & Alma Kyle
Feb. 27, 1929
Mar 5, 1929

Amanda Alice
Dau. of
O. L. & M. L. Bain
Born & died
Mar. 9, 1931
"Weep not Papa & Mama for me,
For I am waiting in glory
for thee."

Frances R.
Daughter of
E. C. & F. E. Sherlin
Sept. 20, 1918
Nov. 23, 1918

J. C. Mitchell
Apr. 18, 1847
Dec. 18, 1918

Everett
Son of
J. R. C. & N. S. Mitchell
Aug. 23, 1912
June 19, 1923
"He was the sunshine of our home."

Amanda Hawkins
1850 - 1929 - Mother

Joseph Albert Hawkins
1880 - 1922
"Our son."

Lorea
Dau. of
Jas. & Annie Robeson
1897 - 1932

James
Husband of
Annie Robeson
1867 - 1919

Philip T. Rawlings
Jan. 2, 1826
Mar. 14, 1872

G. W. Gillespie
Feb. 14, 1849
May 3, 1924

Eugene
Son of
J. L. & L. P. Powell
Died Dec. 28, 1918

Sarah Murphey
1856 - 1927

J. G.
Son of
Earl & Hattie Morrison
Apr. 17, 1929
Aug. 14, 1929

Lizzie Wilkey
Sept. 9, 1863
Feb. 7, 1926
"She believed and sleeps
in Jesus."

Mary A. Scroggins
Dec. 11, 1842
Jan. 14, 1928

George Alfred Miller
Feb. 7, 1867
July 20, 1918

Thomas Conner
Jan. 16, 1835
Mar. 14, 1919

His Wife, Violet
Sept. 11, 1832 - July 19, 1918

Rhea County, Tennessee, Tombstone Inscriptions

BUTTRAM CEMETERY
(Continued)

Virgil G. Johnson
Sep. 9, 1906
Jan. 2, 1918
"Our precious little lamb
is sleeping, safe in the
arms of our Lord."

Evelyn
Dau. of
T. W. & Maud Caudle
July 12, 1914
June 1, 1915

William Gennoe
Died February 29, 1936
Aged 34 yrs.

Dixie Lee
Dec. 24, 1929
Feb. 20, 1932

Jessie Creaba
May 26, 1920
Oct. 19, 1920
(Daughters of
C. H. & Myrtle Brady)

Dorthy
Dau. of
C. B. & A. M. Malone
May 16, 1916
May 16, 1921

John H. Wheeler
May 29, 1876
Feb. 15, 1930
"A light from our household
is gone."

Debla Wheeler
June 7, 1909
Feb. 23, 1930

Marcus Walker McGhee
Son of
W. E. & Emily McGhee
June 25, 1925
June 26, 1925

Daddy - Joseph S. Watson
Jan. 13, 1868
Oct. 10, 1924

L. Tennie Burkett
Wife of
James L. Miller
1849 - 1923

Dorthy T.
Dau. of Taylor & Maggie Brandon
Aug. 18, 1921
July 6, 1922

Lester
Son of
John & Mary Boyd
Apr. 7, 1899
Aug. 26, 1922

Wm. Scarbrough
June 18, 1845
May 13, 1923

Mother - S. C.
Wife of
Wm. Scarbrough
May 10, 1853
Apr. 3, 1921
Age 68 yrs. & 11 mo.

Oza K.
Oct. 31, 1896
Dec. 11, 1924

Earl H.
Dec. 6, 1898
May 3, 1924
(Sons of G. J. & Loretta Green.)

R. T. Howard
1860 - 1925

Amos S. Vaughn
Jan. 16, 1850
Mar. 3, 1923

Leslie A. Morgan
Died May 4, 1924

BUTTRAM CEMETERY
(Continued)

L. G. Nicholson
Aug. 12, 1872
Jan. 15, 1926
"Father."

Jow Wheeler
Son of
W. H. Morgan
Nov. 7, 1899
Mar. 3, 1919
"Those whom God loves,
die young."

Bertha
Wife of
W. H. Morgan
Nov. 2, 1888
Mar. 6, 1919

W. H. Morgan
Jan. 1, 1873
Apr. 18, 1928

"At rest." Wife of
M. G. Schild
Tennie Schild
May 7, 1891
Oct. 19, 1919
"My dear loved one,
why should thou of wearied."

Morgan Schild
July 23, 1889
Sept. 8, 1933

Harold M. Schild
Dec. 2, 1914
Apr. 4, 1928

Winnie Hazel Dickson
Wife of
Lee Hudson, Jr.
Aug. 18, 1899
Jan. 3, 1926

Tookie - James Lee Dickson
Nov. 23, 1922
Aug. 16, 1924

N. P. Frazier
1845 - 1923

J. F. Parham
Mar. 1, 1855
May 31, 1920

Laura Bales
Apr. 17, 1845
Oct. 14, 1917

Isabel Bales
Dec. 29, 1900
Mar. 18, 1920

Chester Mitchell
July 15, 1903
Oct. 3, 1904

Martha
Wife of
N. A. Haines
Feb. 27, 1851
Aug. 8, 1902
"Mother sleepeth."

Salena E. Franklin
Aug. 9, 1859
Mar. 19, 1911
"She was a fond Mother
and a friend to all."

T. L. Rogers
Co. K - 1 Tenn. Inf.
Jan. 27, 1843
Feb. 6, 1904

Homer Owen
Son of
F. O. & R. M. Rodgers
Dec. 3, 1907
Sept. 5, 1908

Dorothy
Dau. of
F. O. & R. M. Rodgers
Feb. 26, 1913
Jan. 2, 1918

Harbeck - Mary Susan Gennoe
Wife of
S. Harbeck
1864 - 1916

BUTTRAM CEMETERY
(Continued)

Sheldon Harbeck
1857 - 1917

J. G. Wallingford
1854 - 1919

David E. Baker
1858 - 1927

Chas. Warren Baker
1924 - 1925

Ellen Maud
Dau. of
Jas. L. & Odie M. Breedlove
Born & died May 8, 1933

W. C. Coleman
June 24, 1872
Mar. 18, 1908

Lucy Coleman
Wife of
W. C. Coleman
Died Apr. 6, 1908

W. M. Coleman
Mar. 17, 1845
Apr. 4, 1912
"Father."

Mrs. C. P. Crawford
Wife of
W. M. Coleman
Sept. 25, 1846
Apr. 13, 1924
"Mother."

James M. Brooks
Sept. 19, 1903
Age 86 years.

Musn. A. Brumagim
Co. C. 10 Mo. Inf.

Sarah E. Brumagim
1854 -
June 30, 1926

Kary Emma
Dau. of
Rev. J. J. & S. E. Brooks
June 30, 1908
Jan. 21, 1911

J. F. Shelton
Died 8-7-1935
Aged 78 years

Cordie Shelton
Oct. 16, 1883
May 21, 1903

Susan F. Henderson
1870 - 1922

John W. Hudson
1861 - 1916

J. E. Ewers
Co. L - 116 Ohio Inf.
Oct. 20, 1842
Oct. 13, 1906

Mother - Martha M.
Wife of
John E. Ewers
Oct. 23, 1841
Apr. 12, 1931

J. R. C. Gitwood
Jan. 25, 1900
Mar. 25, 1900

Wanneta
Dau. of
N. Q. & O. M. Purser
Nov. 16, 1905
May 31, 1907

Elizabeth Purser
Nov. 12, 1833
Dec. 27, 1909

Rachel Clark
Apr. 8, 1838
May 4, 1912
"Gone to a better land."

BUTTRAM CEMETERY
(Continued)

Emma Clark
July 30, 1873
May 30, 1904
Age 30 yrs. 10 mon

William Clark
Dec. 14, 1914
Age 77 yrs.

James P.
Little son of
A. B. & L. Carney
July 12, 1903
July 9, 1904
"Gone so soon."

J. D. Burkhalter
1863 - 1927

Dr. E. M. Allen
Mar. 6, 1869
Feb. 27, 1905
"None knew thee, but to love thee,
None named thee,
but to praise thee."

Mary Mae
Wife of
Will J. Thomison
May 30, 1884
Mar. 1, 1914

Thos. J. Harris
Mar. 28, 1874
May 23, 1907
"Our loved one gone,
but not forgotten."

Mother - Tennie F. Harris
Apr. 15, 1852
Mar. 10, 1925

Father - Samuel Harris
Oct. 6, 1842
Dec. 29, 1907

Kate, Wife of
Robt. Boyd
1887 - 1930

Margaret
Dau. of
R. & K. Boyd
1910 - 1929

Louise
Dau. of
R. & K. Boyd
Apr. 12, 1914
Jan. 28, 1915

Emily King
Wife of
V. C. Allen
1845 - 1925

V. C. Allen
1842 - 1915

John C. Jennings
June 25, 1857
Aug. 3, 1914

Emma Jennings
July 31, 1867
Feb. 7, 1895

MEALER

Robert B.
Son of
C. L. & Lucy Mealer
Feb. 17, 1894
Mar. 21, 1896
Age 2 y's. 14 days.
"Sleep on sweet babe
and take thy rest.
God called thee home.
He thought it best."

Charley L. Mealer
Apr. 12, 1868
Aug. 26, 1929

Bessie Mealer
Feb. 5, 1881
June 27, 1929

Rhea County, Tennessee, Tombstone Inscriptions

BUTTRAM CEMETERY
(Continued)

B. F. Mealer
Feb. 16, 1838
Jan. 20, 1913

Martha Mealer
Aug. 6, 1840
Oct. 10, 1915

M. B. Hicks
Oct. 22, 1903
Age 38
"May he rest in peace."

Rev. G. W. Brewer
Mar. 19, 1842
Jan. 27, 1924 - Father

Mary J. Brewer
June 17, 1846
Feb. 1, 1919 - Mother

Mrs. Ruth C. Moon
Aug. 27, 1936
Aged 64 years

Dixie Brewer
Sept. 23, 1900
July 7, 1903

Abner W. Frazier
Oct. 11, 1821
June 15, 1893

N. M. Hensley
Dec. 5, 1867
Dec. 18, 1915

Infant son of
N. M. & Carrie Hensley
Feb. 1, 1902
Mar. 1, 1902

Infant Dau. of
N. M. & Carrie Hensley
Oct. 1, 1904
Nov. 15, 1904

DODD

Carl Dodd
Jan. 11, 1902
Jan. 13, 1902

Rittie Dodd
June 3, 1898
Sept. 5, 1899

Jessie Dodd
June 2, 1885
Sept. 3, 1899

Woodmen of the World Memorial -
William Bailey Williams
Dec. 25, 1861
Jan. 30, 1914

Genevieve
Dau. of
Dr. W. B. & T. E. Williams
Aug. 13, 1903
May 27, 1907

Maud Williams
Wife of
W. H. Cofer
Aug. 7, 1884
Jan. 29, 1907
"Her spirit smiles
from that bright shore,
and softly whispers,
weep no more."

Walter O. Williams
Sep. 10, 1882
Mar. 23, 1904
Age 21 yrs. 6 mos. 21 days.
"God be with you 'Till we
meet again." "Nearer my God
to thee. In the arms of Jesus.
Good bye." (His last words.)

Arthur H.
Son of
Z. & E. Cofer
June 19, 1878 -, Jan. 15, 1908
Age 29 yrs. 7 mo.

Rhea County, Tennessee, Tombstone Inscriptions

BUTTRAM CEMETERY
(Continued)

Robert Emmett
Son of
W. J. & Mattie Lowry
June 9, 1900
Feb. 19, 1901

Father - U. S. Ellis
Sept. 3, 1858
Dec. 28, 1921

Mother - G. Jane Ellis
Feb. 7, 1861
May 4, 1935

E. A. England
(?)

Parentha
Wife of
Wm. Whitlock
Dec. 13, 1832
Aug. 30, 1908
"A precious one from us
has gone, a voice we
loved is still; a place
is vacant in our home,
which never can be filled."
God in his widdom has recalled;
the boon his love had given
and though the body slumbers
here, the soul is safe in Heaven."

Lieut. Wm. Whitlock
5 Tenn. Inf.
Oct. 2, 1834
Feb. 19, 1925

In memory of
Our sister and Aunt
Caroline McDonald
July 29, 1829
Nov. 3, 1907

Eleanor Catherine
Infant Dau. of
F. A. & J. C. Kyle
Died Aug. 26, 1898

Father - David Kyle
Jan. 2, 1831 - Oct. 6, 1897

Mother - Ellen McDonald
Wife of
David Kyle
Aug. 4, 1836
July 7, 19b4

Catherine
Wife of
F. M. Morrison
Jan. 25, 1842
Mar. 29, 1908 - Mother

F. M. Morrison
Jan. 4, 1840
Sept. 12, 1909 - Father

Henry A. Crawford
Oct. 2, 1835
Dec. 30, 1911

Anna N.
Wife of
H. A. Crawford
Mar. 14, 1842
Nov. 20, 1905

Harry Crawford
Feb. 19, 1880
Feb. 20, 1920

John R. Crawford
June 18, 1882
Feb. 20, 1920

H. L. Reynolds
1852 - 1932

Royal R. Reynolds
July 29, 1876
Dalton, Ind.
Nov. 7, 1907
Phila., Pa.

Mary A. Bradshaw
Apr. 15, 1826
June 23, 1901

Alta Buttram
(?)
Raymond Buttram
(?)

BUTTRAM CEMETERY
(Continued)

Albert T.
Son of
A. C. & S. F. Bennett
July 5, 1866
July 26, 1903

Beulah
Dau. of
S. W. & E. A. McDonald
June 9, 1904
Jan. 31, 1905

SMALL

C. F. Small
May 24, 1886
Sep. 7, 1899

G. M. Small
Aug. 12, 1855
Dec. 18, 1894

Oley Small
Feb. 7, 1880
Jan. 2, 1909

Felix V.
Son of
Dr. J. G. Thomison
1893 - 1917

Jean G. Thomison
Aug. 7, 1891
Aug. 26, 1913

Lena R.
Wife of
Dr. J. G. Thomison
Nov. 24, 1868
May 7, 1900
"Rest Mother, rest in
quiet sleep,
while friends in sorrow
o'er thee weep."

James C. Thomison
June 24, 1890
Mar. 26, 1933

Mary Craighead
Mar. 10, 1808
Nov. 9, 1891

Mary B.
Wife of
M. G. McDonald
Oct. 21, 1864
Sept. 8, 1886

Theodore Moench
Feb. 10, 1856
Apr. 1, 1902
"'Twas hard to give thee up,
but thy will O' God be done."

Louisa J. McDonald
Wife of
John McDonald
Sep. 16, 1834
Sep. 7, 1912

John McDonald
Apr. 30, 1834
May 7, 1910

John Daniel Morgan
June 9, 1847
Jan. 14, 1905

Mary Crayton Elder
Wife of
Dr. John D. Morgan
Sept. 19, 1851
Jany. 4, 1929

Henry Elder Morgan
Jan. 29, 1883
Dec. 20, 1895

Little sister
Dau. of
J. D. & M. C. Morgan
Feb. 26, 1880
Mar. 11, 1880

Asbury Buttram
June 25, 1862
Feb. 27, 1911

Rhea County, Tennessee, Tombstone Inscriptions

BUTTRAM CEMETERY
(Continued)

Orton J. Buttram
Sept. 3, 1894
Dec. 19, 1917

James G. Buttram
Feb. 18, 1825
July 22, 1876

Lucy E. Buttram
Jan. 14, 1896
Mar. 16, 1909

Edmund Norville Gannaway
June 17, 1833
Jan. 20, 1924

Mary J. Gannaway
Dec. 21, 1851
Aug. 22, 1900

Claudie
Son of
J. C. & T. Millican
May 6, 1900
July 7, 1900

In memory of
Jas. A. Howard
Sep. 7, 1855
Mar. 28, 1900

Alice Howard
Aug. 21, 1871
July 15, 1918

W. A. Howard
Mar. 23, 1849
Mar. 24, 1918

Emma
Wife of
W. A. Howard
Oct. 30, 1848
Sept. 18, 1912

Joe Lufoy Morgan
Mar. 13, 1884
Jan. 23, 1909

Ella Howard
Jan. 16, 1882
Nov. 20, 1895

Fred W. Thomison
May 3, 1884
Sept. 27, 1924

Nannie Clair Thomison
Aug. 27, 1888
July 10, 1889

Ella Kyle
May 19, 1870
July 4, 1919

In memory of
Our Father,
Robert Kyle
Apr. 5, 1821
Feb. 13, 1904

Lavinia Kyle
Oct. 29, 1827
Sept. 18, 1891

Harriet A.
Daughter of
Robert & Lavinia Kyle
Dec. 23, 1861
Aug. 16, 1872

Edwin
Son of
D. & E. Kyle
Aug. 19, 1868
July 20, 1872
"How many hopes lie buried here."

Virginia E. McDonald
Sept. 23, 1833
Oct. 31, 1862

Lou E.
Daughter of
R. F. & O. J. McDonald
Aug. 7, 1867
Aug. 26, 1867

Rhea County, Tennessee, Tombstone Inscriptions

BUTTRAM CEMETERY
(Continued)

Roland Foster McDonald
Nov. 12, 1824
Jan. 10, 1898 - Father

Orpha Jane McDonald
June 19, 1834
Feb. 5, 1891

In memory of
My Husband,
W. T. Purser
Nov. 9, 1848
Aug. 11, 1891

S. P. Viles
Co. D - 4 Tenn. Vols.
Mex. War.
Mar. 4, 1826
Jan. 8, 1900

Lucy Blanch Vilas
July 10, 1854
May 7, 1907

Charles Gibbs Gillespie
Sept. 26, 1870
Oct. 3, 1898
"Alas! we search for the touch of a vanished hand. A whisper from a voice forever stilled."

Mary Gillespie
1880 - 1918

Dr. James R. Gillespie
1868 - 1923

A. P. Haggard
1862 - 1932

Rena Clark
Wife of
A. P. Haggard
1869 - 1923

Andrew Haggard, Jr.
1897 - 1899

Floyd Jewell
Aug. 30, 1873
Dec. 20, 1895

Louisa F.
Wife of
Sam'l. Jewell
June 3, 1848
July 31, 1881

In memory of
Our Mother,
Nancy McDonald
Aug. 29, 1836
Oct. 6, 1904

In memory of
My husband,
Lewis F. McDonald
Sept. 3, 1826
Mar. 17, 1901
Aged 74 yrs. 6 mo. 14 d's.

Bryan R. McDonald
May 17, 1797
Feb. 7, 1874
Burried in Botetourt County, Va.

Elizabeth
Wife of
Bryan R. McDonald
Sept. 27, 1805
May 19, 1871

J. E. Sawyer
Dec. 25, 1821
May 16, 1905
Burried in White Oak Cemetery, Chattanooga, Tenn.

Mary E.
Wife of
J. E. Sawyer
May 18, 1834
Dec. 14, 1914

Infant of
B. R. & E. M. McDonald
(?)

Rhea County, Tennessee, Tombstone Inscriptions

BUTTRAM CEMETERY
(Continued)

Son of
R. F. & V. E. McDonald
Born & died
March 15, 1861

Lilly
Daughter of
R. F. & V. E. McDonald
March 13, 1860
March 18, 1860

In memory of
Wm. McDonald
July 5, 1795
May 6, 1858

Nancy
Wife of
Wm. McDonald
Jan. 23, 1804
Jan. 26, 1883

N. M. Keith
Mar. 12, 1848
Aug. 29, 1903

Margaret A. Hindman
June 17, 1898
Age 61 yrs. 11 m. 8 d.

D. H. Hindman
July 31, 1827
May 25, 1896
Age 68 y's. 8 mo. 24 D's.

Mary J.
Daughter of
John & L. J. McDonald
April 8, 1853
Oct. 6, 1854
Age 1 year, & 7 months
"This was a bud,
too bright to bloom
in a world of sin and vice."

John P. Howard
Sept. 4, 1894
Oct. 25, 1894

G. W. Goodrich
Nov. 27, 1831
June 14, 1905

T. W. Goodrich
June 6, 1857
Aug. 25, 1917

John M. Howard
Mar. 30, 1851
July 11, 1919

Hamil H. Howard
Jan. 31, 1852
Dec. 22, 1927

John Howard
Son of
C. L. & Dora Hayes
June 12, 1898
July 7, 1902
"Sunshine of our home."

James Harris
Oct. 17, 1878
Mar. 31, 1902
"My loved one is gone,
his voice is stilled,
His place at home
cannot be filled."

Sarrah Adline Harris
May 4, 1879
Mar. 28, 1907

Austin Gibson Miler
July 3, 1894
Was taken away March 1, 1901

Vivian
Dau. of
J. S. & E. Watson
Feb. 16, 1908
April 30, 1908
"Darling, we miss thee."

Harriet O. McDonald
Wife of
S. W. Leuty
Apr. 13, 1828
July 31, 1902

Rhea County, Tennessee, Tombstone Inscriptions

BUTTRAM CEMETERY
(Continued)

Geo. Alexander McDonald
Dec. 21, 1844
Sept. 7, 1915

Dr. W. E. Wheeler
Aug. 21, 1869
Mar. 3, 1899

Floyd Leuty
Son of
G. W. & M. E. Johnson
Oct. 27, 1881
Dec. 16, 1895

Infant of
E. & B. Waterhouse
Feb. 2, 1907

W. B. Moore
Died Nov. 15, 1898
Age 55 Y's.

Adda Templeton
May 1, 1852
Apr. 5, 1881

Sarah Templeton
Aug. 29, 1844
Jan. 7, 1869

My Sister
Mary Templeton
Dec. 20, 1849
Feb. 17, 1924

J. C. Marney
Adopted child of
W. A. & B. J. Templeton
Mar. 12, 1894
May 17, 1894

J. G. Templeton
Jan. 1, 1825
May 4, 1857

W. A. Templeton
Oct. 10, 1846
Nov. 4, 1913

Beckie J. Templeton
May 24, 1853
Dec. 30, 1928

Dr. J. C. Morgan
June 11, 1850
Sept. 6, 1914

Erected in memory of
Walter James Paton
Died June 28, 1908
Age 23 years

In memory of
Gaylord N. Tingley
Mar. 21, 1863
Aged 28 yrs. 4 mos. & 16 days.

Geo. W. Earhart
Feb. 28, 1882
May 28, 1908

Wm. O. Earhart
Aug. 16, 1846
Mar. 26, 1896

Maggie Denton
May 9, 1898
May 19, 1900

Young Colville
1845 - 1912
Private Co. C - 16 Tenn. Bat.
Cav. C. S. A.

Father - J. W. Williamson
Mar. 21, 1831
Oct. 21, 1912

Mother - Eva Williamson
July 26, 1836
Apr. 18, 1911

W. W. Hutsell
Co. C - 8 Tenn. Cav.
Nov. 28, 1845
July 5, 1899

Nancy Johnson
Died Dec. 1, 1882

Rhea County, Tennessee, Tombstone Inscriptions

BUTTRAM CEMETERY
(Continued)

N. Templeton
1842 - 1843

Sarah Templeton
1791
Aug. 1844
Age 53 yrs.

J. L. Templeton
1838 - 1850

J. H. Templeton
Apr. 10, 1815
Dec. 12, 1858

Mary Templeton
July 18, 1818
May 6, 1866

Catharine C.
Wife of
Dr. S. J. Wheeler
May 29, 1849
June 19, 1871

Fred D.
Sept. 8, 1852
Nov. 6, 1855
Son & Daughter Of
Wm. B. & M. G. Johnson

Armintha P.
July 27, 1861
Nov. 19, 1890

Martha Irene
Jan. 8, 1864
Feb. 7, 1884
(Daughters of Wm. B. &
M. G. Johnson.)

Gertrude
Daut. of
J. F. & Montie Johnson
Sept. 4, 1886
Sept. 16, 1888

Wm. B. Johnson
Feb. 28, 1823
Feb. 2, 1868

Martha G.
Wife of
Wm. B. Johnson
Feb. 7, 1821
Aug. 23, 1892

F. D. Chattin
Feb. 20, 1824
Feb. 25, 1897

Isabelle Elderidge
May 23, 1827
Dec. 24, 1898

Ella Zora
Dau. of
J. H. & Margaret Horton
Nov. 29, 1867
Oct. 23, 1896

Claud Matthews
Apr. 1, 1896
June 9, 1896

Virginia C.
Wife of
Dr. A. C. Blevins
1851 - 1920

Dr. A. C. Blevins
May 27, 1830
June 25, 1905

Ladie A.
Dau. of
A. C. & V. C. Blevins
Feb. 6, 1881
Aug. 27, 1897

Rachel Newman
Wife of
John Day
Oct. 15, 1817
June 8, 1874

William Wooddy
April 27, 1871
June 6, 1899

Robert Nelson
Son of Mr. & Mrs. W. M. Morgan
Feb. 26, 1894 - Nov. 5, 1894

Rhea County, Tennessee, Tombstone Inscriptions

BUTTRAM CEMETERY
(Continued)

Susan C.
Dau. of
W. H. & L. C. Morgan
Mar. 22, 1907
Apr. 29, 1908

Lula C.
Wife of
W. H. Morgan
July 28, 1876
May 1, 1908

Mother - Sophronia J. Brown
June 27, 1839
Sept. 9, 1910

Charlie Ross
Son of
John & Sallie A. Morgan
May 30, 1886
Sep. 1, 1887

Matilda Morgan
1849 - 1885
(Sister of Wm. N. & John Morgan.)

Belle Smith
Sept. 20, 1830
Mar. 22, 1908

William F. Douglass
June 1, 1839
Jan. 5, 1907

Nancy Margaret
Wife of
W. F. Douglass
May 21, 1843
April 26, 1919

In memory of
Bednego Hale
Feb. 25, 1766
Sep. 3, 1841

Laban Haworth
Dec. 11, 1817
Nov. 5, 1894

Mary M.
Wife of
L. Haworth
Jan. 7, 1827
Sep. 28, 1896

L. C. Dickson
Feb. 10, 1880
July 19, 1901
"Remember me as you pass by,
as you are now, so once was I,
as I am now, so you must be,
therefore prepare to follow me."
Dennis Dickson
Ray Dickson

B. F. Kennedy
Aug. 22, 1843
July 16, 1904

Little Ruth Agnes
Dau. of
J. M. & D. A. Purser
May 10, 1900
Jan. 15, 1901

Little Brother
Born & died
Sept. 4, 1897
(Child of Mike & Martha Schild.)

Alfred
July 7, 1902
Nov. 29, 1905
"A precious boy from us is gone,
a voice we love so well,
a vacant place is in our home,
which never can be filled."
(Child of
Mike & Martha Schild.)

Mother - Martha Schild
May 15, 1870
June 11, 1929

Julia Anna Shankle
Daughter of
P. H. & R. N. Shankle
Apr. 1, 1878 - Oct. 27, 1902
(Continued)

BUTTRAM CEMETERY
(Continued)

Julia Anna Shankle
Daughter of
P. H. & R. N. Shankle
Apr. 1, 1878
Oct. 27, 1902
"'Tis hard to break
the tender cord,
when love has bound
the heart, 'tis hard,
so hard, to speak the
words, "we must forever
part.".

Dearest love one, we
must lay thee in the
peaceful grave's embrace,
but thy memory will be
cherished, 'till we see
thy heavenly face."

S. L. Janow
Feb. 1, 1853
Jan. 22, 1897

Charles S. Madaris
Sep. 10, 1831
Jan. 17, 1908

Stephen Scott Godsey
Jan. 31, 1878
Mar 25, 1900
22 y's. 2 m's. & 22 D's.

KEITH
Laura Keith
Born 1877
Oct. 16, 1899
Age 22 yrs.

Jack Keith
1865 -
Aug. 14, 1911

Cathrine Keith
Died Jan. 24, 1897

Nancy Keith
Oct. 16, 1830
Oct. 20, 1915

Glovr Keith
Died Feb. 18, 1906

Jack Keith
April 15, 1823
Sept. 25, 1896

Ellen E.
Wife of
L. A. Daniels
Aug. 17, 1827
Dec. 25, 1900

L. A. Daniels
Apr. 7, 1822
Apr. 7, 1886

Our Father - J. W. Brandon
June 3, 1866
Nov. 12, 1901

U. T. Brandon
Aug. 21, 1834
Mar. 15, 1904

Ruby Rogers,
Dec. 30, 1902
Sep. 23, 1904

RHEA COUNTY

TOMBSTONE INSCRIPTIONS
CITY CEMETERY

Located 2 miles south of Dayton, on left hand side of old Dixie Highway. This Cemetery is in Back Valley Community and near the Mountain View Methodist Church. The property is owned by the city, and is adjoining property of Mr. Joe F. Benson.

Isaac Johnson
Co. A - 51 Ohio Inf.

Adda Mae Dyer
Apr. 18, 1889
Jan. 25, 1928

Maggie
Wife of
Louis Rhea
Jan. 5, 1923
Aged 65 yrs.

Joe Hampton
June 19, 1868
Apr. 4, 1918

Rhoda K. Lowry
Sep. 18, 1934

Mother - Lillie M. Kellogg
Oct. 24, 1884
July 24, 1929

Juanita Smith
Nov. 4, 1911
Aug. 23, 1928

Bert N. Holman
July 3, 1882
May 29, 1931

Emma
Wife of
G. F. Holman
June 10, 1872
Sept. 10, 1899
Age 27 yrs. 3 mo.

Pauline
Wife of
G. F. Holman
June 23, 1883
April 22, 1909 - Aged 25 yrs.

Annie
Wife of
Guy Holman
Feb. 20, 1903
Aged 63 yrs.

Addie Stanfor
Sept. 14, 1887
May 3, 1935

Geo. Gormany
Jan. 20, 1835
Nov. 11, 1900

Willie Roddy
Sep. 9, 1877
Dec. 20, 1895

Bessie Williams
Dec. 25, 1885
Nov. 24, 1933

Tom Williams
July 15, 1890
Nov. 20, 1932
(Janitor's Relief Club.)

Oscar Broyles
Sept. 12, 1890
Sept. 4, 1932

Maryl
Daughter of
Albert & Sarah Broyles
May 23, 1895
Jan. 22, 1897

B. M. Pickle
Co. C - 10 S. G. H. A.

Horace Watts
3 mos. 3 days.

Roselee Higdon - July 3, 1883 - Jan. 15, 1897

Rhea County, Tennessee, Tombstone Inscriptions

CITY CEMETERY

Maggie Clark
1 yr. 10 mos.

Lucy
Wife of
Wm. Jones
Oct. 11, 1895
Aged 25 yrs.

Alice M.
Daut. of
J. F. & Sarah Dosson
June 3, 1870
Sept. 14, 1889

Margaret Louise Doffey
Apr. 12, 1906
June 22, 1906

In memory of
Our Mother, Sarah Hutcheson
Dosson
June 18, 1842
June 10, 1911

Our dear Mother,
Synthia, Wife of
G. W. Fann
June 12, 1889
Aged 75 years

Maggie E. Burns
Wife of
J. D. Burkhalter
Nov. 21, 1867
Oct. 19, 1890

Jennie
Wife of
A. P. Petty
Oct. 24, 1865
June 29, 1890

Gertie
Dau. of
James & Florence McJunkins
Oct. 4, 1885
Aged 8 yrs. 2 mos. 4 days

Vance
Infant son of
R. L. & A. A. Coates - Feb. 16, 1897

Gracie Maud
Dau. of
J. D. & R. E. Young
Apr. 21, 1899
Apr. 12, 1900
11 mo. 22 ds.

Charley G.
Son of
J. D. & R. E. Young
Dec. 24, 1897
Apr. 8, 1900
3 yrs. 3 mo. 15 d's.

Frances Louise
Dau. of
Levi & Minnie Hoback
May 3, 1915
Apr. 6, 1922

W. A. Lovelace
1891

James A.
Son of
H. H. & A. T. Wilson
Aug. 9, 1886
Sept. 3, 1887

Katie
Wife of
T. M. C. Williamson
1834
June 3, 1887
Age about 53 years

Rosa Lee Gibson
Apr. 21, 1934
Aged 53 years, 3 mo. 7 days

Mrs. Ida Cofer
April 26, 1936
Aged 40 years

Frederick Doll
May 10, 1859
Nov. 27, 1900

Cassie G. Gallagher
Aug. 14, 1852
Feb. 10, 1918
"Jesus, Mary & Joseph,
I give you my heart and soul."

Rhea County, Tennessee, Tombstone Inscriptions

CITY CEMETERY
(Continued)

Grace McNelis
Feb. 1, 1894
May 10, 1899

Catherine A. Cunningham
May 13, 1875
Aug. 21, 1913
"Into thy hands of God
I commend my spirit, Lord
Jesus receive my soul."

P. Cunningham
May 31, 1891
Age 35 years
"His words were kindness,
his deeds were loved,
his spirit humble.
He rests above

J. C. Gallagher
Dec. 14, 1898
Age 51 yrs.

In loving remembrance
Catherine Gallagher
May 1, 1855
Dec. 3, 1927 - Mother

Mary Gallagher
July 24, 1878
June 21, 1930
"May she rest in peace."

Edna
Dau. of
J. W. & Vica King
Oct. 3, 1906
May 7, 1908

Sarah
Wife of
Jno. Townsend
Oct. 10, 1880
Mar. 12, 1902
Age 21 yrs. 5 m. 7 ds.
"Our darling one hath gone
before, to greet us on the
other shore."

Frances L. Melton
Mar 4, 1924
Mar. 26, 1924

James Leon
Son of
Mr. & Mrs. A. F. Melton
June 26, 1927
Dec. 21, 1927

Dora Lucile
Dau. of
W. D. & Nannie Cole
Dec. 8, 1926
Jan. 27, 1927

Our Mother
Jane Snoden
Aug. 19, 1857
Oct. 14, 1921

Thomas Snoden
June 12, 1820
Sept. 7, 1903

Phebe Organ
1862
Nov. 10, 1929

Pearl Riddle
Jan. 6, 1898
July 3, 1900
"A precious one from us
has gone, a voice we loved
is stilled, a place is vacant
in our home which never can
be filled."

David G. Hudson
May 8, 1859
Jan. 11, 1905

Sarah Jane
Wife of
David G. Hudson
Jan. 13, 1860
Jan. 20, 1894

Rhea County, Tennessee, Tombstone Inscriptions

CITY CEMETERY
(Continued)

Harold Hayeslton
Son of
T. A. & E. A. Tyler
May 9, 1891
Aug. 13, 1891

Maude
Daughter of
John & Alice B. Lord
July 31, 1894
Sept. 12, 1894

Elizabeth
Wife of
J. M. Millican
May 4, 1841
Mar. 5, 1903

Mara G.
Daughter of
Pat & Mary Haughey
Dec. 26, 1886
Apr. 12, 1900

Francis A. Pierott
Sept. 7, 1879
Oct. 8, 1894

Bettie J. Miller
Dec. 12, 1846
Feb. 9, 1911

F. J. Miller
Apr. 2, 1828
Sept. 2, 1871

Jessie D. Riddle
May 24, 1896
Mar. 16, 1921

John S. Riddle
Feb. 8, 1887
Oct. 15, 1928

Daught. of
K. M. & Edna G. Benson
Dec. 4, 1899
Dec. 7, 1899
"Of souls is the Kingdom of heaven."

Caroline Stephens
1854 - 1910

Ike Stephens
1848 - 1909

Warren K. Jones
June 25, 1928
Age 76 years

Father - Walter J. Organ
1859 - 1926

Margery Reynolds
Oct. 19, 1802
Aug. 4, 1889

Solomon Reynolds
June 20, 1886
Feb. 2, 1890

George L. Hosfore
Apr. 30, 1886
Jan. 7, 1890

Nancy Logan
Sept. 25, 1933
Age 69 years

Jonnie
Son of
John Sohorlotte McArthur
Oct. 9, 1887
Nov. 6, 1892

G. F. Holman
June 9, 1871
May 19, 1926

Robert L.
Son of
S. & H. Holman
Jan. 13, 1908
Mar. 19, 1908

Ike Angle
Aug. 29, 1923

Howard Johnson
(?)

5
CITY CEMETERY
(Continued)

Mother - Margaret L.
Wife of
W. M. Foust
Oct. 13, 1858
May 19, 1910

F. L. Cunnyngham
Apr. 5, 1845
Oct. 12, 1894

H. Minerva Tucker
Wife of
W. W. Cunnyngham
Dec. 18, 1866
Sept. 9, 1892
"A true christian,
a devoted wife,
an affectionate Mother."

S. M. Dofsett
May 6, 1896
Age 84 years

Mary F.
Wife of
J. W. Weaver
Dec. 26, 1837
Mar. 14, 1894

Jessie F. Stargel
May 14, 1917
Sept. 7, 1917

James McJunkins
July 3, 1860
Nov. 22, 1929

Charlotte
Wife of
B. B. Buck
Oct. 15, 1844
Oct. 24, 1890

Nicholas --
March 6, 1875
14 yrs. 7 mo. 20 d's.

1

RHEA COUNTY

TOMBSTONE INSCRIPTIONS
COOK(DR) PRIVATE GRAVEYARD

There are only two graves, that of Dr. Cook and wife, formerly on the Dr. Cook farm. Go north from Dayton on the State Highway to Yellow Creek Church about 14 miles. Turn east at the Church and continue ½ mile to the old Gaine's home. This plot is enclosed by a strong iron fence, and a granite shaft is at the head of the graves. Dr. Cook was probably the practicing Physician for more than forty years. No definite history was at hand.

Dr. Robert F. Cook	Charlotte
May 27, 1805	Wife of
Dec. 1, 1872	Dr. Cook
67 years.	Jan. 11, 1811
	Jan. 8, 1894
	83 yrs.

Rhea County, Tennessee, Tombstone Inscriptions

1

RHEA COUNTY

TOMBSTONE INSCRIPTIONS
COLLEGE HILL CEMETERY
(Continued)

Located 2 blocks off main State Highway No. 41 in Suburb, College Hill. College Hill in in South Dayton, and on the city limit line, located in 4th. District of Rhea County. Public.

BANKS

Viola
Dau. of
W. J. & N. S. Banks
Dec. 12, 1887
Dec. 24, 1913
"Amiable, she won all,
Intelligent, she charmed all,
Fervent, she loves all,
and she sadens all."

Alvint
Son of
W. J. & N. S. Banks
Feb. 15, 1867
July 19, 1882

Marth A
Wife of
G. H. Smith
June 13, 1861
Apr. 20, 1905

Esther -
Died Nov. 29, 1892
Aged 7 weeks

Keever -
Died Nov. 3, 1893

Dan'l. Helton
Co. C - 9th. Tenn. Cav.
(?)

W. J. Baker
Mar. 18, 1858
Nov. 21, 1899

Gertrude
Dau. of
W. J. & Mary J. Baker
June 5, 1894 - Mar. 24, 1898

Robt. C. Wheeler
1859 - 1929

Rommie F.
Son of
Robt. C. & Laura Wheeler
Apr. 21, 1894
Sept. 14, 1895

Penelope J.
Wife of
R. T. Howard
July 9, 1825
Apr. 25, 1906

Rev. R. T. Howard
May 9, 1826
Feb. 8, 1891
"A light from our household gone,
A voice we loved is stilled,
A place is vacant in our hearts,
That never can be filled."
"He followed virtue as his truest
guide, Lived as a christian, as a
christian died."

Margaret A.
Dau. of
J. C. & R. L. Carney
Feb. 11, 1878
Aug. 2, 1883
Aged 5 yrs. 6 mos. & 3 days.

Miss Lucy A. L.
Daughter of
T. L. & R. A. Franklin
Feb. 14, 1866
July 15, 1883

Alice Gray Askin
Wife of
John B. Brooke
Dec. 3, 1856 - Feb. 1, 1891

Rhea County, Tennessee, Tombstone Inscriptions

COLLEGE HILL CEMETERY
(Continued)

GIBSON

E. S. Gibson
June 28, 1919
Age 87 yr. 10 mo. 9 da. - Father

Mary A. Gibson
June 28, 1920
Age 84 yr. 4 mo. 5 da. - Mother

Catharine
Dau. of
E. S. & M. A. Gibson
Jan. 20, 1859
Dec. 5, 1912
Age 53 years, 10 mos. 15 days.

Henry C.
Son of
E. S. & M. A. Gibson
June 27, 1880
May 9, 1890

Louana Amelia Black
Dau. of
W. & S. E. Thomas
Mar. 26, 1855
Married Oct. 4, 1877
Died Nov. 12, 1888

Susan Elmira Howell
Wife of
Webster Thomas
April 17, 1831
Married July 8, 1852
Died Nov. 9, 1905
"Her life was an unselfish ministration for others, as a ministering spirit her heart was ever open to needy, suffering humanity."

Samuel A. Thomas
Oct. 12, 1864
May 31, 1886
"Weep not Father and Mother for me, for I am waiting in glory for thee."
Lodge No. 3630 - K. of L.

Cecil Rose
Infant son of
B. E. & Elmira Walker
Jan. 29, 1888
May 9, 1888

G. T.
Son of
John P. & Sarah Walker
July 6, 1865
Sept. 1, 1885

Cap't. J. P. Walker
Oct. 22, 1826
Apr. 3, 1889

Delilah C.
Wife of
S. D. Broyles
Oct. 31, 1818
Oct. 14, 1905
"Having finished life's duty, She now sweetly rests."

"Boss" Alfred
Son of
S. D. & D. Broyles
July 19, 1855
Oct. 6, 1882
Age 27 yrs. 2 mos. 16 days.
"Meet me in Heaven."

S. D. Broyles
Feb. 15, 1824
Mar. 18, 1892
"Gone to bloom in the garden of Heaven, to dwell with the happy and blest."

Mother - Flora Broyles
Dec. 6, 1855
Jan. 14, 1925

Father - A. C. Broyles
Jan. 6, 1851
Sept. 9, 1925

Rhea County, Tennessee, Tombstone Inscriptions

COLLEGE HILL CEMETERY
(Continued)

"In Heaven." Charlie W.
Son of
H. C. & Lizzie Rose
Oct. 13, 1877
Jan. 3, 1895
Aged 17 yrs. 2 mo. & 20 d's.
"So much of love, so much of joy,
Is buried with our darling boy."

"Only sleeping." Mary Elizabeth
Broyles,
Wife of
H. C. Rose
May 18, 1858
July 7, 1912

H. C. Rose
May 16, 1850
July 3, 1922

Ansley, William E.
1893 - 1918 - Oct. 18
25 yrs. 8 mos, 20 days.

Rev. J. H. Hale
Nov. 26, 1845
Nov. 21, 1909

Malinda Lodermilk
May 2, 1814
Apr. 23, 1887

MOORE
Dora R. Moore
Wife of
Dick Hill
Sep. 21, 1873
Feb. 9, 1893

Walter Moore
June 2, 1887
July 9, 1887

Warren G. Moore
Mar. 28, 1892
July 19, 1892

Mrs. Amanda Moore
Died April 22, --?
Age 72 years.

Ida
Dau. of
Percival & Eva Johnson
April 7, 1888
June 12, 1888

J. L. Daniel
1854 - 1925

Wed Preston
Son of
Joseph L. & Flora G. Daniel
Mar. 13, 1889
Mar. 14, 1898

GREER
Orpha Greer
May 7, 1833
Feb. 5, 1902

Moses Greer
Sep 3, 1829
Feb. 12, 1914

Dora S.
Wife of
R. T. Greer
Jan. 3, 1856
Oct. 22, 1881

Smith
Son of
R. T. & Dora S. Greer
Born Oct. 18, 1881

Myrtle
Dau. of
R. T. & Sue Greer
(?)

Mary A. Stranahan
Wife of
J. A. Foster
Apr. 8, 1843
Jan. 5, 1907

Infant of
J. R. & Edith Walker
July, 1891

Rhea County, Tennessee, Tombstone Inscriptions

COLLEGE HILL CEMETERY
(Continued)

AULT

Mary Emily Ault
Mar. 25, 1873
Jan. 24, 1910

Willy N. Ault
Sept. 29, 1828
June 25, 1897

Margaret A. Ault
Sept. 27, 1846
Jan. 8, 1916

Ruth A.
Dau. of
W. A. & H. A. Autl
May 11, 1892
Sept. 17, 1899
"She was too good,
too gentle and fair,
To dwell in this cold
world of care."

JOHNSON

Wm. A. Johnson
Jan. 8, 1850
Apr. 4, 1906
Age 56 yrs. 2 mos. & 27 days.
"At rest."

Asa Johnson
Apr. 25, 1843
Aug. 27, 1923
C. S. A. 1861 - 1865

Susan Catherine Johnson
Aug. 19, 1848
Nov. 11, 1933

Ettie
Dau. of
A. & S. C. Johnson
Oct. 11, 1875
Nov. 19, 1889

Aubry
Son of
J. S. & Minnie Hardin
Mar. 13, 1907
Mar. 18, 1907

John S. Hardin
Sep. 19, 1864
Aug. 12, 1915

G. W. Storie
May 29, 1881
June 5, 1910
"Gone but not forgotten."

John M. Storie
Aug. 27, 1867
Dec. 17, 1905

W. T. Broyles
Aug. 1, 1849
Jan. 7, 1935

Melia Johnson
Wife of
W. T. Broyles
Nov. 17, 1852
Mch. 30, 1902
Age 49 yrs. 4 m's. 18 d's.

Samuel H. Fleming
Jan. 10, 1875
Apr. 23, 1904

James T. Fleming
Sept. 29, 1871
Dec. 6, 1890

Infant dau. of
Sam & Mary Reed
Born & died
Feb. 21, 1903

Charles H.
Son of
N. D. & M. T. Reed
May 5, 1876
Nov. 18, 1878

Nathan D. Jr.,
Son of
N. D. & M. T. Reed
Sept. 12, 1881
May 5, 1882

Rhea County, Tennessee, Tombstone Inscriptions

COLLEGE HILL CEMETERY
(Continued)

John F. McKinley
Born Douglas, Scotland
April 4, 1874
Jan. 3, 1902

Mattie C
Wife of
J. D. Stansbury
May 8, 1863
Jan. 16, 1902

Johnnie Herbert
Son of
J. D. & M. C. Stansbury
Dec. 6, 1893
Jan. 11, 1894
"Plucked from earth
to bloom in Heaven."

John F.
Son of
G. W. & N. L. Stanfield
Dec. 25, 1867
June 13, 1886

G. W. Stanfield
July - 1836
Aug. 6, 1899
Age 63 years
"Our home is dark without
thee. We miss thee every
where."

Nancy Lee Stanfield
July 27, 1842
April 19, 1925 - Mother

Bertie Lilian
Dau. of G. W. &
Alice Gibson
Apr. 5, 1895
Oct. 2, 1895

Roy E.
Son of
G. W. & Alice Gibson
Nov. 30, 1888
May 18, 1908

Geo. W. Gibson
April 27, 1866
November 6, 1921

May
Wife of
F. A. Bandy
Aug. 15, 1878
Feb. 8, 1909

My husband
N. F. Morgan
Sept. 6, 1851
Sept. 15, 1885
Aged 35 yrs. 9 d's.

Sarah F.
Wife of
N. M. Keith
Mar. 24, 1847
Mar. 25, 1893
Afflictions sore for years
I bore, Physicians were in
vain, at length God pleased
to give me ease, and freed me
from my pain.

Samuel F.
Son of
S. D. & L. C. Bridgman
Mar. 27, 1887
Age 11 mos. 14 days.

Will Lillard
Feb. 13, 1854
May 8, 1891

Minnie Lillard
Sept. 4, 1860
May 29, 1887

Eddie Lee
Son of
J. L. & M. A. Bridgman
Jan. 1, 1886
July 31, 1887

Oscar A. Holland
Aug. 15, 1876
May 29, 1924

COLLEGE HILL CEMETERY
(Continued)

HOLLAND

Father - James F. Holland
Oct. 3, 1869
Feb. 2, 1933

Thomas E.
Son of
Mr. & Mrs. J. F. Holland
Nov. 21, 1929
Nov. 29, 1929

Adolphis G.
Son of
Mr. & Mrs. J. F. Holland
April 30, 1828
Nov. 20, 1829

"Our Darling." Nahoma A.
Dau. of
G. F. & M. G. Holland
Mar. 30, 1925
Dec. 3, 1925

Robert P. Hol.
Nov. 9, 1891
Nov. 21, 1894

Infant son of
C. & I. B. Bridgman
Jan. 10, 1908
Jan. 12, 1908

Jennie L.
Wife of
T. M. Williams
Aug. 9, 1859
Mar. 24, 1896
Age 36 yrs. 7 mos. 15 days.

Stewart (?)
July 31 1893
July 20, 1898

F. L. Bridgeman
Feb. 7, 1866
Sept. 25, 1930

Infant of
G. C. & N. N. McKenzie
Oct. 1897

Burfard Hughes
June 30, 1921
Feb. 5, 1923
"Darling we miss thee."

G. W. Ault
Jan. 10, 1824
June 17, 1908

M. T. Ault
Died Feb. 13, 1907
Age 63 yrs.

Mary E. Lloyd Rogers
Aug. 31, 1860
Dec. 5, 1917

F. R. Rogers
Sept. 25, 1857
May 19, 1906

Martha Kirkland
Wife of
J. H. Rogers
Nov. 13, 1828
Dec. 28, 1901

John H. Rogers
Mar. 17, 1826
Dec. 17, 1895

Martha J.
Wife of
G. M. D. Spence
April 21, 1840
June 16, 1888
"Rest Mother, rest in quiet sleep,
while friends sorrow o'er
thee weep."

Cap't. John W. Fout
Feb. 26, 1818
Feb. 11, 1889

Mary
Wife of
Cap't. John W. Foust
Feb. 26, 1818
July 30, 1891

COLLEGE HILL CEMETERY
(Continued)

Tate Martin
Feb. 14, 1881
Jan. 14, 1903

Wm. M. Shannon
Aug. 12, 1836
May 25, 1885
Aged 48 yrs. 9 mos. & 13 dys.

Margaret L. Baker
Wife of
Wm. M. Shannon
June 12, 1851
Jan. 6, 1927

Little Johnnie
Son of
R. N. & E. F. McGill
Dec. 29, 1888
Age 1 mo. 2 days

"Gone Home." Ida May
Wife of
Chas. H. Robertson
April 5, 1866 (?)
April 5, 1885 (?)

E. S. Larmer
Feb. 12, 1845
Jan. 4, 1929

Callie L.
Wife of
R. L. Thomison
Mar. 25, 1865
Jan. 9, 1887

Walter B.
Son of
R. L. & C. Thomison
Jan. 2, 1887
July 9, 1887

Ada R.
Wife of
R. L. Thomison
Mar. 25, 1865
Nov. 20, 1902

John S. Spence
Feb. 8, 1867
Oct. 27, 1930

Harry Edward
Son of
T. A. & M. C. Barton
Feby. 18, 1891
Oct. 12, 1895

T. A. Barton
Apr. 12, 1863
Jan. 13, 1903

In memory of
Thomas A. Allen
Apr. 14, 1838
Entered into eternal life
Dec. 3, 1897
Aged 59 y's. 7 m's. 19 d's.

Sarah Peak Allen
Wife of
T. A. Allen
Confederate Soldier
Oct. 13, 1924

Jennie
Wife of
Ted S. Greer
Aug. 16, 1865
Oct. 21, 1906

Roland
Son of
J. A. & E. A. Loyd
Sept. 2, 1887
Nov. 12, 1891

Lizzie
Daughter of
H. D. Chambers
Nov. 16, 1878
Mar. 1, 1907

Rosa Chambers
Aged 30 yrs. 11 mos.

Harry
May 9, 1913
June 3, 1913

COLLEGE HILL CEMETERY
(Continued)

Kitty Elizabeth
July 6, 1911
Sept. 17, 1912
(Children of
John & Rosa Chambers.)

Edward Roy Barton
Feb. 21, 1889
Mar. 7, 1891
"A little time on Earth
he spent, till God for
him, His angel sent."

Father - Elijah B. Hudson
Apr. 9, 1825
Dec. 25, 1906

Mother - Nancy Ann Hudson
May 8, 1827
Aug. 8, 1900

Willie
Son of
L. S. & E. S. Kessler
Mar. 14, 1886
Sept. 21, 1889

Also infant
Jan. 30, 1885

Amos L. Smith
November 14, 1935
Aged 85 years, 10 months, 13 days.

Nancy W. Smith
July 4, 1936
Aged 81 years, 7 mos, 28 days.

L. N. Wilson
Oct. 2, 1879
Oct. 7, 1884

Eddie Madge
Daut. of
J. G. & E. E. Allen
Feb. 29, 1892
July 5, 1892

Emma E.
Wife of
J. G. Allen and
Daughter of
H. & M. M. Rogers
Sept. 2, 1870
Mar. 6, 1892

Emma Mildred
Infant daughter of
J. G. & E. E. Allen
Feb. 29, 1892
Mar. 1, 1892

Margaret
Wife of
Robt. F. Tallent
Feb. 8, 1849
May 26, 1903

Robert F. Tallent
Oct. 10, 1852
Mch. 2, 1899

Edward F. Tallent
Mar. 4, 1855
Aug. 24, 1885

Edward F.
Son of
E. F. & S. J. Tallent
Mch. 4, 1886
Mch 29, 1909

Edwin
Son of
D. L. & L. E. Beall
July 5, 1847
Feb. 22, 1886

Rev. Joseph Waldorf
Jan. 21, 1821
Mar. 8, 1893

Hettie
Daughter of
C. J. & Ella Barnard
Oct. 28, 1885
July 15, 1888

COLLEGE HILL CEMETERY
(Continued)

Abigail
Wife of
P. S. Burkhatt
Aug. 1, 1887
Age 63 y's. 2 D's.

In loving memory of
John H. Ferguson
Oct. 8, 1840
June 19, 1888

J. W. Bennett
Nov. 2, 1864
Dec. 20, 1895

John D. Gwilliam
Sept. 26, 1866
Feb. 21, 1899

In loving memory of
Ada M. Ruffles
Who died
June 15, 1895
Aged 11 mo's.

Roger Gwilliam
Oct. 21, 1904
Sept. 13, 1907

Mother - Caroline Gwilliam
Wife of
Rees Gwilliam
Jan. 9, 1888
Aged 51 years.

Rees Gwilliam
Mar. 16, 1828
Mar. 13, 1906

Ella
Born & died
Oct. 24, 1885

Nellie
Born & died
Oct. 24, 1885
(Infant daughters of
A. C. & Flora Broyles.)

RHEA COUNTY

TOMBSTONE INSCRIPTIONS
CONCORD CEMETERY

The Concord Cemetery is twelve miles northeast of Dayton. Follow Highway No. 27. From Dayton go three miles north of Evensville leaving the Highway, take the gravel road east and going by the Concord Union Church. Take the old road turning north. It is about one quarter of a mile from the Church to the Cemetery. There are ninety unmarked graves. The land was given by Isaac West.

Arminda Chambers
July 31, 1848
Sept. 17, 1915
"A tender mother and faithful friend."

H. T. Neal
June 5, 1879
April 17, 1931

Knight, Ida Adelia
Wife of
S. W. Knight
June 23, 1875
Feb. 18, 1913
"At rest."

W. R. Caraway
1827 - 1932

W. M. D. McCulloch
Co. F - 2 Tenn Cav.

Mary E. Kennedy
Wife of
Daniel Kennedy
Jan. 22, 1828
Marc. 3, 1907

Daniel Kennedy
Jan. 12, 1821
Apr. 9, 1909

In memory of
Our father who is gone
but not forgotten
J. R. Gannaway
Nov. 20, 1855
Oct. 27, 1896

Harriet C. Miller
Wife of
J. S. Miller
Feb. 9, 1866
Sept. 2, 1907
"Meet me in Heaven."

E. D. Cartwright
Oct. 14, 1899
Age 64
"Gone but not forgotten."

R. R. Lewis
Dec. 20, 1894
Sept. 17, 1895
"Budded on earth
to bloom in Heaven."

H. W. Lewis
June 9, 1901
Lived four hours
"Budded on earth
to bloom in Heaven."

Cecil Clay Jones
Son of
R. J. & Mary Jones
July 27, 1895
Dec. 30, 1907

Benjamin Vaughn
Son of
Chas. O. & Lassie Vaughn
Born & died
July 26, 1904
"Asleep in Jesus
blessed thought."
Our baby --

Rhea County, Tennessee, Tombstone Inscriptions

CONCORD CEMETERY
(Continued)

H. C. Boofer
June 9, 1845
June 6, 1910
"Gone but not forgotten."

J. T. Boofer
Feb. 21, 1848
Jan. 19, 1929

Sarah A. Barnett
Oct. 3, 1839
Feb. 11, 1917

Azza G. McPheeters
Apr. 21, 1888
Feb. 25, 1918
"Not my will
but thine be done."

Lieut. Alf. D. McPheeters
Co. D - 1 Tenn. Inf.

Walter R. McPheeters
Aug. 28, 1875
July 18, 1932
6 U. S. Inf. T - S. A. War

Delilah A. Barton
Wife of
T. J. Barton
Apr. 25, 1847
Feb. 6, 1923
"Here lies one who in
this life was a kind
mother and a true wife."

Della Barton Watson
Sept. 9, 1908
Age 35 yrs.
"She is not dead but sleeping."

Lois Callie Denton
Dau. of
J. Y & S. R. Denton
April 7, 1922
April 1, 1927
"She was the sunshine of our home."

Sarrah Dyer
Dec. 25, 1837
Aug. 25, 1909
"At rest."

E. H. Brown
Oct. 10, 1838
Feb. 18, 1900

Bertha C. Brown
Wife of W. G. Brown
Oct. 15, 1877
Oct. 15, 1902

James Loyd Hamilton
Aug. 10, 1879
Dec. 17, 1910
"Gone but not forgotten."

Margart Hamilton
June 13, 1923
Age 77 yrs.

H. Yong
Feb. 7, 1811
Dec. 15, 1893
"Gone but not forgotten.
We will meet again."

Mamie Watson
Apr. 22, 1883
Sept. 5, 1910

Delia Knight
Wife of
W. B. Knight
Aug. 16, 1873
Oct. 30, 1912

C. H. Knight
Co. H - 73 Ind. Inf.

Rita Irene Chambers
Dau. of
J. A. & Maggie Chambers
Feb. 3, 1913
Mar. 3, 1913
"A sunbeam from the world
has vanished."

Clyde
Son of
J. A. & M. Chambers
Mar. 1, 1900
Aug. 12, 1900
"Only sleeping."

CONCORD CEMETERY
(Continued)

Hetty An McMillan
Born & died
Oct. 30, 1901

Mother -
Mattie Millard
Wife of
W. D. Millard
Jan. 3, 1856
Sept. 15, 1920
"She was a kind and
effectionate wife,
a fond mother and
a friend to all."

C. W. Millard

In memory of
Isaac West
Jan. 23, 1782
April 1, 1826

Mary -
Consort of
Isaac West
May 2, 1790
Aug. 28, 1876

W. R. McDowell
Oct. 17, 1858
Jan. 11, 1929
"He is not dead
but sleeping!"

James C. Buttram
Mar. 3, 1829
May 4, 1900
"His spirits smiles
from that bright shore
and whispers softly
weep no more."

Synthia P. Buttram
Aug. 27, 1832

Martha Alice
Wife of
W. A. Buttram
Sept. 28, 1866
Feb. 18, 1901

Gordon Alley
Aug. 10, 1937
Aged 24 yrs. 6 mos. 7 days.

Mr. J. Alley
Nov. 27, 1923
Aged 48 yrs. 3 mos. 27 dya.

Ruey A. Henry
Aug. 16, 1819
Apr. 12, 1902

1

RHEA COUNTY

TOMBSTONE INSCRIPTIONS
CORVIN FAMILY CEMETERY

The Corvin family Cemetery is six miles southeast of Dayton. From Dayton take the Blythe's Ferry road going by the five Point Church which is five miles southeast of Dayton. Leave the Ferry road at the five Point Church taking the road northwest. The Cemetery is one mile from Five Point. The land belongs to the Corvins. There are sixteen graves, only one with marker.

In remembrance of
my beloved husband
O. P. Corvin.

Rhea County, Tennessee, Tombstone Inscriptions

RHEA COUNTY

TOMBSTONE INSCRIPTIONS
COVE CEMETERY
(Cran Moore's)

The Cove Cemetery is two and one half miles west of Dayton. From Dayton take Highway # 30 going to the top of Cove Hill which is two miles from Dayton. Leave the Highway at Cove Hill, taking the gravel road southwest. The land belongs to Mr. Dave and George Morgan. There are two hundred and ten unmarked graves.

Mrs. Jennie Preston
Aug. 29, 1848
Nov. 17, 1932

Ragen A. Blackburn
May 6, 1845
Aug. 16, 1888
"Asleep in Jesus,
blessed sleep."

Elmer Blackburn
Dec. 12, 1869
Oct. 13, 1886
"The golden gates
were opened,
a gentle voice
said "come.""

Meridae Blackburn
April 27, 1879
June 21, 1898

Mary E. Blackburn
April 27, 1879
June 1, 1925
"We loved them,
yes we loved them,
but angles loved
them more."

Rufus Hartbarger
Co. H - 13 Tenn. Cav.

Samantha J. Sullivan
Wife of
Frank Sullivan
Dec. 7, 1869
Mar. 3, 1915
"Asleep in Jesus."

At rest -
W. M. Henderson
Jan. 5, 1856
Dec. 20, 1895
"Have fought a good fight,
have kept the faith."

D. Henderson
Son of
W. M. Henderson
May 3, 1889
Sept. 3 --
"Sweet baby at rest."

Elizabeth Winters
Wife of
Jas. Winters
Jan. 31, 1850
June 3, 1913

Tiza L. Best
Nov. 25, 1890
Nov. 13, 1918
"Gone but not forgotten."

S. D. Gentry, J. R.
(?)

Chas. W. James
Oct. 4, 1867
Feb. 2, 1907

His wife -
Feb. 21, 1864
Jan. 7, 1907

Thersey Morgan
Wife of
White Morgan
Oct. 14, 1859 - Feb. 21, 1909
"Follow me."

COVE CEMETERY

Lieut. W. B. Gothard
Co. B - 6 Tenn.
M. T. D. Inf.

Dump Gothard
(?)

W. A. Burwick
Dec. 18, 1856
Jan. 30, 1886

Arlow Morgan
(?)

Alice Morgan
(?)

Franklin Minton
Aug. 21, 1928
Age 19 yrs.

Vera Knight
4-11-1903
8-3-1925

Cory W.
Son of
Stbanham Morgan
Feb. 8, 1867
Nov. 24, 1889
William Harper
July 15, 1809
Feb. 13, 1888

Hershel Dillard
Feb. 17, 1924
Feb. 20, 1924

Earl Dillard
Feb. 17, 1924
Feb. 21, 1924

Very Anis Shadwick
July 14, 1906
May 10, 1912
"At rest."

Mable Wilson
May 4, 1895
Age 49

William L. Wilson
Feb. 2, 1915
Age 70 yrs.

Mary Ann Henderson
(?)

Thad Henderson
(?)

Ray M.
Son of
W. D. & M. L. Wilson
Jan. 22, 1919
May 24, 1920

1

RHEA COUNTY

TOMBSTONE INSCRIPTIONS
CRAWFORD CEMETERY

The Crawford Cemetery is four miles north of Dayton. Follow Highway No. 27 going three and a half miles. Leave the Highway and take the gravel road west, crossing the Rail Road. The Cemetery is up on top of the hill. The land belongs to Lee Arnold. There are forty or more unmarked graves.

    Martha Crawford
    Apr. 16, 1810
    Dec. 4, 1863

    M. Josephine Crawford
    Aug. 26, 1851
    May 25, 1858

Rhea County, Tennessee, Tombstone Inscriptions

RHEA COUNTY

TOMBSTONE INSCRIPTIONS
CUMMINGS COMMUNITY GRAVEYARD

1st. District. Take the Dixie Highway at Dayton, go north 18 miles to Spring City. Take the Grand View road for about five miles on Walden's Ridge to Grand View, going two miles north from Grand View on the road towards Rockwood. This graveyard has about twenty graves without names or dates.

JEWETT

John Freeman Jewett
Apr. 10, 1862
Oct. 21, 1887

Charles Jewett
Co K - 54th. Mass.
Infantry.
(No dates.)

Mary Nutting Jewett
Sept. 7, 1839
Nov. 15, 1909

S. R. Palmer
Captain Co. C.
Sst. U. S. C. T.

Wm. E. Horton
Memorial Stone.
Woodman of the World.
(Dem Tucet Clamet.)
Feb. 14, 1875
May 13, 1828

Alice Gemoa
Nov. 3, 1898
Nov. 3, 1898
"From God to God."
(Lamb carved on stone.)

(M. E. D. carved on stone.)
J. Meredith
1875 - 1901

Father - Wm. C.
1846 - 1911

Mother - Sarah M.
1849 - 1912

Ferguson --
(No dates.)

S. S. Quick
Feb. 12, 1816
Feb. 21, 1899
83 yrs.
"Mark the perfect man, and behold the right, for the end of that man is peace."

Simeon Woodruff
Mar. 27, 1825
Jan. 5, 1892
67 yrs.
"A little time on earth he spent, 'till God for him His angel sent."

Nelson F. Higby
Born in New Hartford, N. Y.
Oct. 10, 1824
Died in Grandview, Tenn.
Apr. 9, 1901

CUMMINGS COMMUNITY GRAVEYARD

Mother -
Mary Thompson Hilleary
1861 - 1898
(buried near Rhea Springs.)

Father -
Henry C. Hilleary
Aug. 1, 1841
Dec. 15, 1910

Orin Hilleary
His son
Sept. 16, 1890
July 2, 1908
"Upright and just
he was in all his ways,
a bright example in these
degenerate days."

BALDWIN

W. W. Baldwin
July 21, 1836
Sept. 23, 1921

Nancy H. Baldwin
Dec. 1, 1845
Nov. 13, 1909
"A loving wife, a Mother
dear lies buried here!"

CLARK

Clark, son of
W. H. and C. R. Clark
Feb. 9, 1874
Jan. 18, 1890

Father -
Wm. H. Clark
Aug. 26, 1882
June 8, 1911
29 yrs.

Mother -
Celia R. Clark
Feb. 21, 1833
Oct. 11, 1913

Mary E. Wilcox
1835 - 1907
(A M. A. teacher for more
than 30 yrs.)

Lydia Daniels Hall
Apr. 2, 1871
Jan. 7, 1919
"Faithful unto death."

1

RHEA COUNTY

TOMBSTONE INSCRIPTIONS
DANIEL'S FAMILY CEMETERY

The Daniel's family Cemetery is three miles southeast of Dayton. Follow the Grassion road from Dayton going to Daniels home which is three miles from Dayton. There are two graves, those of a father and son. The son was killed by a car. The land belongs to the Daniels family.

    John Robson Edwards
    Jan. 3, 1937
    Age 20 yrs. 6 mos. 3 days.

    Call Edwards
    Age 38 years.

1

RHEA COUNTY

TOMBSTONE INSCRIPTIONS
DAVIS FAMILY CEMETERY

The Davis Cemetery is four miles west of Dayton. Follow Highway No. 30 from Dayton. Leave the Highway at the Cove Hill which is one and one half mile from Dayton, taking the gravel road west. There are three graves.

Rhea County, Tennessee, Tombstone Inscriptions

RHEA COUNTY

TOMBSTONE INSCRIPTIONS
DEVANEY GRAVEYARD

2nd. District. Go north on concrete Highway # 67 about 11 miles to a place called Penvine on the railroad following the Highway, then ½ mile west to the Deveney farm, which now belongs to a Mr. Moyer. There are about thirty unmarked graves.

DEVANRY

Father -
John H. Devaney
Jan. 28, 1822
July 23, 1906

Mother -
In memory of
Mary J. Devaney
Feb. 24, 1828
Apr. 1, 1911

Sara C. Devaney
Apr. 17, 1850
May 31, 1905

Albert
Son of
Jacob and Catherine Devaney
May 16, 1904
May 21, 1904

Alma
Daughter of
B. J. and H. E. Devaney
Jan. 20, 1902
Feb. 11, 1905

Hortie Ferguson
Wife of
J. J. Fegguson
May 10, 1873
Dec. 3, 1913

Eddie L. Dier
July 7, 1836
Feb. 22, 1923
Private Co. A - 11 Regular
Tenn. Cav. Civil War Veteran.

John Coxey
Co. G - 5th. Tenn. Cav.

Terza Jane Gannaway,
ne Ferguson
Wife of
E. N. Gannaway
July 7, 1833
July 21, 1875
42 yrs.
(Concrete slab.)

James Ferguson
Privates Whites Co.
McDonald N. C. Regiment
Revolutionary War.

Jane B. Miller
Dec. 17, 1814
May 19, 1849
35 yrs.
Tho' lost to sight,
to memory dear."

Margaret A.
Wife of
J. T. Ferguson
Nov. 13, 1842
Aug. 8, 1870

Amanda P.
Second wife of
J. T. Ferguson
Apr. 9, 1848
Sept. 8, 1905

J. T. Ferguson
Aug. 12, 1838
Apr. 17, 1917
(Civil War Veteran.)

A. J. Wyrick
Born in Withville, Va.
June 5, 1822
Died in Gadsen, Ala. 1912.
"We shall rise again in the
Resurrection of the last day."
John II, 24

Rhea County, Tennessee, Tombstone Inscriptions

RHEA COUNTY

TOMBSTONE INSCRIPTIONS
DEVAULT CEMETERY

The Devault Cemetery is ten miles east of Dayton. Follow Highway No. 30. From Dayton leave the Highway at the Camp Ground Hill which is one mile from Dayton. Keep the gravel road to the Frazier Grammar School which is five miles from Dayton. Take the gravel road east at the School going to the Devault Place which is four miles from the Frazier Grammar School. It is one mile from the road to the Cemetery. The land belongs to the Devaults. There are twenty or more unmarked graves.

Ann Frazier Allen
Wife of
V. Allen
Nov. 21, 1814
Oct. 18, 1895

Our father -
Valentine Allen
July 13, 1809
Feb. 15, 1889
"An honest man is the
noblest work of God."
Rests here.

Abner F. Allen
Sept. 25, 1846
June 12, 1858

Nancy Agnes Allen
July 3, 1867
"Suffer little children
to come unto me, for of
such is the kingdom of God."

William Vellentine Allen
Dec. 10, 1861
Oct. 6, 1869
"Suffer little children
to come unto me, for of
such is the kingdom of
Heaven."

Virginia Ann Allen
Oct. 7, 1860
Aug. 24, 1861
Suffer little children
to come unto me for of
such is the kingdom
of Heaven."

Thomas W. Allen
Oct. 7, 1871
Nov. 26, 1872

Sacred to the memory of
Beriah Frazier -Sen.
May 4, 1776
Oct. 25, 1858
Aged 82 yrs. 5 mos. 21 dys.
"I am the reserection of life."

Our mother -
Barbara Frazier
April 18, 1789
July 8, 1866

J. E. Whaley, Consort
of H. Whaley
Nov. 28, 1852
Aged 33 yrs. 3 mos. 19 dys.
"Not dead but sleepeth."

M. Louisa Frazier
Sept. 26, 1824
Nov. 30, 1893
"Her life was given to others."

Thomas A. Moore
Jan. 1, 1804
Oct. 13, 1867
"Gone to Heaven."

Our brother -
Ainsworth B. Moore
Feb. 5, 1847
Nov. 18, 1868

Mary E. Moore
June 8, 1839
Aug. 14, 1869

Rhea County, Tennessee, Tombstone Inscriptions

DEVAULT CEMETERY
(Continued)

In memory of
Abner Moore
Aug. 25, 1876
Aged 25 yrs. 5 mos. 19 dys.
"Jesus my stay in death."

Rebecca
Wife of
T. A. Moore
Dec. 10, 1808
Feb. 6, 1883
"O' God my heart is fixed."

A. B. Moore
1847 - 1867

Pauline Julian
1829 - 1857

Mary J. Devault
Daughter of
H. C. & Eliza Devault
Oct. 2, 1867
Jan. 1, 1893

Henry Clay
Son of
T. B. & L. B. Hood
Apr. 27, 1903
Jan. 7, 1907

Rosa Anna
Daughter of
Charles & Ida L. Hood
Sept. 27, 1895
Aug. 10, 1896
"Budded on earth to bloom in Heaven."

RHEA COUNTY

TOMBSTONE INSCRIPTIONS
DYER CEMETERY
(COLORED)

The Dyer Cemetery is two miles east of Dayton. Leave Dayton on Highway # 30 northeast traveling two miles. Shortly befor reaching Bales Hill take the first left road. The Cemetery is eighty five yards from the main Highway. This is a colored Cemetery and the land belongs to Kellys. There are Thirty three unmarked graves.

George William Proctor
July 28, 1927
Age 5 mos.

Ida McDonald
Aug. 3, 1935
Aged 57 yrs 5 mos. 18 days.

Flora Williams
Wife of
Rev. A. Williams
Sept. 9, 1887
Nov. 4, 1930

Guy Riddle
Aug. 21, 1936
Aged 34 years.

Lena Sharp
Wife of
John Sharp
Dec. 10, 1890
June 15, 1929

Tennie Shelton
July 24, 1936
Aged 78 years.

Andy Kelly
Dec. 29, 1936
Aged 84 years.

Gillespie

Mary Gillespie
July 24, 1936
Aged 69 years, 4 mos. 20 days.

1

RHEA COUNTY

TOMBSTONE INSCRIPTIONS
EARLY FAMILY CEMETERY

The Early family Cemetery is nine miles east of Dayton. Follow Highway No. 30. From Dayton leave the Highway at the Camp Ground Hill which is one mile from Dayton. Take the gravel road leading up the hill, keep the main road to the Frazier Grammar School which is five miles from Dayton. Take the gravel road east at the School House going three miles, then take the old gravel road west for one mile to the Early Place. Hannah Minerva Early and her two husbands are buried there. The land now belongs to W. W. Smith.

To the memory of	Rev. A. P. Early
Dr. Nicholass Frazier	Feb. 26, 1818
Aug. 28, 1812	May 26, 1893
May 18, 1850	"I have fought a good fight
	I have finished my course,
Hannah Minerva Early	I have kept the faith."
Aug. 21, 1818	
Nov. 17, 1902	

RHEA COUNTY

TOMBSTONE INSCRIPTIONS
EDWARD'S GRAVEYARD

Go north from Dayton on the Lon Foust Highway to Spring City, then take the Grand View road or No. 68 and go 5 miles to Grand View, then 3 miles west to Chas. Reed's farm which leads from his farm to Johnson Stand School house, going 1½ miles untill this graveyard is reached.

John A. Davenport
Sept. 2, 1884
Sept. 20, 1884

Thomas Davenport
May 22, 1881

Johnse Davenport
Born and died
Apr. 10, 1883
(Sons of
W. J. and Ann Davenport.

18 unmarked graves.

In memory of
our loved ones at rest.

Sarah Lytle
Aug. 1, 1862
Sept. 22, 1902

Cora Lytle
Sept. 19, 1902
Oct. 2, 1902

Ed Evens
No dates.

Mack Edwards
No dates.

Harrison Edwards
1891
Mar. 1905

Edith McFalls
No dates.

Anna Mary Edwards
"Baby."

Azariah Larry
(?)

RHEA COUNTY

TOMBSTONE INSCRIPTIONS
EVENS CEMETERY

Located about 1½ miles south of Evansville, and about 5½ miles north of Dayton, on the State Highway No. 41, on right side of road traveling North. Property belongs to a family by the name of Evens, and the Cemetery is a private family-owned Cemetery.

EVENS

H. H. Evens
Wife of T. H. Evens
May 29, 1865
Oct. 16, 1919

T. H. Evens
Jan. 10, 1935
Aged 78 years, 11 months, 7 days.

Winnie D.
Dau. of
T. H. & H. H. Evens
Feb. 13, 1888
Oct. 17, 1896

Joseph S. Evens
Oct. 27, 1819
Nov. 30, 1884

Sarah J.
Wife of
J. S. Evens
Dec. 4, 1822
Oct. 19, 1896

Robert Floyd
Son of
J. S. & S. J. Evens
May 13, 1865
April 27, 1885

J. H. Evens
Feb. 20, 1853
Jan. 10, 1885

James G. Evens
April 15, 1847
Nov. 13, 1887

J. E. Evens
March 17, 1856
June 26, 1913
"All is well."

James B. Thompson
Nov. 1, 1861
Aug. 28, 1885

Samuel W. Thompson
Jan. 17, 1856
May 18, 1884

Mary Thompson
Aug. 24, 1834
Feb. 3, 1896

J. Haws
Son of
T. H. & H. H. Evens
Oct. 22, 1894
July 23, 1895

Nancy Jane
Wife of
Thomas Hall
May 19, 1837
June 29, 1908

N. W. Cunnygham
Mar. 23, 1888
Nov. 28, 1919

RHEA COUNTY

TOMBSTONE INSCRIPTIONS
EVENS CEMETERY

The Evens Cemetery is ten miles northwest of Dayton. Follow Highway No. 30 from Dayton. Go to the top of mountain which is five miles from Dayton. Leave the Highway at the top of mountain and take the gravel road west, going to the Morphy farm which is five miles from the main Highway. There are seventeen unmarked graves. The land belongs to Miss Gladys Morphy.

Stephen R. Bradshaw
Jan. 1, 1879
Age 42 yrs. 5 mos. 20 dys.

Rhea County, Tennessee, Tombstone Inscriptions

1

RHEA COUNTY

TOMBSTONE INSCRIPTIONS
EWING COMMUNITY GRAVEYARD

Go north from Dayton to Spring City 18 miles on the Dixie Highway. Turn east on Rhea Springs road on Highway 68. Go east past Rhea Springs water mill, going south about 3 miles, then turn west on road to Geo. Crosby, or Ewing's old farm one mile. This Cemetery is ¼ mile north of George Crosby's home. This Crosby farm was formerly owned by J. G. Ewing. About 107 graves without names or dates.

Chattin

Fine large gray
granite - Highly
polished stone.
Father -
John D. Chattin
Oct. 22, 1807
Aug. 12, 1869
62 yrs.

Mother -
Susan Chattin
May 9, 1825
Aug. 1, 1908
83 yrs.
"At rest."

John Cook Chattin
Jan. 21, 1848
Dec. 18, 1862
14 yrs.

Mary E. Chattin
Mar. 24, 1865
Apr. 29, 1906
41 yrs.

Family plot, iron fence
and concrete walk around walk.
Six graves in this plot.

Louella
Wife of
G. L. Crosby
Jan. 16, 1871
Apr. 14, 1915
(Crosby top of stone.)

Jacob E. Ewing
Nov. 9, 1853
Nov. 16, 1908
55 yrs.
(Ewing on top of stone.)

James P. Ewing
July 24, 1824
Oct. 27, 1890
66 yrs.
(Mason.)

Martha Elizabeth
Daughter of
J. W. and Annie Vineyard
Jan. 15, 1887
Nov. 8, 1889

Iron fence around this plot.
This graveyard is well kept,
and in very good condition.

Rhea County, Tennessee, Tombstone Inscriptions

2

RHEA COUNTY

TOMBSTONE INSCRIPTIONS
EWING GRAVEYARD

District No. 2. This is part two of the Ewing graveyard and is located on a hill on the Geo. Crosby farm about ¼ mile northwest of Geo. Crosby's home. Go north on the old Stage road about 15 miles to a road that turns east toward Tenn. river, then go east 1 mile to the Geo. Crosby home.

Monument by the Woodman
of the World -
Dum Taget Clamat -
Three logs cave on top.
Five logs in upright
position.

Oscar F. Riggs
Feb. 25, 1888
Apr. 13, 1914
"O' be ready when
the bridegroom comes."
(Riggs on bottom of stone.)

Jessie M. Riggs
May 11, 1852
Sept. 15, 1912
(Riggs bottom of stone.)

Father -
J. P. White
Feb. 11, 1840
Aug. 2, 1926

Mother -
Eliza
Wife of
J. P. White
Aug. 5, 1911
Age about 72 yrs.
"Although they sleep,
their memory doth live."

Chinie R. Mintie Ballard
Feb. 18, 1875
July 13, 1900

Wm. M. Clack
May 2, 1817
Feb. 14, 1910
93 yrs.
(Mason.)

Isabella G. Wilson
Wife of
Wm. M. Clack
May 13, 1819
Dec. 30, 1895
76 yrs.

John S. Clack
Mar. 2, 1831
Aug. 21, 1884
53 yrs.
(Mason.)

In memory of
Margaret
Wife of
M. E. Clack
June 5, 1796
Sept. 10, 1877
81 yrs. 3 mos.

About four graves within
iron fence. No names or dates.

Isabella Wilson
Wife of
John S. Calck
Nov. 19, 1839
Oct. 7, 1875
36 yrs.

Philo T. Clack
Son of
W. M. and G. T. Clack
Apr. 23, --
Dec. 3, 1857
8 mos.

In memory of
Misouri Clack
Apr. 4, 1806
Nov. 12, 1856
50 yrs.

Rhea County, Tennessee, Tombstone Inscriptions

EWING GRAVEYARD
(CONTINUED)

In memory of
Sterlina G. Clack
Jan. 7, 1826
May 29, 1849
26 yrs.

Inmemory of
Martha Clack
Oct. 16, 1787
Apr. 20, 1857
70 yrs.

In memory of
Rollo Clack
Jan. 4, 1772
Dec. 16, 1842
"Gone home."
70 yrs.

Geo. Hale
1762
(Dead 175 yrs.)

In memory of
Elizabeth Hale
Apr. 11, 1845
Age 46 yrs.

Susan L.
Daughter of
Harmon and Jane Mahaffy
July 26, 1819
Dec. 22, 1850
31 yrs.

John W. Hawkins
Son of
J. H. and C. Hawkins
Sept. 11, 1843
Aug. 20, 1855
12 yrs.

Martha Hawkins,
Apr. 7, 1853
Aug. 26, 1855
2 yrs. 3 mos.
"Gone home."
(Holy bible engraved.)

Hugh W. Baldwin
July 23, 1841
Mar. 14, 1881
40 yrs.

Addison M. Broyles
Jan. 15, 1853
Sept. 28, 1930
77 yrs.
"He went about doing good."

HARWOOD - Top of stone.
Sol Harwood
Jan. 23, 1853
Jan. 7, 1919
66 yrs.

Mary M. Harwood
Nov. 11, 1856
(Still living.)

BROYLES

Nile M. Broyles
May 1, 1819
Dec. 22, 1894
75 yrs.

Eleanor C. Broyles
Wife of
Nile M. Broyles
Mar. 20, 1828
Mar. 5, 1893
(These two graves enclosed
by iron fence.)

John H. Riggins
Dec. 21, 1831
Jan. 11, 1873
42 yrs.
(Above grave enclosed
by pickett fence.)

Edith Fugate
Dec. 20, 1889
Feb. 21, 1909
Age 19 yrs. 2 mos. 1 dy.

Rhea County, Tennessee, Tombstone Inscriptions

EWING GRAVEYARD
(CONTINUED)

M. Ora
Daughter of
W. F. and M. R. Baskett
Sept. 18, 1912
May 16, 1913
"Sleep on sweet babe
and take thy rest,
God called thee home,
He thought it best."

Lewis Fugate
Co. B - Mounted Inf.
Civil War - No dates.
"In God we trust."

Eliza J.
Wife of
J. D. Patton
Feb. 5, 1863
July 24, 1885
22 yrs.
"Here rests a
faithful friend.
A wife dear.

J. H. Russell
Jan. 22, 1926
Feb. 27, 1926
Two Mos.

A. G. Russell
Dec. 8, 1931
July 15, 1935
"I've anchored my soul
in the Haven of rest."

Claybom Harwood
May 12, 1850
Nov. 18, 1902
52 yrs.

John D. Harwood
Aug. 7, 1844
Apr. 26, 1885
"Gone, but not forgotten."

James Knox
1799 - Mar. 9, 1859
Age 60 yrs. A volunteer
in Jackson's War.

Elizabeth Knox
Mar. 17, 1802
July 2, 1875
73 yrs.

Selah Benton
Wife of
Benjamin Knox
Nov. 18, 1819
Mar. 13, 1859
40 yrs.

Elizabeth C.
Daughter of
B. & S. Knox
Aug. 9, 1853
10 yrs.

Charley Wilson
Mar. 27, 1884
Jan. 12, 1885
15 Mo.
"Gone so soon."

David Wilson
Apr. 7, 1865
Oct. 12, 1885
20 yrs. 6 mos.
"All is rest."

Father -
F. S. Fugate
July 6, 1844
Nov. 5, 1914
70 yrs.

Aska Ann
Wife of
E. S. Fugate
May 5, 1858
Mar. 28, 1902
44 yrs.
"Gone, but not forgotten."

Mrs. Pearl Baskett
Daughter of
Sol Howard
Nov. 11, 1891
July 9, 1913
22 yrs.
"Gone, but not forgotten."

EWING GRAVEYARD
(CONTINUED)

Mother -
Nancy J. Collins
Nov. 1, 1841
Feb. 22, 1903

Ella G.
Daughter of
J. S. and Celia Wright
Born & died
May 9, 1904

Sarah C.
Wife of
Ben Smith
Mar. 8, 1873
Apr. 30, 1900
"Gone, but not forgotten."

Rhea County, Tennessee, Tombstone Inscriptions

RHEA COUNTY

TOMBSTONE INSCRIPTIONS
FAIRVIEW CEMETERY

The Fairview Cemetery is six miles south of Dayton. From Dayton, take Highway # 27. This Cemetery is by the Highway six miles south of Dayton on the right going south. The land was given by the advent people of Graysville. There are thirty six unmarked graves.

Juliet Schatzel
1848 - 1920

Cyntha Jane Dodd
Died Aug. 15, 1936

Norman B. Dowlen
Dec. 1912
June, 1918

Susan G. Condra
Sept. 3, 1870
Sept. 28, 1936
Age 66 yrs.

Lynn White
(?)

S. E. Lindsley Pierce
Wife of
H. W. Pierce
Feb. 5, 1844
May 3, 1914
"Waiting."

Sturdevant
Charles E. Sturdevant
1859 - 1916
"Resting."

Oliver L. Thorpe
Kansas PVG - 29 MGBN
10 Div.
Sept. 26, 1934

Helena A. Richardson
1904 - 1922

Lula B. Gruze
1893 - 1917

Alice Beatrice Light Keith
Aug. 5, 1890
May 28, 1920
"At rest."

Sister -
Mary J. Cozart
May 10, 1863
Oct. 27, 1916

Father - Mother
M. S. Small
Sept. 3, 1850
Oct. 25, 1923

Mrs. M. J. Small
May 26, 1850
Sept. 22, 1920

Mrs. Medie Price
July 13, 1844
Oct. 22, 1924
Grandmother -

Tennie Crockett Taylor
1850 - 1924

W. H. Taylor
1837 - 1917

Mother -
Nancy E. Johnson
Oct. 24, 1850
July 9, 1918

Elizabeth Van Voorhis
Wife of
H. C. Harrison
Apr. 29, 1891
Jan. 13, 1913
"At rest."

Rhea County, Tennessee, Tombstone Inscriptions

FAIRVIEW CEMETERY

Van Voorhis

Sherman H.
1864 - 1928

Ida A.
1860 - 1936

Jimmie O.
1859 - 1935

FOX

Mildred Swearingen
Wife of
Will H. Fox
1894 - 1924

Hall

Flora M. Hall
Oct. 1850
May 18, 1920

James M. Hall
Feb. 27, 1849
Apr. 8, 1922

HILDEBRAND

Minnie L.
1867 - 1917

Lawrence D. Van Voorhis
1887 - 1936

CLOUSE
John W. Clouse
Feb. 9, 1842
June 22, 1921

Mitchell - Father
1848 - 1923

Barbara Ellen Reel
Died June 18, 1926
Age 3 mos. 29 days.

Thelbert Dodd
Died April 1, 1934
Aged 3 mos.

COULTER
Robert J.
Apr. 18, 1890
Jan. 25, 1923

Maurice
Aug. 17, 1918
Aug. 24, 1918

Robert
Born & died
Aug. 17, 1918

Father -
Charles L. Coulter
Sept. 29, 1867
March 11, 1925

Lewis Owen Coulter
Died Feb. 26, 1937
Aged 40 yrs. 5 mos. 14 days.

BOWER
Virginia Rains
Wife of
F. M. Bower
Sept. 16, 1850
July 13, 1925

F. M. Bower
July 15, 1849
Dec. 28, 1928

CROSS
Sarah M.
Wife of
J. H. Cross
Aug. 7, 1844
Aug. 24, 1935
(A member of the church for 50 years and lived it until death.)

BABER
Father -
Granville H.
1852 - 1936

MCDONALD
Mrs. Dora E. McDonald
Died July 8, 1937
Aged 51 years, 10 days.

Rhea County, Tennessee, Tombstone Inscriptions

FAIRVIEW CEMETERY

LOWRY
James Ernest Lowry
Jan. 3, 1937
Aged 50 yrs. 6 mos. 20 days.

WILSON
John Wilson
April 7, 1842
May 26, 1926
"Dear friends as you pass by, as you are now, so once was I, as I am now, soon you must be, prepare for death and follow me."

LEA
Thomas J. Lea
1848 - 1927

JACOBS
Father-
S. M. Jacobs
1846 - 1927

RIDEOUT
Arthur
1851 - 1925

INGRAM
Edward
1909 - 1926

JENKS
Ena A.
Wife of
H. A. Jenks
Oct. 22, 1877
Feb. 4, 1931

Rose
Mother - Lenora Ferguson
Nov. 14, 1884
Apr. 1, 1933

BARGER
John H. Barger
March 18, 1937
Aged 25 yrs. 8 mos. 6 days.

Thomas Ray Barger
1906 - 1936
Age 30

HENDERSON
Riller Henderson
Jan. 1, 1872
Feb. 2, 1936

ANDREWS
Mrs. Mary S. M. Andrews
Sept. 28, 1934
Aged 58 yrs.

PHILLIPS
Wanda Jean
Daughter of
J. L. & Lucille Barger Phillips
Oct. 18, 1930
Mar. 15, 1935

HATFIELD
Mrs. W. B. Hatfield
Feb. 20, 1935
Aged 46 years.

ALEXANDER
H. M. Alexander
1873 - 1931

Mother - Eliza E. McNett
1851 - 1926
"Resting in hope of a glorious resurrection."

Father - Joseph W. Franklin
1859 - 1934

James L. Hickman
Son of
Mr. & Mrs. Raleigh Hickman
July 26, 1911
Mar. 27, 1928
"Gone but not forgotten."

Anna Hickman Dortch
Aug. 1886
Aug. 1927
"asleep in Jesus."

FAIRVIEW CEMETERY

Anna M. Degraw
1844 - 1934
Age 90.

Hassell Eugene Davis
Feb. 27, 1936
Aged 23 days.

Brooks - Brother -
Wallace R. Brooks
Sept. 17, 1914
Aug. 12, 1933
"He was the sunshine
of our home."

Mrs. Sudie Elsea
July 9, 1937
Age 50 yrs. 11 mos. 6 days.

W. M. R. Holt
1857 - 1924

Sarah E. Holt
1870 - 1928

Donna Sue Thomas
April 28, 1937

Walker, Samuel Walker
Feb. 23, 1861 -
Feb. 23, 1935
Age 74 yrs.

1

RHEA COUNTY

TOMBSTONE INSCRIPTIONS
FARLEY CEMETERY

The Farley Cemetery is fourteen miles northwest of Dayton. Follow Highway No. 27 from Dayton. Go to Evensville which is six miles north of Dayton. Leave the Highway and take the mountain road going eight miles. There are seven unmarked graves. The land belongs to the Jones.

J. T. Farley	A. P. Jones
Mar. 6, 1840	Aug. 1836
June 5, 1900	May 1, 1893
"Gone home."	
	G. L. Chatman

1

RHEA COUNTY

TOMBSTONE INSCRIPTIONS
FERGSON CEMETERY

The Fergson Cemetery is thirteen miles northwest of Dayton. Follow Highway No. 30 from Dayton going to the top of the mountain. Leave Highway and take the road southwest. The land belongs to Alridge. There are six unmarked graves.

Fergson
J. N. Fergson
Died May 6, 1878

Rhea County, Tennessee, Tombstone Inscriptions

1

RHEA COUNTY

TOMBSTONE INSCRIPTIONS
FOUST GRAVEYARD

In first District on Burnett farm. Get on the Dixie Highway at Dayton, come north 18 miles to Spring City, go east on the Rhea Springs road 2 miles. At Rhea Springs take the Muddy Creek road and go 2½ miles to the Burnett farm. There one half mile north of Burnett home on Cedar Hill is the Foust graveyard.

Jacob McDowell
Dec. 2, 1815

Lucy P. Eldridge
Feb. 27, 1865
May 1, 1882
17 yrs.

Harriett E. Eldridge
Dec. 6, 1839
Oct. 19, 1881
42 yrs.

Albert E. Eldridge
Jan. 21, 1859
Jan. 1, 1877
18 yrs.

In memory of
Sara Ann
Daughter of
James I. and E. N. Cash
Wife of
G. P. Roddy
Dec. 13, 1867

In memory of
Ann Cash
Feb. 25, 1807
Dec. 5, 1842
35 yrs.

In memory of
Delila June Thompson
Daughter of
E. M. & E. R. Thompson
Oct. 6, 1856
Nov. 23, 1856

In memory of
Ann B.- First wife of
Rev. James I. Cash
Feb. 25, 1801 - Dec. 1842

In memory of
Second wife of
Rev. James I. Cash
Nov. 22, 1810
Mar. 24, 1875
65 yrs.

Rev. James I Cash
Feb. 18, 1801
Mar. 10, 1885
84 yrs.

In memory of
Hanna J. Cash
Apr. 5, 1829
Aug. 27, 1886
Lived 57 yrs.

Robinson, (R) engraved
David F. Robinson
Aug. 22, 1849
Jan. 23, 1901

(Foust) "Asleep in Jesus."

Docie E. Foust
Wife of
D. F. Robinson
Jan. 7, 1873
Sept. 23, 1893
20 yrs.
"I have fought a good fight,
I have finished my course,
I have kept the faith."

In memory of
John T. Foust
Mar. 8, 1861
June 14, 1892
32 yrs.

FOUST GRAVEYARD

In memory of
Wm. M. Foust
Feb. 5, 1829
Jan. 12, 1877
48 yrs. (Mason.)

Mother – Margaret McPherson
Wife of
Wm. Foust
Sept. 27, 1835
Oct. 2, 1920
85 yrs.
"Yea though I walk thru
the valley of the shadow
of death, I will fear no
evil; for thou art with me,
thy rod and thy staff,
they comfort me."

Deborah R.
Daughter of
Wm. M. and M. Foust
Nov. 2, 1876
Apr. 5, 1877

Mauda May Foust
Daughter of
J. M. and L. A. Foust
Sept. 12, 1897
July 9, 1899

In memory of
Elizabeth A. Ribble
Wife of
J. M. Foust
Nov. 18, 1868
Jan. 10, 1904
36 yrs.
Holy Bible engraved on
top of stone.
"A precious one from us has gone,
a voice we loved is stilled,
a place is vacant in our home,
which never can be filled."

(Iron fence around Foust and
Robinson family plot. Other graves
in woods, probably 35 not cared for.

RHEA COUNTY

TOMBSTONE INSCRIPTIONS
FRENCH CEMETERY

Located about 1 mile west of Dayton, about 2 blocks off the highway from Dayton to Pikeville. Public owned property. Located in the suburb, Sawyer's Hill.

Garbie Lelia
Dau. of
J. W. & Lula Travis
July 16, 1893
May 6, 1896

J. R. Denton
Aug. 14, 1836
Mar. 15, 1917

Dock Smith
May 27 1901
Aged about 23 yrs.

Perry Smith
May 27, 1901
Aged about 21 yrs.

Willie J.
Son of
T. J. & M. K. Mathis
Oct. 3, 1883
May 27, 1901

Walter McGhee
Son of
C. C. And Angebin McGhee
May 5, 1882
Dec. 30, 1923
"Gone but not forgotten."

Mattie A. Rudd
Wife of
J. G. Rudd
July 8, 1843
Mar. 9, 1913
"Our loved one."

Melba Rose
Wife of
Edward Kaylor
May 11, 1910
June 19, 1928
"A precious one from us has gone,
A voice we love is stilled,
A place is vacant in our home,
Which never can be filled."

Willie Hale
(?)

Chroshie Smith
June 20, 1908
Mar. 9, 1931

Maud Lambert
Apr. 25, 1893
Apr. 8, 1920
"Gone Home."

Eva Patten
1887 - 1932 - "Mother."
"She was the sunshine of our home."

Thomas H. Alexander
Jan. 3, 1874
Mar. 7, 1917

Sylvanie
Wife of
B. T. Black
Dec. 11, 1884
Jan. 30, 1915
"She was a kind and affectionate wife, a fone Mother, and lived a true christian."

Rhea County, Tennessee, Tombstone Inscriptions

FRENCH CEMETERY

W. Jerome Elder
Apr. 1, 1936
Aged 66 yrs. 9 mo. 27 das.

Frank Sexton
Died Nov. 10, 1933

John C. Pressnell
Sept. 14, 1860
July 22, 1926

M. M. Lewallan
Oct. 25, 1896
Oct. 15, 1921

Will M. Holmes
Aug. 22, 1888
May 5, 1927

Creed Wilkey
(?)

Nancy C. Wilkey
July 8, 1833
May 27, 1905

Della Jeffres
Wife of
Edgar Pressnell
Aug. 10, 1892
July 31, 1913

Mary J.
Wife of
A. Purser
Apr. 18, 1865
June 16, 1908

Infant son of
A. & N. J. Purser
Dec. 16, 1906
Dec. 17, 1906

Thomas Hughes
Mar. 14, 1910
Sept. 14, 1924
"Darling, we miss thee."

Hazel Hughes
Jan. 14, 1902
Oct. 28, 1919

J. H. Hughes
Nov. 2, 1874
Mar. 30, 1918

O'Lena Keen DeBlieux
April 21, 1867
Feb. 18, 1916
"Her music lives to bless the world."

Willie Mae Daugherty
Sept. 21, 1915
Sept. 30, 1918

Mary Schill
Age 63 yrs.

Dellie Daugherty
June 22, 1891
Mar. 29, 1925

Dillard, W. J.
Nov. 1855
July, 1922

Mrs. Mary Dillard
Oct. 14, 1935
75 years old.

Martha Jolly
Nov. 16, 1886
Nov. 15, 1935

Thomas E. Lane
Dec. 20, 1895
Aged 40 yrs. 6 mos. 10 days.

William H. Lane
Dec. 20, 1895
Aged 19 yrs. 4 mo. 4 days.

J. L. Hunter
Mar. 24, 1867
Mar. 31, 1902

Pearl
Dau. of
J. H. & M. J. Hughes
Apr. 15, 1906
May 23, 1907

Rhea County, Tennessee, Tombstone Inscriptions

FRENCH CEMETERY
(Continued)

B. G. Best
May 28, 1878
May 21, 1907

James Revis
Mar. 23, 1913
Age about 35 yrs.

Infant Dau. of
J. & M. K. Revis
Born & died
June 18, 1912
"Gone to be an angel."

T. W. Morgan
July 15, 1853
Jany. 22, 1907

WASHBURN
Claudie Washburn
Mar. 5, 1906
Feb. 25, 1908

Wallace Washburn
July 18, 1901
June 2, 1911

Elizabeth
Wife of
J. W. Washburn
Feb. 22, 1883
Nov. 9, 1926

Dick L. Hoge
Son of
J. J. & Mary Hoge
June 1, 1887
July 20, 1908

L. P. Yather
Died 1910

Andy Wilkey
Oct. 5, 1873
Dec. 5, 1918

Beulah
Wife of
Walter Clingan, Daughter of
Mr. & Mrs. E. A. Norris
Dec. 28, 1909 - May 24, 1928
"Safe in the arms of Jesus."

Henry M.
Son of
M. R. & L. C. Gibson
Aug. 15, 1893
Feb. 2, 1909

Nola Walker
Aug. 15, 1895
Aug. 16, 1907

George Hughes
Nov. 24, 1901
Age 69 yrs.

Mrs. Anna Hughes
Dec. 11, 1926
Age 77

John Morton
Sept. 27, 1827
June 2, 1903

Infant of
Mr. & Mrs. John Hughes
Died Jan. 25, 1921

Etta Mae Hughes
Dec. 28, 1912
Age 3 yrs. 9 mo. 7 days.

Mrs. Caroline Holmes
Sept. 23, --
Age -- years

Thomas Holmes
Sep. 12, 1842
June 19, 1908
"Good Father, we miss thee."

Della Lowry
Mar 24, 1912
Age 23 yrs. 5 mo. 2 Da.

Bethel Hubbs
Mar. 15, 1890
Apr. 10, 1901

J. H. Jewell
1844 - 1924

Rhea County, Tennessee, Tombstone Inscriptions

FRENCH CEMETERY
(Continued)

Willie E.
Son of
Sam & Evin McJunkins
(?)

Coy
Son of
N. W. & D. E. Steelman
Nov. 15, 1897
Jan. 12, 1901

Carl
Son of
Joe & Flora Pogue
July 17, 1903
Sep. 12, 1904

Nancy C.
Wife of
R. S. Mason
Mch. 28, 1860
Apr. 11, 1895

J. E. Hawkins
Feb. 4, 1859
May 27, 1901

H. P. Best
Feb. 18, 1862
Nov. 21, 1899

Daughter of
J. L. & J. T. Hawkins
Jan. 19, 1892
Mar. 21, 1892

Lee E.
Son of
W. T. & L. A. Revis
Mar. 23, 1900
April 4, 1900

Alda May
Dau. of
R. J. & F. A. Hoge
Aug. 20, 1901
Sept. 20, 1901

Maggie
Wife of
R. G. Newman
Jan. 10, 1869
Apr. 28, 1906

J. H. Best
Jan. 13, 1859
Jan. 6, 1833

Infant of
Martin & Pearl Burrell
(?)

Martha L. Burrell
July 28, 1888
May 5, 1910

Mrs. Gladys Green
April 16, 1936
Aged 23 years

Rachel A. Gray
Feb. 16, 1847
July 14, 1914

George W. Gray
Aug. 30, 1847
July 2, 1909

Harry T. Swicegood
Mar. 10, 1906
Oct. 15, 1909

Pete Schill
1875 - 1929

Ellen Childress
Wife of
A. J. Holden
Apr. 17, 1867
Dec. 13, 1929

Bill Dodd
1896 - 1934

R. A. Davis
April 13, 1837
Mar. 25, 1911

Rhea County, Tennessee, Tombstone Inscriptions

FRENCH CEMETERY
(Continued)

Walter Davis
2 - 12 - 1871
5 - 26 - 1917

Mary Ann Daugherty
Mar. 29, 1880
Nov. 4, 1925
"To die is gain."

Morgan
Son of
U. S. & V. J. Wilson
June 2, 1922
Jan. 10, 1923
"Weep not Mother & Father,
for I am waiting in glory
for thee."

Mrs. Elvira Hunter
1-26-36
Aged 77 years.

George Kiker
June 15, 1874
Dec. 2, 1909

Mrs. Sarah Dodd
Died June 7, 1935
Aged 74 yrs.

Mallie Davis Wyrick
(?)
Joe Pogue
Sept. 15, 1867
June 6, 1924

J. G.
Son of
Earl & Sylvia Pogue
Dec. 8, 1923
Jan. 26, 1924

Blanche Marler
Dec. 23, 1875
Sept. 30, 1921
"She was the sunshine
of our home."

Margret Lowry
Aug. 1, 1859 - Aprl. 12, 1900

Billey R. Clingan
April 7, 1930
Aged 1 yr. 5 mo.

Travis

Thos. C. Travis
June 18, 1831
July 23, 1906

Neal M. Travis
Feb. 25, 1918
Feb. 26, 1918

Nany Travis
Nov. 29, 1834

Joseph H. Travis
Died Apr. 24, 1935
71 years

Gothard, Thomas
Dec. 20, 1878
Dec. 13, 1909

Kenneth Lee Gothard
Oct. 4, 1934
Aged 17 yrs.

Louis A. Neal
Jan. 29, 1829
Jan. 28, 1912

Sarah G.
Wife of
John Neal
July 6, 1873
July 19, 1909

Helen
Dau. of
H. G. & Nannie A. Morgan
Oct. 15, 1895
May 1, 1898

R. T. Clining
Mar. 23, 1878
Jan. 26, 1913

FRENCH CEMETERY
(Continued)

Mettie
Dau. of A. F. &
Bettie Blankenship
Nov. 23, 1900
April 19, 1905

Ada Boyd
Mar. 25, 1900
Feb. 10, 1920

H. H. Hawkins
Jan. 19, 1829
July 30, 1898

H. K. Hamilton
Feb. 26, 1858
May 29, 1913

J. M. Hamilton
Mar. 29, 1830
Sept. 25, 1919

Leslie
Husband of
Mettie Graham
Oct. 4, 1878
Oct. 6, 1917

Freddie Majors
Aug. 31, 1910
Age 1 yr.

Susan L. Majors
Sept. 1, 1840
Mar. 25, 1909

PHILLIPS

Robert C. Phillips
May 26, 1905
Nov. 23, 1905

Lena Phillips
Dec. 28, 1900
Aug. 15, 1909

Carter Phillips
Feb. 16, 1935
Aged 85 yrs.

Thomas A. Smith
June 22, 1855
Sept. 29, 1910

Mrs. Martha Potter
Feb. 29, 1936
Aged 64 yrs.

Edgar
Son of
Edgar P. & Nancy Typton
Died Sept. 26, 1896

Nancy J.
Wife of
E. P. Typton
May 16, 1861
Sept. 20, 1912

Cora B. Shelton Alley
Jan. 10, 1869
June 16, 1909

Silas Potter
Mar. 7, 1865
Sept. 28, 1922

Sam Potter
Aug. 7, 1890
Feb. 27, 1912

Mae
Dau. of
G. A. & Ina Kiker
May 19, 1908
July 1, 1909

Girtrude C. Davis
Dau. of
W. A. & Lellis L. Davis
Feb. 10, 1909
Aug. 29, 1910

Della Wiener
Mar. 9, 1898
April 12, 1926

Clyde
Son of J. G. & E. B. Henderson
Mar. 3, 1921 - Sept. 14, 1924
"Budded on earth to bloom in Heaven."

Rhea County, Tennessee, Tombstone Inscriptions

FRENCH CEMETERY
(Continued)

Lillian L.
Dau. of
H. C. & M. A. Sexton
Oct. 28, 1927
Nov. 19, 1934
"Our darling."

Morgan B. Best
Feb. 9, 1916
Sept. 2, 1917

Ondous
Son of
O. B. & B. Best
Feb. 15, 1889
Aug. 20, 1897

Clay
Son of
O. B. & B. Best
Oct. 15, 1894
Dec. 5, 1895

Earnest Best
Apr. 26, 1886
Feb. 11, 1918

Ida
Dau. of
L. T. & H. M. Powell
Jan. 31, 1881
Aged 19 yrsl

J. A. Iverster
Dec. 25, 1856
Dec. 20, 1895

A. W. Hughes
Co. L - 4th. Tenn. Cav.

Elizabeth
Wife of
B. C. Smith
Aug. 24, 1841
Mar. 18, 1897

Susie E.
Wife of
A. J. English
Dec. 28, 1853
Feb. 7, 1895

Nellie Marie Black
Jan. 3, 1905
Nov. 5, 1906

Infant son of
B. T. & Silvanie Black
Oct. 12, 1903

Henry C.
Son of
A. L. & J. E. Newman
Mar. 16, 1896
Apr. 6, 1896

Harry D. Martin
Nov. 23, 1848
Aug. 4, 1901

Elizabeth McMillen
Aug. 29, 1885
July 12, 1899

Irvir Arthur McMillen
July 26, 1885
Dec. 20, 1895

Hazel E. Best
Mar. 9, 1907
July 29, 1907

Lou A.
Wife of
T. A. Smith
1863 - 1933

L. Myers
1820 - 1876

Infant Dau. of
F. & M. S. Holland
May 1, 1904

Odist Phillips
Jan. 4, 1935
30 years

Lelia M. Phillips
Nov. 15, 1900
Mar. 3, 1903

Eliza J. Wyrick
Apr. 9, 1875 - Sept. 3, 1903

Rhea County, Tennessee, Tombstone Inscriptions

FRENCH CEMETERY
(Continued)

Arthur Rose
Aug. 8, 1902
Aged 22 yrs. 3 mos. 8 days.

Velma Lillian
Dau. of
S. L. & B. L. Umbarger
May 7, 1901
Feb. 17, 1902

Willie Hughes
Oct. 10, 1899
Oct. 17, 1899

Edenia
Dau. of
W. R. & A. L. McClendon
Jan. 24, 1907
May 13, 1907

Edeth May
Daut. of
O. J. & M. M. Green
Born & died
Jan. 14, 1894

Richard Arthur
Son of
W. M. & N. F. Johns
Feb. 16, 1881
Apr. 17, 1893

Sarah Foust
Wife of
Phillip Foust
Oct. 12, 1871
June 16, 1811

In memory of
Phillip Foust
Feb. 8, 1773
Aug. 20, 1855

Nancy A. Foust
Feb. 20, 1825
Mar. 17, 1904
By the children.)

Earl
Son of
T. H. & E. A. Alexander
Mar. 23, 1893
Apr. 6, 1893

J. J. Merrill
Co. H - 2nd. Mo. Cav.

Henry N. Morgan
Jan. 30, 1873
Apr. 17, 1826

Philip T. Foust
Dec. 19, 1816
June 16, 1892
(By the children.)

Bart Hale
Apr. 20, 1865
June 11, 1901

Jas. Roy
Son of
Wm. & S. Craig
Aug. 6, 1897
Nov. 20, 1901

Meda
Dau. of
Joe & H. Jackson
Aug. 22, 1888
Apr. 2, 1902

Clinton D. Hoyl
Apr. 5, 1842
June 19, 1907
"My trust is in God."

Elias H. Morgan
Jan. 18, 1819
Mar. 2, 1896

Tomeasy J. Morgan
Wife of
Elias H. Morgan
Mar. 25, 1824
Aug. 24, 1903

Rhea County, Tennessee, Tombstone Inscriptions

FRENCH CEMETERY
(Continued)

Arva A. Allen
Wife of
Albert A. Morgan
Feb. 8, 1851
Feb. 20, 1925

Elizabeth A.
Wife of
James Allen
Dec. 2, 1821
Dec. 4, 1899

Albert A. Morgen
May 30, 1848
Apr. 8, 1889

T. K. Green
Mar. 13, 1831
Jan. 31, 1907

Jas. K. Love
August 27, 1936
Aged 70 years, 6 months, 20 days

MCMILLEN

Mother – Sarah C. Lewis
Wife of
B. W. McMillen
Jan. 18, 1854
Sept. 7, 1912

George W. McMillen
May 1, 1853
Apr. 2, 1895
"Each of us hopes to join you
at last, on the beautiful
heavenly shore."

Robert S. McMillen
Nov. 5, 1892
Nov. 24, 1894

Bessiee
Dau. of
M. M. & M. A. McMillen
Feb. 10, 1896
Feb. 25, 1896

Z. L.
Son of G. W. & Sarah McMillen
Nov. 14, 1888
June 2, 1889

Bettie Bell
Dau. of
C. N. & E. Ledford
Born in Soddy
June 14, 1884
Died at Dayton
July 14, 1885

Allice
Daughter of
J. L. & M. J. Ledford
July 9, 1886
Nov. 30, 1886

J. Mariah
Wife of
Wm. Morgan
Oct. 2, 1822
June 26, 1882

Martha Jane
Wife of
R. D. Morgan
Aug. 12, 1830
Nov. 24, 1909

R. D. Morgan
June 29, 1832
Oct. 9, 1863

Wm. Gideon
Son of
G. T. & C. M. Morgan
April 26, 1863
July 7, 1863

Sgt. M. S. Riddle
Co. F - 5th. Tenn. Inf.

James R.
Son of
M. S. & S. F. Riddle
Oct. 7, 1864
Aug. 12, 1868

Rhea County, Tennessee, Tombstone Inscriptions

FRENCH CEMETERY
(Continued)

Susan Foust
Daughter of
Jacob Foust
Jan. 22, 1836
June 13, 1857

Susannah Foust
Wife of
Jacob Foust
July 2, 1793
Sept. 5, 1876

Jacob Foust
Apr. 18, 1796
Aug. 25, 1855

Sarah Rudd
Sept. 23, 1846
Dec. 19, 1930

Mother - Mrs. E. A. McDonald
(?)

PURSER
Frank
Son of
John & Lena Purser
1892 - 1924

Grady Purser
(?)

F. Mogene Purser
(?)

Robert Wayne
Son of
R. D. & E. M. Purser
Nov. 29, 1887
Aug. 21, 1899

May
Daughter of
R. D. & E. M. Purser
Jan. 10, 1896
June 14, 1899

R. D. Purser
Nov. 4, 1852
Dec. 21, 1917

Anderson Bryan
Son of
N. L. & J. T. Henry
July 14, 1897
Nov. 25, 1898

Julia T.
Wife of
N. L. Henry
Aug. 12, 1860
Dec. 6, 1901

Elijah L. Rudd
Nov. 17, 1820
Jan. 7, 1905
"He was a true to his God, family & country."

Eliza C.
Wife of
E. L. Rudd
June 19, 1824
Sept. 25, 1903

Robbie Lillard
Sept. 6, 1884
Apr. 8, 1896

Zoa E.
Daught. of
B. F. & E. Lillard
Mar. 27, 1885
July 18, 1888

Robert
Son of
B. F. & E. Lillard
Feb. 26, 1887
June 20, 1888

AYERS

Eliza Jane Ayers
Oct. 14, 1901
Mar. 18, 1902

Charley S. Ayers
May 23, 1903
Feb. 27, 1904

FRENCH CEMETERY
(Continued)

Claudie
Son of
W. E. & L. E. Ayers
Aug. 20, 1906
Oct. 30, 1906

C. R. Wilson
Co. C - 2nd. Tenn. Cav.

Ellen
Wife of
C. R. Wilson
June 9, 1849
April 11, 1919
Her last words,
"Heaven, sweet heaven,
I long for thee."

Paul Lewis
Infant son of
H. A. & L Deblieux
(?)

H. A. Deblieux
Jan. 25, 1863
Dec. 30, 1907

Lola Bell
Daughter of
J. W. & Lola Troutman
Dec. 5, 1898
June 24, 1899
Age 6 mo. 19 days.

Provy
Wife of
Frank Ervin
Sept. 9, 1880
Nov. 15, 1909

John H. J.
Son of
F. & P. Ervin
Feb. 1, 1903
Dec. 3, 1905

Lou P.
Wife of
T. A. Smith
Aug. 24, 1863
June 23, 1903

Charlie Frank Thurman
May 16, 1926
Sep. 23, 1928

Cora Lee Johns
July 30, 1893
Age six weeks

Thomas E. Lane
Dec. 20, 1895
Aged 40 yrs. 6 mos. 10 days

William H. Lane
Dec. 20, 1895
Aged 19 yrs. 4 mo. 4 das.

The Church of God -
Mandy C. Lane
(?)

Emaline
Wife of
B. H. Harris
Dec. 20, 1834
July 3, 1894

Eliza J. Hawkins
Mar. 1, 1836
Nov. 15, 1888

Mary M. Denton
Nov. 8, 1841
Nov. 1, 1909

Abner Witt
Son of
T. M. & Low Whaley
Nov. 28, 1894
Mar. 16, 1897

Lou
Wife of
T. M. Whaley
Jan. 8, 1859
Nov. 29, 1896
"She was too good, too gentle
and fair to dwell in this
cold world of care."

Rhea County, Tennessee, Tombstone Inscriptions

FRENCH CEMETERY
(Continued)

Roy Dodd
Aug. 3, 1934
Age 32

Thomas Lee
Son of
W. A. & L. T. Dodd
Aug. 27, 1904
Sept. 18, 1906
"Darling, we miss thee."

Artie Lenia
Dau. of
W. A. & L. T. Dodd
Apr. 5, 1898
Sept. 27, 1899
"She was the sunshine
of our home."

Abbie May
Dau. of
W. A. & L. T. Dodd
Sept. 28, 1896
Mar. 26, 1897

Ella
Wife of
J. B. Dodd
Mar. 24, 1832
Oct. 2, 1894

Lucy Rhea
Dau. of
J. B. & L. J. Dodd
June 25, 1873
Oct. 12, 1875

John S. Whaley
Co. C - 16 Tenn. Batt.
May 28, 1832
Killed in battle at Chickamauga
Sept. 12, 1863

Ethel May
Dau. of
N. B. & S. C. Brady
Mar. 30, 1887
Sept. 7, 1888

N. B. Brady
June 2, 1855
Oct. 7, 1910

1889 - 1918 -
Sgt. Fred W. Brady
Co. C - 105 Field Sig. Bat.
killed in action at Estrees, France
last words - "Have done my best."

Mackinney Stewart
Oct. 1847
W. F. S. Nov. 14, 1842

Jonis McDonald
Son of
Wm. McDonald
Dec. 7, 1837
Age 10 days

Hugh Andrew
Son of
J. M. & Della Head
Jan. 18, 1892
Feb. 5, 1892
"I am a little angel now."

Albert W.
Son of
C. B. & Ella Morgan
July 8, 1889
Aug. 6, 1890
"Sleep on little Albert and take
they rest. God called thee home.
He thought it best."

Freddie T.
Son of
J. F. & S. A. Sharp
Sept. 12, 1892
Apr. 23, 1894
"Only sleeping."

Robert A.
Jan. 10, 1887
July 19, 1887

Walter F.
Apr. 15, 1888
Aug. 4, 1889
(Children of J. A. & L. E. Holden.)

Rhea County, Tennessee, Tombstone Inscriptions

FRENCH CEMETERY
(Continued)

J. B. Sneed
July 10, 1852
Feb. 2, 1904

Cynthia E.
Wife of
J. R. Burnett
Apr. 27, 1846
Oct. 20, 1887

Lula Grace Burnett
(?)

Teddie Burnett
Sept. 27, 1887
Sept. 30, 1887

William Reed
(?)

Effie Nash
Jan. 13, 1860
July 22, 1911

Johnnie
Son of
J. W. & Effie Nash
June 2, 1891
Apr. 11, 1905

Bennie
Son of
J. W. & E. Nash
July 5, 1894
Aug. 8, 1895

Father - John W. Nash
Nov. 11, 1848
Jan. 6, 1915

Brother - W. H. Nash
June 8, 1888
Mar. 25, 1916

James L. Nash
Aug. 13, 1885
Apr. 9, 1918 - Woodman

Calvin Morgan
Mar. 6, 1822
Jan. 21, 1901

P. C. Morgan
Mar. 21, 1860
Oct. 10, 1893

Sarah L.
Wife of
Calvin Morgan
Oct. 30, 1828
Apr. 12, 1915
"The golden gate stood open,
A gentle voice said come,
And with farewell unspoken,
They calmly entered home."

Margaret S. Benson
Mar. 4, 1841
Dec. 18, 1876

G. W. Presley
Nov. 27, 1816
May 27, 1901

Posey
Son of
J. H. & Sallie Best
Dec. 18, 1894
Apr. 7, 1895
"Our darling sleeps."

Luther
Son of
Wm. & S. Best
Jan. 28, 1891
Oct. 22, 1893

M. F. Best
Wife of
E. P. Best
Mar. 15, 1870
Dec. 25, 1894
"Gone Home."

Myrtle M.
Dau. of
J. J. & M. T. Hoge
Nov. 9, 1894
July 7, 1895
"One little angel more."

J. H. Hoge
Sept. 7, 1849
Aug. 5, 1901
May Brackett - Feb. 11, 1895

RHEA COUNTY

TOMBSTONE INSCRIPTIONS
FRIENDSHIP GRAVEYARD

Go out 5 miles from Dayton out to Washington. Take State Highway from Washington to past Dock Smith's water mill, turn north east on Toe String road. Go about 4 miles to Friendship Church. Here you will find the above named graveyard just a few steps up the hill in sight of the Church. About 80 graves without names or dates.

Garrett Tallent
May 6, 1826
Mar. 3, 1903
77 yrs.

Nancy Tallant
Mar. 1, 1829
Jan. 22, 1886
59 yrs.

Mother - Margaret Smith
Nov. 10, 1843
Jan. 9, 1892
49 yrs.
"Gone but not forgotten."

Father - Colman Smith
Jan. 23, 1833
May 21, 1914
81 yrs.

Vesta Ella Mitchell
Apt. 17, 1882
Aug. 2, 1886
"Gone, but not forgotten."

GARRISON

John W. Garrison
Son of
James & Mary Garrison
Mar. 12, 1895
Feb. 8, 1899
"Our Darling son."

Eugene Garrison
Feb. 15, 1840
Aug. 3, 1900
60 yrs.

"Her home in Heaven."
Bertha Jane Garrison
Daughter of
James & Mary Garrison
Mar. 8, 1904
Feb. 14, 1905
"Our Darling baby."

Geo. W. Garrison
Nov. 5, 1863
Oct. 15, 1929
"Gone, but not forgotten."

BELL

James W. Bell
Aug. 10, 1839
Nov. 21, 1911
"God's finger touched him, and he slept."

Mother - At rest.
Mary A.
Wife of
James W. Bell
Nov. 10, 1848
Mar. 3, 1921
"A tender Mother, and a faithful friend."

Rollo Clyde
Son of
E. R. & M. A. Bell
Mar. 1, 1914
May 28, 1918
"Darling, we miss thee."

Willie T. Bell
Aug. 12, 1893
May 17, 1903
"Budded on earth, to bloom in Heaven."

Rhea County, Tennessee, Tombstone Inscriptions

FRIENDSHIP GRAVEYARD

Timothy M. McNutt
Jan. 28, 1855
Jan. 17, 1931

Rebecca L. Harmon
Nov. 18, 1856

Andrew Harmon
Jan. 25, 1859

Sina A. Harmon
Apr. 19, 1864
Dec. 19, 1921

Father and Mother Harmon
(No dates.)

Manning, J. S.
May 20, 1880
Feb. 8, 1926
"Beloved Father, farewell."

Ethel
Wife of
J. S. Manning
July 27, 1893

Cyrene Emily Long
Apr. 18, 1853
July 3, 1933
"I know that my Redeemer liveth."

Rebecca Paul
Nov. 20, 1816
Feb. 10, 1886
70 yrs.

Leander W. Clark
Apr. 2, 1848
May 23, 1897
49 yrs.

Sarah E. Clark
Apr. 11, 1855
May 27, 1899

(Beautiful marble stone. No name or dates.)

Edward
Son of
Mr. & Mrs. Emmert Wright
Aug. 11, 1925
Sept. 9, 1926
"Gone to be an angel."

Dortha Blanch
Daughter of
S. H. & C. L. Keylon
Feb. 28, 1911
Jan. 28, 1912
"Darling, we miss thee."

Mattie Hestella
Daughter of
M. B. & L. E. Keylon
July 12, 1909
Aug. 16, 1910
"Gone, but not forgotten."

Ina Grace
Daughter of
S. H. & C. L. Keylon
June 20, 1903
Dec. 31, 1918
15 yrs.
"Gone, but not forgotten."

Gordon B. Keylon
May 16, 1903
Apr. 1, 1928
25 yrs.
"Again we hope to meet thee,
when the days of life are fled,
and in Heaven with joy to
greet thee, where no farewell
tears are shed."

S. H. Keylon
May 2, 1877
July 9, 1926
54 yrs.
"Beloved Father, farewell."

BOLES

Muriel Boles
Oct. 30, 1916
Dec. 6, 1935
19 yrs.

FRIENDSHIP GRAVEYARD

Burke Wright
Nov. 27, 1915
Dec. 6, 1935

Our daughter
Arzona Gladman - At rest.
July 23, 1883
Jan. 12, 1913
"She sleeps with Jesus."

Father - Wm. Gladman
Mar. 23, 1840
Aug. 9, 1913
"At rest. My husband
dwells with the Savior."

Arch Boyd Boles
Aug. 19, 1918
Aug. 5, 1934
16 yrs.
"A sunbeam from the world,
has vanished."

Pearl
Daughter of
M. A. & Betty Granfill
Feb. 23, 1893
Jan. 31, 1923
"Weep not Father and Mother
for me, for I am waiting in
glory for thee."

NEWMAN

Carder M. Newman
Dec. 1, 1927
Mar. 21, 1928
(More than 3 mos.)
"Gone to rest."

Austel M. Newman
May 22, 1906
Mar. 4, 1929
23 yrs.
"Gone, but not forgotten."

Eastland, Henry L.
1857 - 1922
65 yrs.

Wm. R. Clack
Feb. 4, 1839
Apr. 25, 1919
80 yrs.

Sabria C. Clack
Apr. 5, 1849
"Father and Mother,
Heaven has claimed me."

WILSON

Geo. Thomas Wilson
Nov. 27, 1887
July 8, 1911
24 yrs.

Amanda M. Brown
Wife of
Dr. W. M. Wilson
Apr. 1, 1848
Dec. 8, 1929
81 yrs.
"Her children rise up and
call her blessed."

Dr. W. M. Wildon
Oct. 1, 1831
Dec. 26, 1909
78 yrs.

John Franklin
Son of
Dr. W. M. and Amanda M. Wilson
Apr. 25, 1876
June 17, 1890
14 yrs.

Sallie
Wife of
J. R. Wilson
Jan. 10, 1889
Apr. 15, 1919

Baby
Born and died
Apr. 15, 1919

Rhea County, Tennessee, Tombstone Inscriptions

FRIENDSHIP CEMETERY
(Continued)

CUNNINGHAM

Laura Cunningham
Nov. 17, 1872
June 25, 1905
"We will meet again."
33 yrs.

James Cunningham
Feb. 28, 1832
Oct. 26, 1902

Catherine Cunningham
Aug. 15, 1843
Feb. 15, 1909
"They are gone, yet not forgotten."

J. C.
Son of
C. L. & L. M. Roberson
Sept. 18, 1902
Sept. 18, 1918

Aunt Mary Roberson
Mar. 19, 1835
Nov. 10, 1913
78 yrs.
"None knew thee, but to love thee."

EWING
Father and Mother
A. C. Ewing
Feb. 24, 1837
Mar. 19, 1916
79 yrs.
"Sinner, saved by grace."

Sara Fine Ewing
July 7, 1841
Apr. 17, 1915
"Thy will of God, be done."

PRICE

G. S. Price
Jan. 4, 1848

Mary, wife of
G. S. Price
Nov. 7, 1848 - Mar. 26, 1920

Father and Mother McCuiston
(No dates.)

Dolly McCuiston
Oct. 5, --
Aug. 15, --
Age 10 mos. 9 das.

Nellie McNeal
Oct. 21, 1886
United in marriage to
Caleb McCuiston
May 1, 1903
Dec. 19, 1918
32 yrs. old
(She wanted the children to meet her in Heaven.)

A. J. Stinecipher
July 20, 1867
Mar. 15, 1924
55 yrs.
"Gone, but not forgotten."

Amanda J.
Wife of
A. J. Stinecipher
Mar. 4, 1877
Mar. 18, 1917
40 yrs.

Walter
son of
Smith & Harriet Brady
Jan. 13, 1879
Aug. 23, 1906
27 yrs. old.
(Mason.)
"tho' lost to memory dear come ye blessed."

Will Brady
Son of
Smith and Harriet Brady
Feb. 18, 1870
Apr. 11, 1906
"Gone, but not forgotten."
Age 36

Rhea County, Tennessee, Tombstone Inscriptions

FRIENDSHIP CEMETERY

Harriet Brady
Wife of Smith Brady
Apr. 29, 1838
Dec. 19, 1918
Age 80 yrs. 7 mos. 20 dys.
"Asleep in Jesus,
Blessed sleep from
which none ever wake
to weep."

Smith Brady
Jan. 11, 1827
Aug. 5, 1904
Age 77 yrs.

Jack Smith
Infant son of
Charles and CleoButter
June 31, 1916

C. L. McElwee
Oct. 4, 1849
Jan. 9, 1931
82 yrs.

Mary A. Gibson
His wife
Apr. 22, 1858

Mattie McElwee
Wife of
Frank Sedman
(Holy Bible engraved.)
Jan. 3, 1883
Sept. 14, 1908
25 yrs.
"Thy will be done."

John R.
Son of
C. L. and Mary McElwee
May 28, 1886
Jan. 22, 1909
23 yrs.
"Thy will be done."

Moss, Lillie May

McElwee, Moss
May 2, 1891
Jan. 19, 1925
34 yrs.
"She was the sunshine
of our home."

Bessie L.
Wife of
Martin Brown
Aug. 24, 1886
Apr. 5, 1911
25 yrs.
"Gone, but not forgotten."

BROWN

Maudie L.
Daughter of
Martin and Bessie Brown
Jan. 9, 1909
July 25, 1911

Marie
Daughter of
Martin and Bessie Brown
Dec. 21, 1907
Apr. 9, 1908

Margaret Lee
Daughter of
Martin and Mae Brown
July 3, 1913
July 24, 1913

Bessie
Daughter of
Martin and May Brown
Nov. 12, 1914
Dec. 14, 1914

Eugene Franklin
Son of
Martin and May Brown
Feb. 28, 1920
Sept. 20, 1920
"Our darling."

RHEA COUNTY

TOMBSTONE INSCRIPTIONS
GARGAN CEMETERY

The Gargan Cemetery is five miles south of Dayton. Follow the old Graysville Highway, going to Graysville which is five miles south of Dayton. Cross the Railroad at Graysville between the Railroad and the creek on the left hand side of the road. There are forty unmarked graves. The land belongs to Russells.

RHEA COUNTY

TOMBSTONE INSCRIPTIONS
GARRISON CEMETERY

Located 5 miles southeast of Dayton in suburb Garrison. In the 4th. District of Rhea County. Leave main Highway at Sanitary Grocery store in South Dayton; go east, traveling on Blythes Ferry road. This Cemetery is about ½ mile off this road and on the left hand side of road, opposite what is known as "Garrison Bluff." It is about 1½ mile beyond the Garrison School house. A great number of the graves have no tombstones, and is grown over with vines and shrubbery.

Martha Dunn
April 12, 1891
June 21, 1917
"Gone but bot forgotten."

Albert Stice Dunn
1912 - 1930

Sarah H. Gill
Wife of
W. A. Gill
April 10, 1886
Nov. 30, 1914

Lucy Roberts
(?)

Mrs. W. H. Wampler
Died May 2, 1934

E. S. Cox
Nov. 25, 1860
Sept. 11, 1925

Dixie C.
Wife of
W. F. Jewell
Dec. 12, 1895
April 18, 1930

Agnes Genevia Swafford
May 1, 1923
Feb. 15, 1924
"Safe in the arms of Jesus."

Alvin Gill
April 19, 1895
Tennessee Prot., 4 Pioneer Inf.
Oct. 12, 1918

John Gill
(?)

Crockett Corvin
April 27, 1927
Aged 68 years

Robt. Turner
Jan. 29, 1928
Aged 19 yrs. 10 mos. 18 days

Mrs. Savana McClandon
Jan. 20, 1928
Aged 69 yrs.

Oleva
Wife of S. E. Turner
Sept. 23, 1890
Dec. 13, 1918

Steve Edward Turner
Oct. 23, 1936
Aged 53 years.

William D.
Son of
Henry & Narcis Starns
Aug. 30, 1863
Aged 1 yr. 10 ms. 1 day

Infant son of
Henry & Narcis Starns
Jan. 1, 1864
Aged 4 ms. & 3 ds.

Nancy Jane Sexton
Wife of
J. P. Sexton
Maryed Nov. 8, 1879
Dyed March 10 --

2
GARRISON CEMETERY

Martha E. Sexton
Wife of
J. P. Sexton
Mared May 16, 1880
Jan. 29, 1895

Ellen
Wife of
J. P. Sexton
Mairyed Jan. 9, 1896
Dec. 25, 1922

Corp'l. Robt. T. Sexton
135 Co., U. S. C. A.
Corps
July 30, 1887
Aug. 13, 1913

Chas. W. King Smedley
Feb. 10, 1897
Feb. 5, 1899

Carl H. Smedley
April 26, 1893
March 28, 1896

Mamie B. Smedley
March 5, 1895
Nov. 16, 1895

RHEA COUTNY

TOMBSTONE INSCRIPTIONS
GASS FAMILY GRAVEYARD

Formerly Gass Farm, now owned by Brown Spears, second District. Get on Dixie Highway at Dayton, come 13 miles north, crossing Clear Creek, about 1 mile north of Clear Creek is the Brown Spear's Farm. Right in front yard at his home is the family graveyard. Col. W. T. Gass, an old Civil War Veteran is buried there. After the close of the Civil War, Col. Gass practiced Law in Rhea County for 30 or 40 years. His office building now stands in the front yard of the Brown Spear's home. Brown Spears married the Col's. daughter and she is also buried there. Two graves covered over with limestone slabs. No names or dates. Probably 6 graves unnames or dated.

Col. W. T. Gass
Civil war Veteran
Southern Soldier
or Col. (Mason.)
Sept. 5, 1921
Apr. 17, 1906

Bessie
Daughter of
J. B. and Adelia C. Spears
      (?)

Jacob A.
Son of
J. B. and Adelia C. Spears
Double tombstones.

1

RHEA COUNTY

TOMBSTONE INSCRIPTIONS
GASS COLORED GRAVEYARD

Old slaves and children of slaves buried there. This graveyard is ¼ mile back south of Spear's home in Cedar Hill. Probably 25 graves undated or marked.

Rhea County, Tennessee, Tombstone Inscriptions

RHEA COUNTY

TOMBSTONE INSCRIPTIONS
THE GIBSON GRAVEYARD

1st. District on the Burns farm. Get on the Dixie Highway at Dayton, go north 18 miles to Spring City, continue north about 3 miles to the Parham or Burns farm. Back in a little hill near the mountain, you will find the Gibson Graveyard.

Top of stone - "At rest."
Jesse Parham
Nov. 9, 1855
Jan. 3, 1929
74 yrs.
"Gone but not forgotten."

Martha C.
Wife of
Jesse Parham
June 5, 1859
June 12, 1923
64 yrs.
"A devoted christian wife and Mother, her work lives on."

DAVENPORT

Moses Davenport
Mar. 20, 1865
July 11, 1927

Lucy Davenport
May 6, 1880
July 9, 1926

Lucinda C.
Wife of
E. S. Evans
Jan. 27, 1845
Aug. 29, 1873

GIBSON

Jacob Gibson
June 4, 1814
Nov. 12, 1862
48 yrs.

Mary Ann
Wife of Jacob Gibson
Mar. 16, 1814 - Jan. 16, 1866
52 yrs. old

Earnest S.
Son of
C. C. and J. E. Gibson
Sept. 17, 1882
Dec. 22, 1884
2 yrs.
"And they shall be mine, saith the Lord of Hosts in that day, when I make up my jewels."

G. C. Gibson
Nov. 15, 1838
Mar. 14, 1888
50 yrs. old.

Jane Gibson
Mar. 29, 1846
Mar. 7, 1898

Wm. W. Cash
1821 - 1896
75 yrs. old

In memory of
Lucinda S.
Wife of
Wm. W. Cash
June 3, 1826
Nov. 29, 1885

Sarah Ann
Daughter of
Wm. W. Cash & Lucinda Cash
Mar. 15, 1859
June 23, 1878
"In my hand, no price I bring, simply to thy cross I cling."

Canzada Dorton
Wife of
J. C. Gibson
July 20, 1874
July 4, 1910
"Gone, but not forgotten."

THE GIBSON GRAVEYARD

Lorinda J. Cantrell
Wife of
T. E. Gibson
Dec. 8, 1865
Dec. 11, 1890
25 yrs. old
"Gone, but not forgotten."

Ollie Theodore
Daughter of
T. E. and L. J. Gibson
Aug. 2, 1886
Jan. 3, 1887
10 mos.
"A little bud of love,
to bloom with God above."

Probably 20 unmarked graves in this graveyard. Grave yard in fairly good condition.

1

RHEA COUNTY

TOMBSTONE INSCRIPTIONS
GILE'S FAMILY GRAVEYARD

Go north from Dayton on the State Highway to Carp Schoolhouse about 15 miles, turning west on the old Stage road. Continue for about a mile to the Mitchell farm, now owned by Tom Mitchell. There are about 8 graves, and has been abandoned for several years.

RHEA COUNTY

TOMBSTONE INSCRIPTIONS
GILBREATH CEMETERY

The Gilbreath Cemetery is five miles southwest of Dayton. Follow Highway No. 30 from Dayton one and a half mile. Leave the Highway and take gravel road south for three miles taking road west one half mile to Gilbreath Cemetery. There are five unmarked graves. The land belongs to Clifts.

RHEA COUNTY

TOMBSTONE INSCRIPTIONS
GILLESPIE GRAVEYARD

On river road, one mile north of Iron Hill Church, about 22 miles north of Washington Ferry, go north from Dayton on the State Highway to Jinney Wallace farm, turning east on the river road. Continue up Tennessee river 1 mile north of Iron Hill Church. Turn to the right ¼ mile to a large gate on the hill. Five Prehistoric mounds stand nearby in the field. This was a family graveyard, and was abandoned years ago. A strong iron fence surrounds it, underpined by heavy limestone posts and limestone base at gate and corners. One of the most famous families in Rhea County is buried there. No one has been buried there for eighty years. It was formerly the Gillespie farm.

GILLESPIE

Sacred to the memory of
Thos. J. Gillespie
Apr. 22, 1805
June 30, 1857
Age 52.
"Life's severance is best
eternal union."

Wm. N. Gillespie
July 28, 1803
Oct. 16, 1840
Age 37.

Geo. Gillespie
June 17, 1767
Oct. 18, 1840
73 yrs.

Anna Gillespie
Feb. 1, 1782
Sept. 18, 1840
58 yrs.

Jane H. Blain
Oct. 9, 1809
May 13, 1846
37 yrs.

Thomas G. Blain
July 18, 1833
Oct. 31, 1842
9 yrs.

John R. Blain
Feb. 2, 1836
Apr. 1, 1836
2 mos.

James H. Blain, Jr.
Aug. 6, 1843
Sept. 15, 1844
1 yr. 1 mo.

Jane H. Blain, Jr.
1846 -
July 9, 1846
1 yr.

This graveyard is 24 X 40 ft. Is in very good condition. Two graves with no markers. Beautiful shrubbery and crepe myrtle. Also large cedars.

Rhea County, Tennessee, Tombstone Inscriptions

RHEA COUNTY

TOMBSTONE INSCRIPTIONS
THE GILLIAM GRAVEYARD

Get on the Lon Foust or Dixie Highway at Dayton, go north to Spring City 18 miles, then go 3 miles on the same road to the McCawood crossing, turn east going by the St. Clair Church and school house, then follow the same road and direction for more than another mile. Here, upon a hill to the left of this road, you will find the Gilliam graveyard. Two very large stone slabs over two graves not dated and no names.

Mother -
Margaret, wife of
William Ketchersid
May 31, 1851
Jan. 14, 1920
"She was a kind and
affectionate wife,
a fond mother, and
a friend to all."

Lucinda Marrs
Dec. 26, 1852
July 12, 1913
"She believed and
sleeps in Jesus."

Aaron Marrs
Feb. 12, 1824
Nov. 17, 1914
Age 90
"Asleep in Jesus,
blesses thought."

Delila Marrs
Oct. 23, 1827
Dec. 13, 1912
Age 85

Nancy Ann
Daughter of
Aaron and Delila Ann Marrs
July 1, 1862
Apr. 21, 1905
43 yrs. old - Member of
Rebecca Lodge. Professed
religion at 15 yrs. of age.
Joined the M. E. Church, South
and lived a devoted christian
life, 'till death. "The Lord
giveth, and the Lord taketh away,
blessed be the name of the Lord."

"Come ye Blessed."
Dr. G. R. Brown
Feb. 24, 1831
July 29, 1909
78 yrs.

Francina Mitchell
Mar. 28, 1793
June 17, 1853
Age 60

Chas. Mitchell
Apr. 2, 1786
Aug. 9, 1840
54 yrs.

Three graves covered with large sandstone slabs. No dates or names given.

In memory of
Nathaniel M. Gilliam
Mar. 10, 1790
Nov. 29, 1869
79 yrs.

Sallie
Wife of
N. M. Gilliam
Age 84 yrs.
"Asleep in Jesus."

Sewell A.
Son of
J. D. and S. A. Gilliam
Dec. 25, 1875
Nov. 14, 1876
"Darling, we miss thee."
(Large slab also.)

THE GILLIAM GRAVEYARD

GILLIAM

J. D. Gilliam
Aug. 29, 1824
Nov. 7, 1907
83 yrs.

S. A. Gilliam
Wife of
J. D. Gilliam
Feb. 24, 1841
Jan. 16, 1884
"Weep not for they are at rest."

1

RHEA COUNTY

TOMBSTONE INSCRIPTIONS
GRAVETT FAMILY CEMETERY

The Gravett family Cemetery is three miles and one half north of Dayton. Follow Highway No. 27 from Dayton going to the Thomason farm which is three miles north of Dayton. Leave the Highway at the Thomason farm and take the road east for one half mile to the Gravett farm. There are two graves. The land belongs to the Gravetts.

Noah Gravett

Vinie Gravett

1

RHEA COUNTY

TOMBSTONE INSCRIPTIONS
HALL FAMILY CEMETERY

The Hall family Cemetery is one and a half miles southeast of Dayton. Follow the Armstrong Ferry road. After crossing the Broyles Branch which is in South Dayton, take the road leading south which is called the Mailey Hollow Road. Keep the Mailey Hollow Road which leads to the Hall farm, thereby the Cemetery is located. The land belongs to the Halls. There are four unmarked graves.

Roy Hall P. V. T. 155 Depot Brig. Apr. 13, 1935	Mrs. Minnie Hall F. Hall Died 1920
Mary Hall Died Aug. 5 – Age 43	Lester Hall
Mother – Sally Hall Died Jan. 1, 1933	Mary Hall Died 1913 Age 40 yrs.

RHEA COUNTY

TOMBSTONE INSCRIPTIONS
HERSE CEMETERY

The Herse Cemetery is nine miles northeast of Dayton. From Dayton take Highway # 27 going by Evensville. Take the old Washington road to White Flat, then take left gravel road to Smyrna Church, going by Smyrna Cemetery, traveling two miles to Cat Hollow road. The land belong to the Herses. There are twenty one unmarked graves.

Mr. Lee Smith
Soddy, Tenn.
Mar. 28, 1908
Sept. 15, 1934
Aged 26 yrs. 5 mos. 18 days.

Pelfrey

Ovie Pelfrey
Oct. 7, 1907
April 21, 1911

Little Margaret Burdett
Dec. 12, 1934
Feb. 26, 1937
Age 2 yrs. 2 mos. 14 days.
"Our little darling how we miss you."

T. H. Burdett
Aug. 12, 1875
Oct. 22, 1918

RHEA COUTNY

TOMBSTONE INSCRIPTIONS
HICKEY COMMUNITY GRAVEYARD
(COLORED)

From Rhea Springs, take the State Highway about 3 miles to a colored community called Hickey town. Here you will find what is known as the Hickey graveyard. It is located on Andy Hickey's farm, not far from his residence. This graveyard contains twenty two graves, without names or dates. Is rather new and very well kept.

Florence Wife of G. W. Doughty June 11, 1887 Jan. 16, 1929 "Asleep in Jesus."	Condon Ray Dec. 20, 1914 Jan. 20, 1915
Kendall Hickey May 4, 1904 July 27, 1927 "In his care."	Twin baby – 1 month old buried here.
Froston D. Hickey Feb. 14, 1861 March 28, 1928 "Asleep in Jesus."	

RHEA COUNTY

TOMBSTONE INSCRIPTIONS
HICKMOTT FAMILY CEMETERY

The Hickmott Family Cemetery is three miles and one half west of Dayton. Follow Highway No. 30 from Dayton going to the top of the Cove Hill which is two miles from Dayton. Leave the Highway, going to the Williams place. There is one grave. At the time the person was buried the place belonged to Hickmotts. The land is now owned by Billie Williams.

1

RHEA COUNTY

TOMBSTONE INSCRIPTIONS
HIGH POINT CHURCH GRAVEYARD

2 District. Get on Dixie Highway or Highway 27. Go north 12 miles to Brown Spear's Farm, turn east on High Point road, go east to High Point church and school house. Just back of this church in little lot there are three graves.

Rev. Homer Chambers
July 14, 1881
Aug. 12, 1922 - Graves of two of his children's names and dates are
 not given.

1

RHEA COUNTY

TOMBSTONE INSCRIPTIONS
HILTON CEMETERY

The Hilton Cemetery is twelve miles northwest of Dayton. Follow Highway No. 27 from Dayton going to Evensville which is six miles north of Dayton. Go two miles north of Evensville leaving the Highway and taking the road west. The Cemetery is in the woods. The owner of the land is unknown. There are sixteen unmarked graves.

A. J. Hilton
1849 -
May 8, 1903

Irva Hilton
1843 -
Oct. 6, 1901

Rhea County, Tennessee, Tombstone Inscriptions

RHEA COUNTY

TOMBSTONE INSCRIPTIONS
THE HINDES GRAVEYARD

Get on the Dixie Highway at Dayton, come north 18 miles to Spring City, then two miles further north to the Mullenex farm, west of the Railroad near the mountain, you will find the Hindes graveyard.

A. J. Evans
Nov. 22, 1849
Mar. 16, 1818
"He is not dead, but sleepeth."

Son of
M. & Chas. Evans
Born & died
May 5, 1906
"Budded on earth
to bloom in Heaven."

F. E. Hinds
(Holy Bible engraved.)
Dec. 12, 1853
Feb. 23, 1875
"I have fought a good fight,
I have kept the faith."

S. L.
Wife of
R. D. Hindes
Apr. 20, 1827
Dec. 27, 1904
77 yrs. old.
"Not lost, but gone before."

R. D. Hindes
Aug. 30, 1826
Mar. 31, 1926
Age 99 yrs. 7 mos. 1 da.
"At rest."

(About 30 graves, only 5 or 6 of them dated.)

Hindes Grave yard, very well kept.

1

RHEA COUNTY

TOMBSTONE INSCRIPTIONS
HOLLAND AND GODBY GRAVEYARD

District No. 2. Go north on the Dixie Highway for 13 miles to Clear Creek, then continue north to the Brown Spear's farm, then turn east to the Wolf Creek Road for about 4 miles to the old Allen-Godby farm. Here you will find the Holland and Godby graveyard. There are four unmarked graves. This graveyard is on the old Allen Godby farm.

E. M. Holland 1844 - 1848	Thomas Godby and Wife, Sabilla Taylor
M. A. Holland 1845 - 1869	(No dates.)

RHEA COUNTY

TOMBSTONE INSCRIPTIONS
JOHN HOLLOWAY FAMILY GRAVEYARD

John Holloway and his wife are buried here. No names or dates are inscribed. It is located north of Dayton on State Highway about 14 miles. Turn east on the Dividneg Ridge. On the top of this ridge on the old John Holloway farm and near the old homestead, you will find these graves.

RHEA COUNTY

TOMBSTONE INSCRIPTIONS
HOWERTON CEMETERY

The Howerton Cemetery is seven miles north of Dayton. Leave Dayton on Highway # 27 going by Evensville. It is about one mile from Evensville. This is a very old Cemetery, and there is no road from the Highway to the Cemetery. The land belongs to Darwins. There are thirty one unmarked graves.

Susan J. Hicks
June 26, 1859
Jan. 1, 1877

Joseph Hicks
Mar. 5, 1799
Oct. 1, 1863

Jane Howerton
Apr. 30, 1809
Jan. 16, 1881

Micajah Howerton
Sept. 22, 1793
Aug. 21, 1870

Elizabeth A. Howerton
Dec. 29, 1864
Aug. 2, 1840

Grief Howerton
Feb. 6, 1755
Nov. 21, 1827

Jane Brown
Sept. 15, 1847
Aged 80 yrs.

Prickett

Our Mother-
C. A. Prickett
Mar. 27, 1826
Nov. 17, 1899
"Sleep on dear one
and take thy rest
God called thee home,
He thought it best."

West

Carrie West
Oct. 20, 1936
Aged 45 years.

Rhea County, Tennessee, Tombstone Inscriptions

RHEA COUNTY

HUGHES CEMETERY

Hughes Cemetery is located on the mountain about six miles north of Dayton. Follow Highway # 30 to the top of mountain, turning to the left on the gravel road. Three graves are under a lone pine tree on the Colvin farm. There are three rocks with E. H., one with J. E. A. H. and one with T. Two of those boys were hanged in Scottsboro, Alabama. They were accused of burning a barn. Lawyer Nick Allen went down there to defend them, and the people refused to listen to anything he had to say. The Sheriff had to guard him to the train, so they hung the boys and sent them back to Dayton, Tennessee. They were taken to the mountain on an ox wagon and their father walked. Mr. Hughes wanted to see them, so Mr. Marion Snow opened the casket and took the black caps off their faces. Rev. Howard conducted their funeral services. Later a man confessed he was the one who did the crime. Their sister Ettie is buried by the side of them. Their names were Tobe and Asberry Hughes. It happened about fifty years ago.

COPIED BY;
FLOYD POOLE
RHEA COUNTY
DAYTON, TENNESSEE

Oct. 14, 1937

1

RHEA COUNTY

TOMBSTONE INSCRIPTIONS
HURST GRAVEYARD

District No. 1. This graveyard is on the old Wallace True's farm, and is out in an open field about 200 yards from Wallace True's home on the Toe String road. Go north from Dayton on Dixie Highway about 18 miles to Spring City turning east on Highway No. 68, then go east to ¼ mile past Rhea Springs, turning north on Toe String road. From there it is about 3½ miles to the Wallace True farm, and to this graveyard. There are about 16 graves without markers. No fence and is badly grown up.

Elijah Burnett
May 29, 1828
July 20, 1859
Age 31 yrs.
"Gone, but not forgotten."

Granville Hurst
Sept. 17, 1838
Mar. 2, 1883
Age 45 yrs.
"Gone, but not forgotten."

Mary Elizabeth
Wife of
Granville Hurst
July 15, 1846
Nov. 14, 1848
"Gone, but not gorgotten."

Rhea County, Tennessee, Tombstone Inscriptions

RHEA COUNTY

TOMBSTONE INSCRIPTIONS
INGLE GRAVEYARD

The old Ingle farm now belongs to a person whose name is Steincipher. To reach this graveyard, go north from Dayton on the Lon Foust Highway about 24 miles to Cawood R. R. Crossing, turning east 1 mile to St. Clair Church, then turn south on the Muddy Creek road and go two miles to the Kris Kimmer farm, from there going ½ mile to the Elbert Ingle home.

Jesse J. Ingle
May 17, 1824
July 24, 1890
66 yrs.
(Hand clasp engraved.)
"Farewell, not lost but gone before."

M. A. Ingle
Wife of
Jesse J. Ingle
Feb. 23, 1826
Sept. 22, 1892
(Hand clasp engraved.)
"Asleep in Jesus, blessed thought."

Stella
Daughter of
T. H. and Van Ingle
Nov. 18, 1888
Aug. 21, 1896

Ella
Daughter of
T. H. and Van Ingle
Apr. 2, 1873
Aug. 8, 1891
18 yrs.
"We loved them, yes we loved them, but the angels loved them more, and they have sweetly called them to yonder shining."

Beloved -
S. E. Ingle
Her husband, W. S. Hallock
Captain in Civil War.
Co. e - 13 Mosouri Cav.

E. M. Ingle
June 2, 1859
May 6, 1885
26 years.
"In my hands, no price I bring, humbly to thy cross I cling."

Myrtle Lee Hinds
1900 - 1901
"A good wife and Mother."

Louisa McClendon
June 10, 1857
May 8, 1925
(Was married Aug., 1908
Age 67 yrs. 10 mos.

There are four graves, unmarked.

1

RHEA COUNTY

TOMBSTONE INSCRIPTIONS
IRLAND CEMETERY

The Irland Cemetery is ten miles east of Dayton. Follow Highway No. 30 from Dayton going three miles. Leave Highway and take the graveled road northeast going four miles to the Cemetery. The land belongs to the Montgomerys. There are five unmarked graves.

IRLAND

J. E. Irland
Born 1832
Nov. 8, 1903

Martha A. Irland
1842 –
Jan. 6, 1901

B. W. Irland
1834 –
June 5, 1900

RHEA COUNTY

TOMBSTONE INSCRIPTIONS
JARGAS CEMETERY

The Jargas Cemetery is twelve miles northeast of Dayton. Follow Highway No. 30 from Dayton going four miles. Leave Highway and take the road north. The land belongs to the McCormics. There are five unmarked graves.

Fred Jargas Sept. 1833 Apr. 6, 1895	J. N. McMary
T. E. Marlin Jan. 5, 1795 May 7, 1863	

1

RHEA COUNTY

TOMBSTONE INSCRIPTIONS
JENKIN'S CEMETERY

The Jenkins Cemetery is thirteen miles northwest of Dayton. Follow Highway No. 30 from Dayton going six miles.. Leave Highway and take the road north seven miles. The land belongs to Mr. Housley. There are twelve unmarked graves.

N. E. Jenkins   :   E. A. Jackson
1823 - 1899   :

1

RHEA COUNTY

TOMBSTONE INSCRIPTIONS
JOHNSON CEMETERY

The Johnson Cemetery is five miles south of Dayton. Follow Highway from Dayton which goes to Graysville, going by the Johnson Place. There are five graves or more. The land belongs to Johnsons.

1

RHEA COUNTY

TOMBSTONE INSCRIPTIONS
JONES CEMETERY

The Jones Cemetery is three miles northwest of Dayton. Follow Highway No. 30 from Dayton going to Morgantown which is one mile from Dayton. Leave the Highway at Morgantown and take the gravel road north going to the old T. C. Mines. The Cemetery is a negro Cemetery and is on top of a hill to the right.. There are a few rocks, but none have markers. There are about eighteen or more graves. The land belongs to the Dayton Coal and Iron Company.

RHEA COUNTY

TOMBSTONE INSCRIPTIONS
KERLEY CEMETERY

The Kerley Cemetery is nine miles east of Dayton going out Highway # 30. From Dayton go three miles leaving the Highway taking the Port Ferry road. The Cemetery is near the cotton port Ferry. There are twenty three unmarked graves in this Cemetery. The land belongs to Fariser.

Holy Bible -	Willard F. Kerley
John A. Kerley	Son of
Sept. 21, 1863	D. L. & I. M. C. Kerley
Feb. 10, 1899	Jan. 16, 1878
"Not lost blest thought	May 5, 1878
but gone before, where	"Gone but not forgotten."
we shall meet, to part	
no more."	

Rhea County, Tennessee, Tombstone Inscriptions

RHEA COUNTY

TOMBSTONE INSCRIPTIONS
KIRKLAND COMMUNITY GRAVEYARD

Follow the Lon Foust Highway from Dayton north to White's Creek about 25 miles, turn west a few hundred yards to White's Creek Railroad bridge. Just near the bridge in the woodland, you will find the above named graveyard. This is a very old graveyard and is now abandoned.

John F. Thompson
Feb. 12, 1816
May 8, 1816
"Time how short,
eternity, how long."

Nathan Whittenberg
Dec. 16, 1816
Feb. 25, 1892
76 yrs.

M. J. Whittenberg
Nov. 10, 1862
Nov. 12, 1890
28 yrs.

Kirkland family plot.
Six graves in a row.
Concrete wall around.

KIRKLAND

Mary M.
Daughter of
A. L. & M. M. Kirkland
Sept. 15, 1854
Jan. 22, 1888
34 yrs.

Crawford, H.
Son of
A. L. & M. M. Kirkland
Feb. 14, 1849
July 5, 1873
24 yrs.

Catherine McDaniels
Sept. 17, 1851
Dec. 14, 1932
81 yrs.

A. L. Kirkland
Feb. 14, 1818
June 26, 1900
82 yrs.
"There in no parting
in heaven."

Mary M.
Wife of
A. L. Kirkland
April 4, 1813
May 20, 1883
70 yrs.
"My faith looks up to thee."

Minerva J.
Daughter of
A. L. & M.M. Kirkland
Mar. 24, 1857
May 15, 1888
31 yrs.

Effie Bean
Oct. 17, 1881
Nov. 23, 1882
Age 1 year, 1 mo.

Anna, Daughter of
Joseph & Mala Brandon
Sept. 15, 1886
Dec. 16, 1886
3 mos. 1 da.

George M.
Son of
J. T. & S. Bean
Apr. 2, 1880
Oct. 6, 1882
2 yrs.

Rhea County, Tennessee, Tombstone Inscriptions

2.

KIRKLAND COMMUNITY GRAVEYARD

Infant son of
J. T. & S. Bean
   (?)

Geo. M. Bean
Aug. 8, 1858
July 6, 1880
22 yrs.

Josie Bean
Aug. 13, 1854
Mark - Bean
Dates worn away.

Geo. M. Bean
Aug. 12, 1862

Lizzie Montgomery
Daughter of
D. & M. Montgomery
June 28, 1867
Jan. 5, 1900
33 yrs.

David Montgomery
Aug. 16, 1842
June 19, 1879
37 yrs.

Rachel E. Brandon
Mar. 13, 1844
Mar. 30, 1875
31 yrs.

Judith Ann Brandon
Sept. 18, 1824
Apr. 19, 1870

Twenty graves with large
sand head stones. No
names or dates.

Nancy Parks
Wife of
Robert Parks
May 6, 1873
Dec. 19, 1847

Large sandstone slab on top of rock wall. Slab 6 by 12 ft.

RHEA COUNTY

TOMBSTONE INSCRIPTIONS
KIUKIA CEMETERY

Located about four miles west of Dayton on Walden's Ridge. Situated about 1 mile off, and to the right of the mountain road from Dayton to Pikeville near the Bledsoe and Rhea County line, and in 4th. District of Rhea County. Very well kept and most graves have tombstones. Public Cemetery.

William Jesse Reed
July 18, 1903
Dec. 4, 1935
"Beloved one farewell."

Calvin Gerald
Son of
John & Melvia Reed
Sept. 16, 1935
Jan. 3, 1936

James A.
Son of
N. R. & Lillie Reed
Aug. 13, 1914
Sept. 26, 1920

N. R. Reed
July 15, 1879
Feb. 11, 1932

Darius Franklin Morgan
March 3, 1884
March 26, 1936
"His toils are past, His work is done, He fought the fight, the victory won. United mine workers of America. 5899.

J. T. Elder
(?)

J. T. Wright
April, 1871
May 27, 1901
"He was faithful and God has said, He that endureth to the end shall be saved."

J. H. Williams
June 7, 1857
March 17, 1912

Henrietta
His wife
Nov. 25, 1836
March 24, 1914

OLINGER

Henry B. Olinger
Jan. 30, 1884
Jan. 12, 1904

Arbell Olinger
Oct. 30, 1840
Nov. 13, 1915

John Olinger
March 27, 1840
Jan. 26, 1916

James Olinger
Jan. 4, 1934
Age 54 years

Sarah R.
Wife of
E. M. Tallmadge
Aug. 28, 1846
Jan. 10, 1903
"Rest in peace."

S. L. Houser
May 12, 1890
Oct. 1, 1912

GOTHARD

James F. Gothard
June 1, 1883
May 27, 1901

Albert E. Gothard
Jan. 7, 1885
May 27, 1901

Rhea County, Tennessee, Tombstone Inscriptions

KIUKIA CEMETERY

MORGAN

Mrs. Martha Morgan
July 10, 1934
Aged 84 years, 6 months, 20 days.

John Morgan
Tennessee P. V. T. 105(?) Engrs.
May 14, 1932

J. W. Curtain
June 19, 1928
Age 50

WALKER

B. H. Walker
Feb. 22, 1891
Oct. 28, 1918

W. M. G. Walker
Sept. 22, 1837
June 12, 1913

Alsie Jane Walker
July 13, 1849
Dec. 29, 1902

Walker, R. F.
Feb. 11, 1877
Feb. 22, 1891

Eddie
Son of
W. H. & Lizzie Walker
May 27, 1905
Oct. 15, 1906

Jessie
Son of
W. H. & Lizzie Walker
July 4, 1895
Oct. 15, 1896

Samuel Burwick
June 18, 1868
May 27, 1901
"Beloved one farewell."

Infant son of
S. H. & M. J. Burwick
Born & died
Aug. 22, 1891

Mrs. Effie Johnson
Nov. 14, 1936
Aged 46 years, 8 months, 28 days.

REED

Wm. H.
Son of R. L. & Alice Reed
Born & died
Feb. 17, 1902

Love (?) R. L. Reed
April 11, 1877
Nov. 6, 1909

CARTER

D. T. Carter
March 11, 1887
May 21, 1901

Tommy Carter
March 11, 1889
May 27, 1901

WALKER

O. F. Walker
Sept. 25, 1852
May 27, 1901

J. F. Walker
Sept. 25, 1856
May 27, 1901

C. A. Walker
May 11, 1816
Jan. 22, 1892

PICKETT

C. F. Pickett
May 1, 1891
Jan. 18, 1892

M. D. Pickett
Wife of
J. F. Pickett
July 24, 1853
Nov. 20, 1905

ROGERS

Oscar Rogers
Jan. 5, 1878
May 27, 1901
"May he find joy in the life everlasting."

Rhea County, Tennessee, Tombstone Inscriptions

KIUKIA CEMETERY

L. G. Rogers
June 10, 1851
May 27, 1901

Mrs. I. J. Oldham
April 24, 1840
June 25, 1873

Emma C. Childress
Wife of
J. M. B. Headler
July 5, 1865
March 3, 1922

Robert Earl Headler
Sept. 3, 1891
Aug. 13, 1898

Louisa Headler
May 31, 1853
Feb. 4, 1904

1

RHEA COUNTY

TOMBSTONE INSCRIPTIONS
LAWSON FAMILY CEMETERY

The Lawson Cemetery is eleven miles northwest of Dayton. Follow Highway No. 30 from Dayton going six miles. Leave the Highway and take road north going five miles to Cemetery. There are five or more unmarked graves. The land belongs to Lawson.

Dave L. Lawson
1796 - 1853

Annie Lawson
1803 -
June 7, 1854

Rhea County, Tennessee, Tombstone Inscriptions

RHEA COUNTY

TOMBSTONE INSCRIPTIONS
LEUTY GRAVEYARD

This is a very old graveyard in District No. 2, on the Chas. Wassom farm. A number of stones are broken and torn down, and same has not been well kept. No burials here of late date. Probably 75 unmarked graves. Go one mile east from Spring City to Midway.

Maggie Jones
Daughter of
M. M. and G. W. Jones
Oct. 18, 1884
Apr. 12, 1905
"Maggie is gone,
but not forgotten.
She is resting with
the angels."

Cora H. Fillers
Daughter of
G. W. and M. M. Jones
June 19, 1878
May 3, 1902
(Verse not visible.)

Little Gay
Daughter of
G. W. and M. M. Jones
Nov. 8, 1899
Sept. 24, 1903
"Safe in the arms
of Jesus."

PERKINSON

Joel Perkinson
Husband of
H. M. Perkinson
Dec. 23, 1828
Dec. 14, 1892
64 yrs.
(Mason.)
"I have fought a good fight,
I have finished my course."
II Timothy, 4:10

Nancy J. Perkinson
Wife of
W. H. Perkinson
Oct. 1, 1845
Feb. 8, 1914
"Blessed are the pure in heart,
for they shall see God."

Hester
Wife of
James How
June 7, 1883
Dec. 4, 1891

Concrete wall around four graves.
Kelly family plot. No marked
stones.

Maggie C.
Daughter of
Lucy Parks
Nov. 14, 1864
May 1887

T. H. Robinson
May 21, 1842
Dec. 4, 1914

Sarah A. Bryson
Wife of
T. H. Robertson
Aug. 16, 1844
Mar. 16, 1908

Geo. Samuel
Son of
David E. and Sarah E. Gillespie
Aug. 30, 1855
Mar. 27, 1856
7 mos.

UNITY GRAVEYARD

Harvey Robertson
Sept. 19, 1814
Apr. 22, 1889

Mahala Pearson
Wife of
Harvey Robertson
May 17, 1812
Nov. 13, 1905
93 yrs.

Rufus B. Shirley
Dec. 26, 1827
May 7, 1871

Ephraim Kirklin
Son of
R. B. and Malinda Shirley
May 26, 1851
Apr. 18, 1859
8 yrs.

Wm. A. Thompson
Jan. 18, 1848
Aug. 9, 1873

Our Father —
John Thompson
June 4, 1822
Nov. 23, 1883
61 yrs. 5 mos. 19 dys.

Our Mother —
Francis
Wife of
John Thompson
June 14, 1824
Mar. 3, 1888
63 yrs. 8 mos. 19 dys.

E. C. Wright
Feb. 22, '98
July 8, 1898

Wife of
J. M. Wright
Apr. 23, 1872
Jan. 14, 1901

Daniel Broyles
June 10, 1803
Mar. 23, 1881
77 yrs.

Wife of
Daniel Broyles
Sept. 9, 1819
July 21, 1897
77 yrs. 10 mos. 12 dys.
"At rest."

Two infants of
I. N. and M. P. Broyles
(No dates.)

Mary P. Gannaway
Wife of
I. N. Broyles
Jan. 12, 1851
Oct. 13, 1904

Wm. Dagley
Aug. 15, 1818
Dec. 28, 1888
70 yrs.

Amanda Dagley
Mar. 20, 1824
Jan. 15, 1890
56 yrs.
"At rest."

Olive Lyon
Dec. 30, 1807
June 11, 1890
83 yrs.

In memory of
Bertie Barnwell
Age 1 yr. 9 mos.
"Sleeping in Jesus."

Maggie E.
Wife of
J. H. Thomas
Nov. 22, 1862
Oct. 16, 1882
20 yrs.

Rhea County, Tennessee, Tombstone Inscriptions

LENTY GRAVEYARD

Iron fence around Lenty lot. One fourth of graveyard plot.

Burton Virginia Lenty
Daughter of
J. B. and Will Lenty
Mar. 29, 1907
Dec. 14, 1920
13 yrs.
"Sleep sweetly on."

Infant
(New grave. No dates. Number of marked slabs torn down.)

Virginia A. Lenty
Wife of
Burton Lenty
Nov. 5, 1832
Nov. 5, 1902
70 yrs.
"Blessed are the pure in heart, for they shall see God."

Son of
B. M. and M. A. Lenty
Dec. 16, 1861
Mar. 23, 1862

Daughter of
Mar. 16, 1864
Feb. 12, 1866

MCPHERSON

Thomas H. McPherson
Apr. 1, 1831
Jan. 10, 1894
"Rest in peace."

Son of
W. P. and S. A. McPherson
June 2, 1897
Aug. 6, 1898
1 yr. 2 mos.

James D. McPherson
Jan. 18, 1810
Aug. 19, 1892
82 yrs.

Juliett Ann McPherson
July 13, 1811
June 17, 1885

Eddie Lee Foust
Dec. 4, 1874
Aug. 7, 1875
"Sleep on dear babe
and take thy rest,
God called thee home,
He thought it best."

James E. Foust
July 20, 1867
Sept. 4, 1890
"Since thou canst no longer
stay to cheer us with thy face,
we hope to meet thee again,
in yon bright world above."

Geo. W. Foust
May 6, 1844
Mar. 5, 1903
59 yrs.
"Dear one thou hast left us,
yet we hope again to meet,
where no mourning tears are shed."

Mother -
Emma
Wife of
G. W. Foust
Dec. 5, 1845
Sept. 24, 1917
"Asleep in Jesus."

FRANKLIN

B. C. Franklin
Aug. 16, 1804
Jan. 18, 1882
"Sleep on dear husband,
and take thy rest, God called
thee home, He thought it best."
78 yrs.

4

LIBERTY GRAVEYARD
(CONTINUED)

Lydia A.
Wife of
B. C. Franklin
Aug. 3, 1808
Dec. 5, 1893
85 yrs.
"I have fought a good fight,
I have finished my course,
I have kept the faith!"

J. A. Abernathy
Nov. 11, 1849
Sept. 24, 1895
44 yrs.
"Come unto me, all ye
that labor and are
heavy laden, and I
will give you rest."

Permelia G.
Wife of
J. A. Abernathy
July 5, 1852
Nov. 11, 1881
(Mason.)

Rev. Wm. Wiley Neal
Aug. 12, 1824
Jan. 24, 1878
(Licensed to preach
Oct. 6, 1850. Member
of Holston Conference
M. E. Church south for
28 yrs.)
"Servant of God well done."
Holy bible engraved on stone.
Suffered much persecution at
close of Civil War.

Susan T. Neal
Wife of
Rev. W. W. Neal
Dec. 9, 1831
July 30, 1896
"Blessed are the pure in heart,
for they shall see God."

Father and Mother Saul
Father Saul
1843 - 1922
79 yrs.

Mother Saul
1844 - 1914
70 yrs.

Our Beloved Mother -
(Holy bible engraved.)

Julia A.
Wife of
C. L. Cobb
Apr. 13, 1835
May 14, 1883

ROSE

Our Father -
Wm. F. Rose
Sept. 28, 1835
May 30, 1906
71 yrs.

Wm. Lee Rose
Oct. 20, 1873
May 12, 1875

Amanda Rose
Jan. 5, 1870
May 5, 1875

Our Mother -
N. J. Rose
Mar. 8, 1837

Amanda
Daughter of
J. P. and P. A. Brady
Feb. 1, 1883
Oct. 19, 1904
"At rest."
21 yrs. 8 mos. 18 dys.
(Bird engraved on stone.)

Rhea County, Tennessee, Tombstone Inscriptions

LEUTY GRAVEYARD
(Continued)

Ella T. Brady
Wife of
John C. Pearson
Nov. 8, 1880
Oct. 16, 1917
"She was the sunshine
of our home."

Georgia T.
Daughter of
J. C. and E. T. Pearson
Nov. 27, 1906
Nov. 14, 1909
"Budded on earth
to bloom in Heaven."

Florence
Wife of
E. Earle
Sept. 16, 1886
Dec. 5, 1918
(Monument by Woodman
of the World.)
Circle (Earle)

James K. Polk Brady
Nov. 10, 1848
Aug. 21, 1914

Phoebe Ann Brady
Oct. 1, 1853
Dec. 5, 1917

Father and Mother -
Leland E. Brady
July 25, 1898
Mar. 16, 1919
21 yrs.
"Gods finger touched him
and he slept."

Vivian Wamita
Daughter of
L. E. and Grace Brady
May 18, 1916
Apr. 14, 1918
"Darling we miss thee."

Early Estil
Son of
J. E. and Malissa Meadows
Apr. 17, 1908
July 18, 1911
3 yrs.
"Christ loved him
and took him home."

ABERNATHY

Rev. Berry Abernathy
Departed this life
Nov. 6, 1870
86 yrs.
"I have fought a good fight,
I have finished my course
I have kept the faith henceforth there is laid up for me
a crown of righteousness
which the Lord, the righteous
judge shall give me at that
day, and not to me only but
to all them that love is ap-
pearing."

Mira
Wife of
Rev. B. Abernathy
Dec. 27, 1893
Age about 90.
"Her children shall rise up
and call her blessed."

Lieut. Col. J. T. Abernathy
10th. Tennessee Cavalry
Civil War.
- -

John Clayton Abernathy
Mar. 30, 1824
Apr. 20, 1911

Infant son of
J. C. and M. M. Wasson
Born and died
Aug. 16, 1863
"In the diadem of Heaven."

Rhea County, Tennessee, Tombstone Inscriptions

LIBERTY GRAVEYARD
(Continued)

Infant son of
J. C. and M. M. Wasson
Born and died
June 8, 1867
"Behold the glorious
setting."

Infant son of
J. C. and M. M. Wasson
Born and died
July 22, 1866
"Heart gems have we
given."

Infant son of
J. C. and M. M. Wasson
Mar. 13, 1863
#3 mos. 11 dys.

Infant son of
J. C. and M. M. Wasson
Dec. 16, 1864

Laura Mellville
Daughter of
J. C. and M. M. Wasson
Feb. 5, 1865
12 dys. 10 hrs.
"Early bright transient
as the morning dew,
exalted to Heaven."

Ida
Twin daughter of
J. C. and M. M. Wasson
Aug. 31, 1875
1 yr. 4 mos. 26 dys.

DAVIS
Our beloved husband and father –
John F. Davis
June 6, 1858
Dec. 3, 1886

Luella, wife of
J. F. Davis and daughter of
J. C. and M. M. Wasson
Mar. 18, 1857
June 30, 1890
"Meet me in Heaven."

Condon Davis
Son of
John and Luella Davis
May 26, 1882
Feb. 9, 1903
21 yrs.
"Them also which sleep
in Jesus, will God bring
with Him."
I Thess. 4:14
Fair as the morning,
bright as the day,
dear ones in glory
looking this way.

Samuel Jeremiah
Infant son of
John and Luella Davis
Born and died
Mar. 6, 1881

Eugene Clayton
Son of
J. C. and M. M. Wasson
Oct. 3, 1877
Apr. 23, 1879
"A fairer bud of promise never
bloomed, he is at rest
in Heaven."

Blanche Louise
Daughter of
J. C. and M. M. Wasson
Dec. 29, 1879
Nov. 18, 1883
4 yrs.
"Weep not Father and Mother for me,
for I am waiting in glory
for thee."

Chapman Wasson
Nov. 17, 1858
Oct. 15, 1914
56 yrs.

Catharine Hood Gay
His wife
July 19, 1865
June 30, 1909
44 yrs.
(Continued on next page)

LEITY GRAVEYARD
(Continued)

Catharine Hood Gay
His wife
July 19, 1865
June 30, 1909
44 yrs.
"Blessed are the dead
which die in the Lord
henceforth yea, saith
the spirit that they
may rest from their
labors, and their works
do follow them."

Rev. Catherine Gay Wasson
Wife of
J. F. Cate
Feb. 7, 1888
Jan. 9, 1909
21 yrs.
"She was worthy to be
clothed with the sun,
to have the moon under her
feet, and on her head a
crown of twelve stars."

Dr. J. C. Wasson
Sept. 20, 1836
July 20, 1914
(Mason.)
78 yrs.

Martha M.
Wife of
Dr. J. C. Wasson
Jan. 31, 1839
Mar. 20, 1906
"Blessed are the dead which
die in the Lord from hence-
forth, yea saith the spirit
that they may rest from their
labors, and their works do
follow them.
Rev. XIV, 18

Ada P. Wasson
Wife of
Chas. Dietzen
Apr. 5, 1874
Feb. 11, 1910

Pope
Son of
L. M. and Ellen Heiskel
June 25, 1858
Sept. 14, 1871

Probably twenty unmarked graves.

Rhea County, Tennessee, Tombstone Inscriptions

RHEA COUNTY

TOMBSTONE INSCRIPTIONS
LOCKE CEMETERY

Located 7½ miles northeast of Dayton and ½ mile east of Washington. 3rd. District of Rhea County. Leaving Garrison's store at Washington, travel east ½ mile. Cemetery located about ¼ mile off this country road, and on left hand side of road. On Locke property. This Cemetery is very old, but most graves have tombstones.

Samuel Robinson
Sept. 8, 1810
June 19, 1866

Mary Robinson
April 6, 1814
Nov. 8, 1898

Sarah
Wife of
Samuel Pugh
March 22, 1803
Sept. 21, 1873

In memory of
Addison Locke
Oct. 23, 1817
Nov. 17, 1870

One Tombstone

Ada White
Sept. 5, 1880
Age 1 yr. 15 days.

Della Wilmont
Aug 2, 1889
Age 1 yr. 5 mos.

Icie Foster
Sept. 28, 1889, Age 4 yr. 7 mo. 17 days.

Bonnie Kate
Aug. 24, 1884
Sept 9, 1896
Children of
W. L..& Linnie Givens.

Locke
Pink Locke
Wife of W. L. Locke
Nov. 4, 1865 - Oct. 1902

In memory of
Adeline Lock
Oct. 22, 1817
Aug. 8, 1887

D. J. Locke
Aug. 9, 1842
Oct. 21, 1906

Leah A. Locke
Oct. 30, 1848
Dec. 23, 1901

John
Son of
R. & N. Locke
Dec. 13, 1813
Sept. 14, 1850

Minerva
Daughter of
R. & N. Locke
July 5, 1810
March 12, 1862

In memory of
Adaline
Daughter of
T. J. & N. H. Locke
April 24, 1859
June 12, 1862

In memory of
Thomas M.
Son of
T. J. & N. H. Locke
Jan. 19, 1864
Oct. 18, 1871

In memory of
Nancy Harris
Wife of T. J. Locke
May 1, 1823 - April 30, 1874

LOCKE CEMETERY

LOCKE

Pliny
Son of
R. & N. Locke
May 1, 1822
March 4, 1848

In memory of
T. J. Locke
June 14, 1824
July 24, 1885

In memory of
Nancy Locke
Died Sept. 29, 1837

David Leuty
June 15, 1795
April 4, 1872

In memory of
Robert Locke
June 11, 1787
Dec. 19, 1838

Adeline Locke
Wife of
James H. Locke
Aug. 24, 1822
Dec. 31, 1871

James H. Locke
Nov. 7, 1815
May 31, 1887

In memory of
Rebecca L.
Wife of
L. J. Givens
June 11, 1824
Dec. 13, 1854

Rhea County, Tennessee, Tombstone Inscriptions

RHEA COUNTY

TOMBSTONE INSCRIPTIONS
LONE MOUNTAIN CEMETERY

The Lone Mountain Cemetery is four miles and ½ south of Dayton on the Graysville Highway. Leaving Dayton, cross the Southern Railroad at the south Dayton Freight Depot, keeping the main road which leads to College Hill, taking the old Highway southwest. The Cemetery is on the left of Highway traveling south. The land belongs to the Hickman heirs and there are seven hundred and six unmarked graves.

James A. Kelly
Nov. 8, 1843
Nov. 8, 1919

Mother -
Martha J. Moyer
1831 - 1925

P. D. Moyers
Oct. 30, 1831
Dec. 30, 1911
"Only sleeping."

Sam Moyers
Aug. 28, 1886
Feb. 20, 1919
"Asleep in Jesus."

Mother -
Mattie J. Finch
Wife of
C. H. Moyers
Dec. 15, 1863
Dec. 9, 1918
"Sweet be thy rest."
Rev. 21: 4

Father -
C. H. Moyers
Oct. 5, 1863
Oct. 2, 1920
"Asleep in Jesus."

P. F. Dagnan
1892 - 1930
"He has gone to his rest after a useful life."

C. M. Capps
Wife of
F. M. Capps
Aug. 14, 1856
"A devoted wife and loving mother."

F. M. Capps
July 31, 1854
March 15, 1919
"Beloved father, farewell."

A. Glispie
1853 -
Mar. 30, 1919
Age 66 yrs.
"Everybody was his friend."

J. L. Rideout
1861 - 1921

W. V. Marler
Nov. 7, 1876
Nov. 12, 1925
"Gone but not forgotten."
We will meet again.

McDavid Holt
Nov. 5, 1926
Age 72 yrs. 9 mos. 20 days.

Lillie Hambrick
(?)

W. M. Sparks
Oct. 22, 1846
Feb. 7, 1924

Dima Sparks
Wife of
J. H. Shaver
Aug. 3, 1898
Apr. 23, 1926

Ralph
Son of
A. H. & L. J. Sparks
Feb. 27, 1902
Nov. 2, 1920

Rhea County, Tennessee, Tombstone Inscriptions

LONE MOUNTAIN CEMETERY

Ruth E. Sparks
Daughter of
A. H. & L. J. Sparks
June 12, 1916
Jan. 12, 1920

Nellie M. Sparks
Wife of
Fred Rudd
Feb. 14, 1889
Nov. 5, 1915
"She has gone from our midst,
the bright star of our home,
our once happy hearts are
now cheerless and lone."

James A. Black
Nov. 10, 1849
Oct. 21, 1931

His wife
Annie M. Black
Feb. 29, 1853
Jan. 6, 1929
(one unmarked by wife's side.)

James C. Calwell
May 9, 1898
Feb. 8, 1916
"We know no sorrow,
knew no grief 'till thy
bright face was missed."

Mother —
Addie McGill
Sept. 19, 1878
Dec. 21, 1934

Carl Clayton Ritchey
Son of
F. S. & V. Gertie Ritchey
June 11, 1910
May 14, 1922

Frances L.
Daughter of
J. E. & T. V. Ritchey
Born & died
Dec. 6, 1927

William T. Barger
Co. E - 4 Tenn. Cav.
Jan. 3, 1845
Feb. 3, 1926

Nancy Queen (?)
1855 -
May 1, 1923
(2 unmarked graves in
the same lot.)

Robert Lee Minton
Feb. 13, 1882
Dec. 18, 1912
"Gone to be an angel."

Will Jorden
(No date.)

J. L. Nichols
June 10, 1857
May 9, 1925

M. W. Nichols
Jan. 14, 1863
July 10, 1928
(Church of God.)

Children of C. & M. A. Walker

Rollie
May 4, 1911
Dec. 7, 1911

Infant
Born & died
June 14, 1919

S. D. Powers
Dec. 25, 1850
Mch. 31, 1910
"Gone but not forgotten."

Mary A. Powers
Mar. 20, 1849
Jan. 14, 1923

Grover Denton
June 24, 1884 - June 10, 1911
"Gone but not forgotten."

Rhea County, Tennessee, Tombstone Inscriptions

LONE MOUNTAIN CEMETERY

Malcolm Paul Frields
June 11, 1909
Sept. 19, 1913

Daughter -
Ida Jane Baker
Aug. 7, 1878
July 8, 1910

Jessie A. Rose
Son of
E. D. & Edna Rose
Dec. 9, 1915
March 15, 1916
"Our darling."

John W. Russell
Aug. 9, 1870
Jan. 28, 1919
"At rest."

Dorman E. Haga
Son of
C. L. & M. E. Haga
Sept. 19, 1888
June 21, 1907
"How desolate our home
bereft of thee."

L. V. Landreth
1862 - 1923
"Asleep in Jesus."

Elizabeth J. Hobbs
Sept. 6, 1853
Aug. 7, 1907
"She sleeps 'till
Jesus comes."

Rachel E. Hobbs Webster
May 28, 1856
May 16, 1912
"She rests 'till
Jesus comes."

E. L. D. T. M.(?) Steward
Nov. 16, 1827
April 21, 1907
2 Tim. 4: 78

Eld. C. A. Hall
1847 - 1904

J. C. Ottinger
Jan. 28, 1856
July 6, 1920

Francis Willard
Jan. 21, 1918
April 23, 1918
(Son of Carl Ottinger.)
"Our darling."

Nora R. Holm
Mar. 10, 1855
May 18, 1916
Woman of Woodcraft.
Courage, hope, remembrance.
"I shall see my Savior
first of all."

Wayne Baker
Son of
A. K. & Laura Baker
Oct. 28, 1904
Age 1 yr. 10 days.

POTETT

M. E. Fousts
Wife of
L. L. Poetett (or Patett?)
Nov. 27, 1858
March 2, 1916
"Thy will be done -
Gone to a better land."

L. L. Potett (or Patett?)
Nov. 18, 1857
Apr. 19, 1932
"Gone to abbetter land."

Everett, Hazel Pearl
Apr. 20, 1916
Dec. 15, 1916
"Darling we miss thee."

Coppinger, R. L.
Son of
C. J. & R. A. Coppinger
Sept. 11, 1903
July 5, 1904

Francis M. Kennedy
Jan. 7, 1837 - Sept. 7, 1911

Rhea County, Tennessee, Tombstone Inscriptions

4

LONE MOUNTAIN CEMETERY

Baby -
Clara Mae Burnett
May 9, 1908
Sept. 30, 1909
"Budded on earth
to bloom in Heaven."

Laura May Carlock
Daughter of
J. W. & Maud H. Carlock
March 4, 1903
July 3, 1904
Age 1 yr. 4 mos. 29 days.
"where I am, there ye may
also."
John 14: 3

Harold C. Nail
July 8, 1911
May 6, 1913
"Lead kindly light."

Baby Nail
Born & died
Feb. 18, 1906
"Suffer little children
to come unto me."

Robt. G. Edwards
Aug. 22, 1846
May 22, 1908
"Absent but not
forgotten."

Father -
J. B. Edwards
Feb. 10, 1878
Dec. 28, 1912

Little H. H. Smith
Born & died
Aug. 16, 1912
"At rest."

Little T. R. G. Smith
Jan. 16, 1910
Jan. 1910
"Asleep."

Little Hope
Son of
T. J. & K. E. Smith
Sept. 5, 1914
July 1, 1915

Haskell Edwards
Son of
W. N. & R. G. Edwards
June 11, 1898
July 23, 1915

Malcom Edwards
Son of
W. N. & Hattie Edwards
Jan. 16, 1915
July 30, 1915

Susan McMillen
July 29, 1856
July 25, 1911
"At rest."

Roy Welch
Nov. 8, 1899
Oct. 29, 1904
"At rest."

Lucinda Greceory
Nov. 7, 1905
Age 73.

Cyrus Hebbred
July 24, 1822
Feb. 19, 1896
"Ever faithful in his home
and with the world."

Op Lenam Messer
Dec. 11, 1898 (Daughter of
July 19, 1900   Mr. & Mrs. P. S. Messer.)

Jennie Vreeland
May 30, 1893
June 14, 1893

Lula H. Vreeland
Aug. 16, 1887
May 11, 1909

Rhea County, Tennessee, Tombstone Inscriptions

LONE MOUNTAIN CEMETERY

Kathryn Peace
Wife of
G. F. Peace
Oct. 7, 1925

William H. Elexander
May 19, 1851
Sept. 11, 1919

Rachel E. Keedy
His wife -
Oct. 12, 1850
July 3, 1919

Edna Alexander
Daughter of
S. H. & Mary Alexander
Nov. 25, 1876
Nov. 14, 1909
"Gone but forgotten."

John L. Alexander
Nov. 18, 1881
Dec. 21, 1907

Estey May Hayes
Wife of
John L. Alexander
May 18, 1884
Feb. 17, 1904

Father - Mother
Stephen H. Alexander
Mar. 20, 1821
May 10, 1887

Mary J. Alexander
Sept. 12, 1842
July 24, 1914

Smith -
Wife of
W. M. Smith
June 15, 1842
Oct. 3, 1901
"one precious to our hearts
has gone, the one we loved
is stilled, the place made
vacant in our home can never
more be filled."

Mrs. Dessie Nothrop
(?)

Infant Daughter of
J. W. & R. A. Britt
Apr. 10, 1901
"Our darling."

J. L. Riley
Co. D - 23 RD Ky. Inf.

Thomas Painter
Oct. 5, 1831
Mar. 6, 1907

Mother -
Peirlee Painter
Dec., 1850
Died (?)
"Death is eternal life,
why should we weep."

Martin Vanburen (Beene?)
Mar. 19, 1841
July 30, 1911
"The hour is coming in the wich
all that are in the graves shall
hear his voice."
John 5: 28

Martha Beene
Dec. 24, 1901
June 1, 1904
"Of such is the kingdom of Heaven."

Harold Wilber Beene
Sept. 23, 1911
July 12, 1912
"Budded on earth
to bloom in Heaven."

W. A. Anderson
Feb. 4, 1839
Oct. 26, 1911
"Asleep in Jesus."

Catherine Anderson
Wife of
A. Anderson
Mar. 18, 1841
Nov. 8, 1899
"Asleep in Jesus, blessed sleep."

Rhea County, Tennessee, Tombstone Inscriptions

LONE MOUNTAIN CEMETERY

John R. Foster
Feb. 20, 1862
Apr. 21, 1901
"Asleep in Jesus, peaceful rest whose waking is supremely bles."

Flora Phillips
Wife of
A. J. Anderson
and infant
Apr. 16, 1905

S. Rosa Fox
1848 -
Nov. 27, 1907
"At rest."

Charley Bacon
Jan. 2, 1866
Died in Denver, Col.
Jan. 7, 1887

F. W. Bacon
May 30, 1842
Mar. 11, 1901

Henry T. Fox
Feb. 13, 1849
Jan. 27, 1925
"At rest."

Alice B. Fox
Wife of
Henry T. Fox
Aug. 18, 1853
June 4, 1904
"At rest."

Minnie M. Sullivan
Wife of
J. D. Sullivan
July 20, 1872
June 1, 1899

Ellen Wade
(?)

J. J. Kelly
(?)

Arthur M. Barger
Son of
R. H. & M. M. Barger
Dec. 29, 1894
Jan. 17, 1895
"Only sleeping."

Infant son of
W. A. & M. M. Hatfield
Born & died
April 23, 1889

W. A. Hatfield
Mar. 28, 1864
Mar. 13, 1889
(Mason.)

J. V. Dugan
Jan. 24, 1875
Feb. 8, 1875

J. T. Dugan
June 22, 1863

Nancy J. Hall
Wife of
Jno. M. Hall
Aug. 24, 1861
Apr. 29, 1901
Aged 39 yrs. 8 mos. 5 days.
"At rest."

Joseph E. Dart
Apr. 19, 1833
Mar. 8, 1908

Exa B. Davis
Wife of
D. D. Davis
Aug. 1, 1882
Feb. 6, 1910
Dear Mother, she made home happy.
"Asleep in Jesus, blessed sleep."

I. R. Nail
Oct. 30, 1847
Apr. 16, 1931
"Gone to a bright home where grief cannot come."

Rhea County, Tennessee, Tombstone Inscriptions

LONE MOUNTAIN CEMETERY

Emma L. Brickey
June 26, 1849
June 13, 1904
"Blessed are the dead
which die in the Lord
from henceforth."

Gaynell Davis
Daughter of
W. A. & Lillis Davis
June 22, 1902
Apr. 1, 1906
"She was but a jewell
lent us to sparkle in
our midst awhile."

Vestie Stelie Mitchell
Daughter of
C. L. & Flora Mitchell
Feb. 24, 1904
Mar. 6, 1904
"Only sleeping."

Lue
Daughter of
D. & Erie Mitchell
April 10, 1902
June 25, 1902

Sam M. Lewis
Son of
S. A. & J. E. Lewis
Feb. 14, 1901
Aug. 26, 1902
"At rest."

Mrs. Belle Jordon
Apr. 29, 1863
Dec. 13, 1907

Julia A. Coulter
Dec. 3, 1848
Apr. 29, 1917

Elsa Nichols
Daughter of
A. T. & M. A. Nichols
July 7, 1890
Dec. 4, 1910

Julia A. Coulter
Dec. 3, 1848 - Apr. 29, 1917

Harry Fox
Son of
Henry T. & Alice B. Fox
Mar. 24, 1887
June 27, 1887

Mary
Daughter of
W. M. & Lilla Fox
Born & died
Aug. 7, 1884
"Of such is the kingdom of Heaven."

John S.
Son of
W. K. & S. A. Gray
June 3, 1872
Oct. 11, 1879

Baby - Sarah A.
Daughter of
James M. & Etta Gray
June 27, 1905
"Sleep on sweet babe and take
thy rest. God called thee home,
He thought it best."

James M. Gray - Husband
Oct. 14, 1880
Nov. 18, 1910
"Though I, with throught the valley
of the shadow of death, I will fear
no evil, for thou art with me, thy
God and thy staff, they comfort me."

Louis Miner Yongs
Born in Chester, Ohio
Geauga Co.
June 4, 1818
Died in Graysville, Tenn.
May 7, 1888.

Stephen Yongs
Born in N. Y.
Aug. 4, 1805
Died in Graysville, Tenn.
1893

R. M. Green
Apr. 25, 1869
(Mason.)

Rhea County, Tennessee, Tombstone Inscriptions

LONE MOUNTAIN CEMETERY

Lida E. Green
Wife of
R. M. Green
Aug. 4, 1878
Apr. 24, 1906
"God be with you
'till we meet again."

J. B. Green
Co. F - 5th. Tenn. Inf.

I. A. Martin
Co. B - 6 Tenn.
M. T. D. Inf.

T. B. Coulter
Dec. 5, 1848
Feb. 3, 1909

Thomas
Son of
T. B. & Julia Coulter
Apr. 20, 1888
Mar. 5, 1899

Frankie
Daughter of
T. B. & Julia Coulter
Apr. 19, 1885
Jan. 5, 1901

Evins, Dewey Essie
Daughter of
A. & Fannie Evins
Jan. 26, 1900
Oct. 27, 1904
"Budded on earth
to bloom in Heaven."

Margareta Helton
Dec. 26, 1913
Oct. 17, 1914
"Our darling, rest in peace."
(A lot with 4 unmarked graves.)

LACEWELL

Infant Daughter of
J. W. & M. E. Lacewell
Oct. 12, 1908
Oct. 21, 1908

Clonce, Effie May
Wife of
P. L. Clonce
May 25, 1888
Mar. 31, 1912
"Our loved one has gone to rest."

George Sharpe
Jan. 18, 1919
Jan. 21, 1919

J. D. Gad
Apr. 6, 1844
Feb. 23, 1903
"A place is vacant in our
home that never can be filled."

Walter Gad
Apr. 9, 1889
Nov. 17, 1910
"Come ye blessed - May he
rest in peace."

Rebekah L. No. 31.
Graysville, Tenn.
Dora E. Foust
Wife of
G. R. Foust
Mar. 11, 1883
Mar. 16, 1908
"At rest."

Grace Woody
Daughter of
Robt. & Ruth Woody
Nov. 12, 1889
June 21, 1893
"Plucked from earth
to bloom in Heaven."

Cyrus Alexander
Dec. 6, 1877
Dec. 20, 1895
"Our darling boy has gone to rest,
to reign with Christ forever blest,
could we but hear his precious
tongue sweetly sing a Heavenly song
we would not wish him back again,
but say "dear Cyrus with Christ remain." Killed in Dayton mines explosin.

Rhea County, Tennessee, Tombstone Inscriptions

LONE MOUNTAIN CEMETERY

Wife of
R. F. Alexander
Apr. 5, 1839
Nov. 5, 1901
Age 62 yrs. 7 mos.
"She was loved by all who knew her."

J. C. Myers
1850 - 1915

Nettie Barger
Nov. 9, 1887
Oct. 7, 1911
"Holy bible, come ye blessed."

R. B. Barger
Born in Elvert Co. Ga.
Aug. 28, 1812
Died in Rhea Co. Tenn.
Apr. 16, 1893

Ellen Barger
Born in Bledsoe Co. Tenn.
July 22, 1812
Died in Rhea Co. Tenn.
Feb. 26, 1901

Bessie May Barger
Dec. 4, 1899
Mar. 3, 1912
"Redeemer liveth."

George Clayton Barger
Mar. 11, 1891
Murdered by his wife in
Dallas, Texas.
Sept. 4, 1916

M. J. Barger
Born in Logan Co. Ky.
July 22, 1851
Died in Rhea Co. Tenn.
June 20, 1889

R. H. Barger
Born in Bradley Co.
Feb. 8, 1849
Died in Rhea Co.
Sept. 15, 1925

Mary M. Barger
Born in Monroe Co. Tenn.
Nov. 8, 1863
Died in Rhea Co. Tenn.
Dec. 3, 1914

Miriam Lucille Barger
Daughter of
A. H. & G. M. Barger
Born & died
Oct. 6, 1918

Wilma E. Barger
Feb. 12, 1909
Sept. 17, 1918
"Darling we miss thee."

Emily Godson Rogers
Aug. 11, 1846
Sept. 8, 1934

Susan Rogers
Oct. 15, 1827
Feb. 4, 1900

Rebecca Rogers
Jan. 30, 1859
Dec. 22, 1911

Maggie Rogers
June 4, 1868
Jan. 29, 1890

Father - John P. Rogers
Mar. 7, 1856
Nov. 10, 1918

Mother - Mary J. Rogers
May 15, 1857
March 17, 1933
"Gone but not forgotten."

Lizzie Gadd
June 21, 1867
Apr. 20, 1905

John B. Gadd
Born Mar. 10, 1862

Rhea County, Tennessee, Tombstone Inscriptions

LONE MOUNTAIN CEMETERY

Mammie L. Green
Daughter of
Alex. & Bertha Green
Apr. 26, 1904
Apr. 25, 1905

MARLER

Erected by Kattie Marler
Wife of
John Marler
May 25, 1872
Jan. 22, 1900
"His words were kindness,
his deed were love, his
spirit humbel, he hests
above."

Mollie Mary Cleft Hall
Wife of
B. R. Dunning
June 28, 1874
Oct. 1, 1917

Claudie N. Field
Son of
W. T. & L. A. Field
Oct. 18, 1889
Jan. 29, 1890
"He can&t come to us,
but we can go to him."

Ray B. Everett
May 12, 1924
Sept. 15, 1926

Johnie Dennis
Son of
Chas. & Bell Dennis
June 8, 1906
Sept. 16, 1916
"Our darling."

Infent daughter of
Chas. & Birtie Dennis
Born & died
Sept. 1, 1898

Jessie Earl Bedwell
Apr. 5, 1918
Apr. 20, 1918
"Budded on earth
to bloom in Heaven."

Julia Lewis
Daughter of
G. L. & A. L. Lewis
Sept. 27, 1899
July 18, 1900

S. H. Helton
Aug. 1, 1821
Apr. 1, 1899
"At rest."

Martha N. J. McBride
Wife of
J. E. McBride
Sept. 11, 1866
March 9, 1896
"Gone but not forgotten."

Maggie McGill
Daughter of
F. H. & Ida McGill
Feb. 16, 1903
July 22, 1904

Mary T. Steele
July 4, 1821
June 12, 1900

William A. Steele
Jan. 30, 1819
Apr. 6, 1894

Susan Jordan
May 5, 1830
Oct. 23, 1899

Francis Bower
Feb. 14, 1827
Apr. 17, 1910
"Let our Father's will be done."

Albert S. Bower
Son of
Francis & Margaret Bower
May 27, 1872
Nov. 19, 1892
"Gone but not forgotten."

George F. Myers
Nov. 17, 1873
Dec. 14, 1896

Rhea County, Tennessee, Tombstone Inscriptions

LONE MOUNTAIN CEMETERY

Sallie Doss
Wife of
John Doss
Feb. 7, 1830
Sept. 4, 1896

Emma Green
Wife of
W. T. Green
Nov. 1873
Nov. 18, 1903

W. D. Bowman
May 28, 1882
Oct. 14, 1902

Isaac Bowman
1852 - 1921
"At rest."

Jennie Bowman
1850 - 1922
"At rest."

Creed Benson
Mar. 14, 1895
Oct. 14, 1898
"At rest."

Paul Benson
July 24, 1899
Oct. 20, 1918
"We will meet again."

W. M. H. Bean
Co. C- 5th. Tenn. Inf.

J. H. Rose
Son of
Joseph & N. Y. Rose
Mar. 26, 1883
Nov. 10, 1888

O. E. A.
Son of
Joseph & N. Y. Rose
June 16, 1886
Nov. 20, 1888
"Of such is the kingdom of Heaven."

Albert
Son of
J. & N. J. Rose
Dec. 7, 1888
Apr. 17, 1923

Creed Rose
(?)

Mr. John Collier
June 5, 1927
Aged 62 yrs. 11 mos. 26 days.

Mrs. Lizzie Collier
Mar. 23, 1932
Aged 64 yrs. 4 mos. 8 days.
(4 unmarked graves in same lot.)

Ethel T. Nowlen
1908 -

Ottinger, Clyde V.
Aug. 31, 1898
Sept. 17, 1902

Fred Ottinger
Aug. 5, 1900
Sept. 19, 1901

Nellie L. Cox
Daughter of
V. G. & M. M. Cox
Born & died
Aug. 26, 1920
"Our darling."

C. L. Swicegood
Son of
R. F. & N. M. Swicegood
Aug. 1, 1920
Feb. 19, 1923
"Gone but not forgotten."

J. W. Rose
Nov. 25, 1878
July 24, 1900
"Gone but not forgotten."

Joseph Rose
Mar. 23, 1837
Oct. 17, 1915

Rhea County, Tennessee, Tombstone Inscriptions

LONE MOUNTAIN CEMETERY

McMurray

Ida C.
Wife of
S. H. McMurry
1884 - 1920

Milo M. Card
Mar. 10, 1878
May 5, 1903
"There was an angel band
from Heaven that was not
quite complete so God took
our darling Milo to fill
the vacant seal."

Edwin R. Wheeler
1856 - 1915
"Resting."

William L. Wheeler
1827 - 1897
"At rest."

R. Alice Wheeler
1826 - 1916
"At rest."

Roy M. Swicegood
Son of
R. F. & N. M. Swicegood
Born & died
Oct. 9, 1915
"At rest."

Eliza J. Hensley
Wife of
H. M. Hensley
Feb. 12, 1847
Oct. 11, 1893
"In Heaven we'll meet -
Gone but not forgotten."

James R. Brown
Aug. 29, 1870
Nov. 1, 1901
"Darling Jim, he has left us,
yes forevermore, but we hope
to meet our loved one on that
bright and happy shore."

Holy Bible -
Martha Riddle
Wife of
J. I. Riddle
Nov. 28, 1819
Apr. 13, 1886

Jashua I Riddle
June 26, 1814
Aug. 15, 1874
Holy Bible -

Mary O.
Daughter of
J. I. & Martha Riddle
Dec. 18, 1842
May 18, 1884

S. G. T. - J/ W. Hoge
Co. E - 11th. Tenn. Cav.

Tressie Duggan
Daughter of
S. & M. S. Dugan
Nov. 3, 1888
Nov. 23, 1888
"Gone but not forgotten."

Virty Bean
Daughter of
C. O. & N. L. Bean
Oct. 16, 1897
Nov. 11, 1915
"Our darling is gone
but not forgotten."

Isham Dennis
Mar. 24, 1832
Feb. 24, 1885
Age 52 yrs. 11 mos.

Lola Edna Nail
Daughter of
I. R. & M. I. Nail
Aug. 7, 1893
Mar. 6, 1897
"Sweet little Edna,
gone to rest. God thought
it best."

Rhea County, Tennessee, Tombstone Inscriptions

LONE MOUNTAIN CEMETERY

Sarah A. Rogers
Nov. 17, 1823
Apr. 11, 1892

MORGAN

Mother - Father
William H. Morgan
Apr. 27, 1843
Apr. 6, 1927
Co. K - 1st. Tenn. Inf.

James E.
His wife
July 13, 1855
Aug. 16, 1927
"We hope to meet
them again."

I. W. Morgan
May 1, 1847
Sept. 21, 1911

Robert N. Bolton
May 6, 1844
June 30, 1917
P. V. T. Co. B -
6th. Tenn. R. E. G.
M. T. D. Inf.

His wife
Sidney A.
Mar. 12, 1842
July, 1912

Ellen Hughes
Wife of
Sam Hughes
July 17, 1855
Aug. 17, 1920

GRIMSLEY

Nannie J.
Wife of
L. M. Grimsley
Feb. 12, 1878
Drowned Sept. 5, 1921
to save another.
"Greater love hath no man
than this."

Weldon O. Smith
Jan., 16, 1897
Jan. 9, 1904
"Safe in the arms
of Jesus."

Sarah Rebeca Grimsley - Mother
Nov. 5, 1849
June 24, 1902

Father - James Monroe Grimsley
Sept. 29, 1841
Nov. 26, 1908

W. H. Hickman
Mar. 1, 1834
Dec. 10, 1894

William T. Parkhurst
Mar. 29, 1825
June 23, 1910

Mary Jane Parkhurst
June, 1829
Died (?)
"They died as they lived,
devoted followers of Christ."

Nail A. Shelton
Apr. 13, 1889
May 4, 1914

Mary J.
Aug. 14, 1855
Apr. 12, 1906
"Resting 'till the
resurrection morn."

Daily A. Green
1863 - 1907

Mary C. Green
1865 - 1903

Emmet P. Green
1885 - 1904

Martin -
Born May 6, 1843
Aug. 8, 1902
"At rest."

14

LONE MOUNTAIN CEMETERY

Pearl Jorden
Daughter of
J. N. & M. J. Jorden
Jan. 1, 1894
Oct. 26, 1895

Infant son of
J. N. & M. J. Jorden
Born &, died
Nov. 26, 1898
"Plucked from earth to bloom in Heaven."

Della
Daughter of
J. N. & M. J. Jorden
Born & died
Jan. 2, 1893

George S. Vreeland -Veerland(?)
Age 82 yrs.
Born 1852
Nov. 30, 1935

GREEN

Holy Bible –
P. G. Rebekah Lodge No. 87.
Graysville, Tenn.
Emma Green
Wife of
W. T. Green
Nov. 1873
Nov. 18, 1903

Rhea County, Tennessee, Tombstone Inscriptions

RHEA COUNTY

TOMBSTONE INSCRIPTIONS
THE LONG COMMUNITY GRAVEYARD

This graveyard is located in the 1st. District. The farm on which this graveyard is located is known as the Kris Kimmer farm. Get on the Dixie Highway or Lon Foust Highway, come 18 miles north to Spring City. Take the Rhea Springs road going east for 2 miles, turn north at Rhea Springs on the Muddy Creek road and go north for about 3 miles to the Kris Kimmer farm. On the left of the road on a little hill in sight from the Muddy Creek road, you will see the above named graveyard.

One Miss Shadden
(No dates.)

Verna McCully
Jan. 29, 1896
Mar. 6, 1929
33 yrs.

Infant of
J. H. & Verna McCully
Apr. 18, 1917
"Budded on earth
to bloom in Heaven."

Eugene McCully
June 27, 1912
Oct. 22, 1914
"Asleep in Jesus."

Wilma Sue Tredway
July 11, 1935
Mar. 12, 1936
"She was the sunshine
of our home."

Lillian Cleo
Daughter of
Fred and Elsie McCully
Aug. 29, 1920
June 8, 1922
About 2 yrs. old

Martha Shadden
(No dates.)

Mary
Wife of
J. T. Long
June 20, 1855
Jan. 5, 1918
"Blessed are the pure in heart,
for they shall see God."

Father - Z. T. Long
Aug. 28, 1847
Nov. 1, 1915
"We miss thee from
our home, dear Father."

Mary Long
Wife of
F. A. McCabe
May 15, 1845
Apr. 7, 1877
"A tender Mother,
and a faithful friend."
32 yrs.

In memory of
Gettie McCabe
Jan. 10, 1875
Dec. 24, 1886
11 yrs.

Nellie Mae Smith
May 18, 1877
July 8, 1904
25 yrs.

Archibald Long
Apr. 10, 1854
Nov. 15, 1889
"Here rests a beloved Husband."

E. K. Pass
Wife of
W. E. Pass
Apr. 23, 1852
Jan. 20, 1880
28 yrs.

N. H. Long
Feb. 21, 1818
Jan. 2, 1872
Age 54

Rhea County, Tennessee, Tombstone Inscriptions

THE LONG COMMUNITY GRAVEYARD

Margaret J. Long
Mar. 30, 1824
Feb. 17, 1884

In memory of
C. G. Dudley
Nov. 1, 1818
Nov. 18, 1872
54 yrs.

Mrs. N. G. Prestwood
May 24, 1845
Feb. 19, 1910
65 yrs.
"We will meet again."

James Gregory
Apr. 6, 1876
Feb. 8, 1921

J. H. Brock
Co. C - 7th. Tenn.
M. T. D. Infantry
(No dates.)

Lizzie Stookie
Oct. 17, 1890
Age 8 yrs. 6 mos. 10 da.

Leander Smith
Feb. 14, 1883
Oct. 29, 1896

CAWOOD
Large sandstone family marker
in midst of five graves, plain
stone - no dates.

Sherman Drake
May 14, 1881
Aug. 8, 1936
55 yrs.

BIRD

L. E. Star Bird
Aug. 3, 1863
Sept. 1, 1918

Probably 35 unmarked graves.

Rhea County, Tennessee, Tombstone Inscriptions

RHEA COUNTY

TOMBSTONE INSCRIPTIONS
LOWE COMMUNITY GRAVEYARD

Dist. No. 2. This graveyard is situated just east of State highway, and south of Rhea Springs water mill. It is found on Jimmy Wallace's farm. Take the old Stage road at Dayton and go north about twenty miles to this graveyard.

In memory of Violett Miller, wife of
Charlie Lowe
Sept. 21, 1868
Mar. 10, 1904
36 yrs.

Mary
Wife of
W. H. Lowe
Aug. 16, 1848
Mar. 16, 1904
56 yrs.
"Blessed assurance."

Lettie W.
Wife of
W. P. Foust
Dec. 18, 1819
Oct. 17, 1883
64 yrs.

Mattie Hill (Mother)
Same as
Mattie E. Hill
July 19, 1878
Oct. 6, 1918
"Just when we learned
to love her, God called
her back to heaven."

S. A. Fugate
(No dates.)

Robert Rivers
July 7, 1833
Mar. 15, 1907
74 yrs.

Mary Rivers
June 12, 1834
(Monument with large ball
on top of head stone.)

One grave enclosed by strong
iron fence. Holy Bible engraved
in top of headstone.

John C. Moss
Nov. 20, 1873
Nov. 18, 1904
31 yrs.
"Can I forget the agonizing
hour, when those loved eyes
were closed to wake no more."

Raymon Fugate
Son of
L. M. & G. Fugate
Nov. 14, 1920
Nov. 1922

Raymon H. Collins
Son of
J. C. & A. D. Collins
Mar. 7, 1906
Mar. 20, 1920
Age about 14 yrs.
"He was a loving son,
and affectionate brother."

Callie P.
Wife of
Albert H. Collins
Dec. 14, 1897
Jan. 28, 1918
21 yrs.
"She was the sunshine of our
home."

Albert H.
Son of
Albert & Dallie Collins
Nov. 12, 1916
Jan. 17, 1917
2 mos., 5 dys.
"Our Darling."

Rhea County, Tennessee, Tombstone Inscriptions

LOWE COMMUNITY GRAVEYARD

Granvil H. Wade
Mar. 24, 1832
Aug. 10, 1916
84 yrs.

Nancy Davis
Wife of
Granvil Wade
Sept. 29, 1926

John Collins
Jan. 17, 1871
Aug. 17, 1924
53 yrs.
(Monument woodman of
the world Memorial.)
"Come ye blessed."

Dessie
Wife of
W. T. Wiggins
May 30, 1905
Feb. 13, 1927
"Asleep in Jesus."

A few graves with plain
stones. No dates.
About 50 graves without
names or dates. Four
graves with large lime-
stone slabs. No names
or dates.
Large family monument.
Wire fence in poor
condition.

John Hardin
Mar. 15, 1870
Sept. 3, 1875
5 yrs.

James Wm. Hardin
July 24, 1867
Dec. 10, 1885
18 yrs.

Jane Elizabeth Hardin
Jan. 1, 1857
Sept. 28, 1880
23 yrs.

FOUST

James IV
Son of
W. P. & I. W. Foust
July 8, 1853
Oct. 7, 1889

Timothy
Son of
W. P. & L. W. Foust
July 17, 1855
Aug. 20, 1876
21 yrs.

Rufus M.
Son of
W. P. & L. W. Foust
May 19, 1847
Aug. 15, 1879
52 yrs.

Wm. P. Foust
Mar. 22, 1818
Apr. 27, 1861
43 yrs.

Sarah J.
Daughter of
W. P. & L. W. Foust
Feb. 5, 1842
Dec. 26, 1864
22 yrs.

Rebecca C.
Daughter of
W. P. & L. W. Foust
Sept. 9, 1843
Oct. 16, 1862
19 yrs.

Wm. T. Foust
July 18, 1851
July 25, 1855
4 yrs.

Andrew J. Foust
Feb. 18, 1849
Aug. 5, 1855
6 yrs.

2
LOWE COMMUNITY GRAVEYARD

In memory of	In memory of
S. W. Lowe	Jane Lowe
Oct. 11, 1840	July 27, 1797
Sept. 18, 1841	Dec. 20, 1855
11 mos.	58 years

S. H. marked on rough sandstone. Grave yard needs cleaning.

1

RHEA COUNTY

TOMBSTONE INSCRIPTIONS
MACEDONIA CHURCH CEMETERY

Dist. No. 1. Take the Dixie Highway Route, go north from Dayton 22 miles. This graveyard is 4 miles north of Spring City, near by Mullenex. Up in the woodland near the pike, you will find the above named graveyard. Very old graves and many headstones are gone. Some unmarked. Probably 50 graves. One marked James Shadden. No dates.

RHEA COUNTY

TOMBSTONE INSCRIPTIONS
MARLER FAMILY CEMETERY

The Marler family Cemetery is five miles and a half southwest of Dayton. Take Highway No. 30 from Dayton going one and half mile. Leave Highway and take graveled road south for four miles to Marler Place. There are three unmarked graves. The land belongs to the Marlers.

RHEA COUNTY

TOMBSTONE INSCRIPTIONS
THE MARS HILL GRAVEYARD

This graveyard is in Dist. No. 1. Come up Dixie Highway 18 miles by way of Wash Cawood's Mill, then turn north and go about 3 miles to Myer's Hill School House out to left of this School House in the Woodland you will find the above mentioned graveyard. It is a very old graveyard, people here say. At least 20 unmarked graves. About 30 A. of ground donated for church and school and burial grounds. A very old graveyard almost abandoned.

Mary Walker
Wife of
Richard Walker
Sept. 1799
Jan. 21, 1855
Member of M. E. Church.
"Gone Home."

Margaret A. Walker
Daughter of R. and M. Walker
Oct. 20, 1827
July 15, 1854
Member of the M. E. Church.
27 years old.

1

RHEA COUNTY

TOMBSTONE INSCRIPTIONS
MARSH FAMILY GRAVEYARD

This is a very old graveyard located north of Wolf Creek Church in the woods. Take the old stage road from Rhea Springs to Washington, going one mile north of Wolf Creek Church. District No. 2.

Rev. E. W. Marsh
Son of
J. L. and Orinda Marsh
Nov. 27, 1847
Mar. 4, 1874
27 yrs.
(Mason.)

In memory of
G. S. Marsh
(Torbitt)
Oct. 25, 1845

Thos. F. Torbitt
Oct. 31, 1830
Nov. 4, 1868

Marye
Wife of
Thomas F. Torbitt
Jan. 31, 1838
Dec. 28, 1897
"When immortal spirits reign, we hope to meet again."

Elizabeth J.
Wife of
J. M. McPherson
1836
1868

Alfred Marsh
June 7, 1800
Oct. 12, 1863
63 yrs.

Gravener S.
Son of
Alfred and Celia Marsh
Apr. 20, 1842
Oct. 17, 1844
2½ yrs.

J. L. Marsh
Sept. 24, 1824
May 9, 1866

Orinda
Wife of
J. L. Marsh
Mar. 14, 1827
Nov. 23, 1873
56 yrs.

Probably one dozen graves unmarked. Five outside with plain slabs.

RHEA COUNTY

TOMBSTONE INSCRIPTIONS
MARTIN FAMILY CEMETERY

The Martin family Cemetery is five miles south of Dayton. Follow Highway No. 27. From Dayton go four miles. Leave the Highway and take the gravel road west for one mile to the Martin Place. There are two unmarked graves. The land belongs to the Martins.

RHEA COUNTY

TOMBSTONE INSCRIPTIONS
MCCALEB GRAVEYARD

Go north from Dayton on the State Highway about 20 miles to the end of Toe String road, going about 4 miles to the Friendship Church, then turn east past Iron Hill church, for about 1 mile. There are about 20 unmarked graves.

Archie McCaleb
Nov. 11, 1818
Aug. 10, 1897
79 yrs.

Nancy J. McCaleb
June 11, 1828
"They steered their course
to the same quiet shore."

Addie Keylon
Wife of
M. J. Keylon
June 28, 1875
Feb. 9, 1904
29 yrs.
"Not parted long,
and now to part no more.""

Elizabeth S.
Wife of
Thomas H. McPherson
Oct. 1, 1829
Oct. 7, 1868
39 yrs.

Archibald McPherson
Son of
T. and E. McPherson
Oct. 30, 1853
Oct. 6, 1856
3 yrs.
(Lamb engraved on stone.)

Infant Daughter of
P. H. and I. J. McPherson
Born and died July 27, 1870

In memory of
Infant son of
Archibald and Jane McPherson
Died Aug. 1, 1819

In memory of
Infant daughter of
Archibald and Jane McPherson
Died Aug. 5, 1850

In memory of
Anna McCaleb
Wife of
Andrew McCaleb
Apr. 30, 1853
58 yrs.

Andrew McCaleb
Dec. 23, 1888
July 9, 1860
72 yrs.

This farm was owned by Archie McCaleb at one time, about 40 years ago. Mr. McCaleb was said to be an honest man, very attentive to the poor and needy of his day.

RHEA COUNTY

TOMBSTONE INSCRIPTIONS
MCCLENDON COMMUNITY GRAVEYARD

District No. 2. Take Highway No. 27 or the Dixie Highway. Go north 18 miles to Spring City. Go ½ mile east of Spring City on Rhea Springs road to Danvin road, going two miles out to Gray farm.

David Matison Mitchel
May 16, 1866
Feb. 28, 1911
45 yrs.

Carrie Louella Mitchell
Mar. 16, 1897
July 8, 1898
1 yr. 4 mos.

Eliza Garrison
June 15, 1929

Amanda Wiggins
Dec. 19, 1921

Bettie J. McClendon
Jan. 27, 1926

Bessie McClendon
Jan. 5, 1931

G. M. Marshall
Mar. 25, 1856
Nov. 10, 1926

Minnie
Wife of
Tom Mitchel
June 15, 1891
Aug. 22, 1930
49 yrs.
"She was a loyal friend, a noble daughter, a devoted wife and Mother."

Two others buried in concrete wall.

Mother
Wife of
J. L. Walker
Jan. 29, 1874
Aug. 4, 1934
Age 57

There are about 60 unknown and unmarked graves.

Rhea County, Tennessee, Tombstone Inscriptions

RHEA COUNTY

TOMBSTONE INSCRIPTIONS
MILLER COMMUNITY GRAVEYARD

Thirteen miles north of Dayton on the Dixie or Lon Foust Highway, one mile north of Penvine and six miles south of Spring City is located the Walter Miller farm. one half mile west of Walter Miller's home is the Miller graveyard.

Weltha A.
Wife of
A. F. Devaney
June 7, 1859
Jan. 15, 1898
39 yrs.
"How desolate our home bereft of thee."

Floyd Marie
Daughter of
W. P. and Mary E. Ferguson
Feb. 13, 1896
Feb. 15, 1900
4 yrs.

Mary E.
Wife of
W. P. Ferguson
Nov. 14, 1868
Apr. 19, 1901

Chas. W. Mitchell
Apr. 7, 1871
Dec. 31, 1897
(Died in Ft. Worth, Texas.)

Emma Mitchell
Jan. 31, 1862
June 4, 1894
"She died as she lived, a christian."

John H.
Son of
W. G. and S. A. Mitchell
Feb. 27, 1866
Dec. 11, 1884
"Johnnie made home pleasant."

Father and Mother -
W. G. Mitchell
July 6, 1844
Aug. 13, 1893 - (Mason.)

Sara A. Mitchell
Jan. 7, 1885

Levy B. Thompson
May 7, 1847
Dec. 20, 1907
"He died as he lived, a christian."

BURDETT
A. A. Burdett
Jan. 21, 1812
Sept. 13, 1899

Rebecca Burdett
Mar. 10, 1816
Dec. 20, 1894

Joseph McMillan
Co. C
7th. Tennessee Inf.

Our Father and Mother -
Samuel B. Ferguson
Oct. 24, 1792
Oct. 26, 1881

Sara B. Ferguson
Mar. 13, 1819
June 19, 1860

L. C. Ferguson
Apr. 27, 1824
Mar. 25, 1893
69 yrs.
"Gone, but not forgotten."

Mollie D.
Daughter of
W. S. and O. J. Miller
Dec. 3, 1867
Aug. 28, 1868
8 mos. 25 dys.

Rhea County, Tennessee, Tombstone Inscriptions

MILLER COMMUNITY GRAVEYARD

Elbert S. Miller
July 18, 1858
May 19, 1878
20 yrs.

Lieut. Peter W. Miller
Veteran of the Revolution
Dec. 16, 1814
Apr. 9, 1863
(Mason.)
Dates wrong.

Tombstone broken
Dates, 1842 - 1871

Mary A.
Wife of
J. T. Boofer
Sept. 9, 1856
Sept. 14, 1917
"The world is better
for her having lived."

Nellie
Daughter of
J. T. and M. A. Boofer
Mar. 9, 1882
Sept. 6, 1903

Susan M. Dismong
Aug. 31, 1840
Oct. 25, 1856
"Rest in peace."

About 50 graves without
dated markers.

L. P. Essex
Aug. 25, 1847
Feb. 6, 1911
"Gone home, the Lord
is my shepherd, I shall
not want."

Harry W.
Son of
J. W. and Mirtle Phipps
May 18, 1903
June 21, 1919
"He was the sunshine
of our home."

Windle P. Graham
May 9, 1912
May 30, 1913

Arnold B. Graham
July 6, 1914
Mar. 20, 1916

Robert E. Graham
Aug. 11, 1916
Aug. 13, 1916

Marian H. Horton
Tenn. Cook, 120 Inf. 3rd. Div.
World War Veteran.
Aug. 29, 1923

Anna May
Daughter of
R. and A. E. Defenderfer
Mar. 1, 1896

G. C. Neal
June 29, 191-
70 yrs.

M. F. Neal
Jan. 1840
Feb. 22, 1921

Marble stone marked
Ferguson. No dated.

1

RHEA COUNTY

TOMBSTONE INSCRIPTIONS
MONROE FAMILY GRAVEYARD

District No. 1. Take the Dixie Highway or Highway No. 27, going two miles north of Spring City, and one mile west of Highway No. 27. There are about twelve graves with blank stones.

A. J.
Wife of
J. T. Monroe
April 28, 1844
Aug. 11, 1882
38 yrs.

Rhea County, Tennessee, Tombstone Inscriptions

RHEA COUNTY

TOMBSTONE INSCRIPTIONS
MONTGOMERY CEMETERY

Located 9 miles northeast of Dayton and 2 miles north of Washington, Tenn. This is an old Cemetery and many graves have no tombstones. Located in 3rd. District of Rhea County, Tenn. Located on Dixie Highway, and on left hand side of road traveling north.

Alfred Carney
March 11, 1921
Age 47 years.

J. H. Boles
(?)

Pearl Wyrick
Wife of
D. L. Kincer
May 7, 1891
March 24, 1929

Iva G.
Dau. of
A. V. & N. B. East
Dec. 4, 1919
Dec. 8, 1920
"Our precious darling."

Mary Magdaline
Dau. of
J. C. & Latitia Carney
Nov. 24, 1894
Jan. 15, 1895

Father - James C. Carney
Oct. 12, 1844
Jan. 12, 1921

Mother - Rebecca L. Franklin
His wife
Oct. 17, 1856
Nov. 13, 1921
"A loved one from us has gone,
a voice we loved is stilled,
a place is vacant in our home,
which never can be filled."

Lucy Tatitia Carney
Oct. 21, 1935
Age 50.

L. J. Hedgecoth
Aug. 22, 1867
Jan. 2, 1890
"A light from our household is
gone, a voice we loved is stilled."
A place is vacant in our home,
that never can be filled.

BRADY
Our loved one - Mrs. S. S. Brady
April 26, 1892
Oct. 28, 1918
"At rest." Till we meet again.

Our loved one - S. S. Brady
June 17, 1892
Aug. 7, 1919
"At rest." Good by Mother till
we meet again.

Infant of
Mr. & Mrs. S. S. Brady
Oct. 26, 1918

Archie E.
Born & died
Feb. 1, 1903

Luther J.
Aug. 1, 1893
May 3, 1897

J. Dott
Dec. 6, 1907
March 28, 1910

Infant son
Born & died
Sept. 15, 1896
Sons & Dau. of J. R. & A. B. Hall.

Mother - Margrett Hall
Sept. 19, 1844
Feb. 28, 1912 - A tender Mother &
faithful friend.

Rhea County, Tennessee, Tombstone Inscriptions

MONTGOMERY CEMETERY

Mother - Belle Hall
Nov. 15, 1872
"There is no sorrow that Heaven cannot heal."

John R. Hall
Feb. 20, 1869
Dec. 11, 1921
"There is no sorrow that Heaven cannot heal."

William King
Sept. 9, 1862
Feb. 4, 1884

Father - John H. King
June 14, 1838
June 21, 1906

Mother - Nancy
His wife
April 27, 1839
Feb. 9, 1915

Edward L. Collins
Feb. 7, 1936
Age 86 yrs. 8 mos.

W. M. Wiggins
May 26, 1921
Age 74 yrs.
"Gone but not forgotten."

James Wiggins,
March 30, 1894
June 5, 1926

Alfred Locke
Dec. 13, 1934
Age 88, 6 mo. 15 days.

Robert Oliver
Son of
J. G. & Sallie Wilkey
Sept. 13, 1904
Oct. 7, 1905

Floyd Edgar
Son of
J. G. & Sallie Wilkey
Sept. 15, 1895
July 2, 1896

Malinda Jane
Wife of
C. C. Wilkey
Sept. 16, 1844
Nov. 23, 1873

WILKEY
Christopher C. Wilkey
Oct 25, 1841
Oct. 25, 1918
"Death is eternal life, why should we weep."

Lucindie Wilkey
Sept. 1858
Oct. 13, 1920
"Thy trials ended, thy rest is won."

Campbell Wilkey
Co. F. 1. Tenn. Inf.
Sept. 28, 1891
Age 49 yrs.

Marion Wilkey
1796 -
April 23, 1900

Roger Wilkey
1813 -
June 7, 1883

Mrs. J. H. Jackson
June 6, 1935
Age 71 yrs. 2 mo. 26 days.

James H. Jackson
Co., J. 19 Tenn. Inf. C. S. A.
James H. Clark
Dec. 25, 1855
Feb. 3, 1914 - Father.

J. C. Perry
July 23, 1910
March 11, 1926
"There is no parting in Heaven."

J. L. Rudd
Died 1932
Age 1 year, 7 months.

Isaac Byrd
Nov. 27, 1935
Aged 88 years, 7 months, 3 days.

Rhea County, Tennessee, Tombstone Inscriptions

MONTGOMERY CEMETERY

BYRD

Nancy Byrd
Born at Jonesboro Union Co. Ill
March 6, 1850
Dec. 1, 1916
"She has done what she could."

A. J. Byrd
Died Dec. 14, 1913

George Dibrel Byrd
Nov. 4, 1880
Oct. 31, 1902
"My trust is in God."

Mrs. Sidney Canady
June 15, 1922
Aged 70 years.

Henry Pearman
Jan. 1, 1854
July 31, 1911

Jocie Locke
Nov. 5, 1861
Nov. 26, 1924

Elsia Rockholt
12.22.1926
Aged 18 yrs. 7 mos.

Charley Shadden
Nov. 21, 1898
May 13, 1922
"Beloved one farewell."

Frank Shadden
Aug. 20, 1928
Aged 35 years.

Newton Locke
March 18, 1813
Aug. 28, 1872
Aged 59 yrs. 5 mos. 10 days.

Judge Franklin Locke
July 2, 1811
Oct. 30, 1874
(He was a Ruling Elder in
the Presbyterian Church.)

Sabella T. Locke
Wife of
Judge F. Locke
Born in Greenville, Tenn
Died at Washington
May 4, 1815
May 24, 1882
"After much suffering, she rests in peace."

CUNNYNHAM

Elvira Cunnynham
May 27, 1856
March 16, 1897
"Servants of God well done. Thy glorious warfare is past."

D. W. Cunnynham
Aug. 14, 1850
July 5, 1894
"One precious to our heart has gone. The voice we loved is stilled."

Elvina Cunnynham
Feb. 6, 1817
Jan. 18, 1900

W. H. Cunnynham
Dec. 11, 1811
Sept. 20, 1862
Aged 50 years, 9 mos. & 9 days.

Infant son of
Jas. R. & M. T. Cunnynham
(?)

Mattie T.
Wife of
Jas. R. Cunnynham
Oct. 22, 1857
April 26, 1880
Aged 22 yrs. 6 mos. & 4 days.

Lorinda Jane
Wife of
T. N. L. Cunnynham
April 25, 184?
Feb. 26, 1883
Aged 40 yrs. 10 mos. & 1 day.

Rhea County, Tennessee, Tombstone Inscriptions

MONTGOMERY CEMETERY

T. N. L. Cunnynhan
Aug. 30, 1840
Sept. 14, 1914

HENRY

W. R. Henry
April 23, 1833
April 14, 1915 - Father

Rachel F. Henry
Dec. 1, 1840
Nov. 5, 1892 - Mother

Oliver
Son of
W. R. & R. F. Henry
Nov. 26, 1866
Aug. 14, 1875

Infant son of
W. R. & R. F. Henry
Born & died
May 1869

Infant daughter of
W. R. & R. F. Henry
Born & died
Aug. 1860

Infant son of
W. R. & R. F. Henry
Born & died
Mch. 31, 1859

Solomon Henry
1812 -
Nov. 11, 1872

Selia Blevins
Aug. 10, 1842
Oct. 22, 1882

Lydia K
Daughter of
Wm. & Mary B. Price
Jan. 11, 1894
Jan. 15, 1894

Imogene Coxey
Dec. 31, 1928
Aged 15 years.

Mother - Hiley Underwood
Aug. 8, 1849
March 6, 1925

Father - J. W. Underwood
Jan. 5, 1848
May 7, 1908

Perry Blevins
March 9, 1893
Aged 7 m's.

In memory of
James Montgomery
May 11, 1874
July the 22nd. 1844

In memory of
Elizabeth Montgomery
Dec. 7, 1779
Aug. 19, 1840

Charles Cox
April 19, 1800
Dec. 7, 1851

Rebecca Cox
Jan. 16, 1809
Oct. 1, 1876
"Their happy souls have winged
their way to one pure bright
eternal day.

Joe Campbell
Nov. 24, 1933
Aged 60 years.

In memory of
William Campbell
March 30, 1813
July 27, 1888
Age 75n years, 3 months, 27 days.

S. L. Wilkey
Oct. 24, 1846
April 21, 1912
"There is rest in Heaven."

Rebecca
Wife of
S. L. Wilkey - April 10, 1839
Sept. 16, 1919

Rhea County, Tennessee, Tombstone Inscriptions

MONTGOMERY CEMETERY

WILKEY

Hugh
Son of
S. L. & Rebecca Wilkey
May 22, 1870
Oct. 18, 1873
"Our loved one."

Samuel Wilkey
Oct. 13, 1871
Aged about 50 years.

Cynthia Wilkey
Oct. 4, 1823
Departed this life
Feb. 24, 1900
Aged 76 yrs. 4 mo. 20 days.

S. E. V. Wilkey
Daughter of
A. L. Wilkey
March 4, 1880
Feb. 1, 1910

MONTGOMERY

J. H. Montgomery
Jan. 4, 1869
May 16, 1876
"All is well."

Cyntha Montgomery
Oct. 2, 1865
July 1, 1866

R. C. Montgomery
Jan. 14, 1816
Aug. 9, 1874
"Heaven has claimed its own."

R. A. Montgomery
March 1, 1844
Oct. 15, 1921

Infant son of
L. A. & R. A. Pierce
1879 -

Martha Lou Montgomery
Nov. 26, 1935
Aged 40 years, 5 months, 9 days.

Margret Houston
(?)

Lillie
Wife of
Geo. Paul
Nov. 20, 1892
Jan. 22, 1923
"In Heaven."

Little son of
George Paul
Born & died
Feb. 19, 1914
"Our loved one."

Lorenda Dobbs
Dec. 1935
Aged 51 years.

A. H. Dobbs
May 31, 1934
Aged 73 yrs.

Sam J. Owens
Oct. 1, 1936
Aged 52 years.

Husband - Paul Dunn
April 29, 1894
April 27, 1922

Winford
Son of
Mr. & Mrs. T. E. Dodd
Oct. 11, 1915
Nov. 3, 1916

Infant son of
Mr. & Mrs. T. E. Dodd
(?)

Warren
Son of
Mr. & Mrs. T. E. Dodd
Jan. 26, 1911
Feb. 14, 1913

Abner Wilkey
1861 - 1910
Eliza - His wife - 1861 - 1912
Father & Mother.

6

MONTGOMERY CEMETERY

Dellie May Collins	W. F. Burnett
June 7, 1881	Dec. 1, 1934
	Aged 74 years, 11 months, 15 days.

RHEA COUNTY

TOMBSTONE INSCRIPTIONS
MOORE CEMETERY

The Moore Cemetery is eighteen miles north of Dayton. Follow Highway No. 27 from Dayton going two miles north of Dayton. Leave the Highway and take graveled road east going six miles. The land belongs to Ritchey. There are eight unmarked graves.

C. T. Moore Jan, 2, 1860 Aug. 5, 1906	Moore A. J. Moore Died March 7, 1895
Joephes Anderson 1843 - April 6, 1901	

RHEA COUNTY

TOMBSTONE INSCRIPTIONS
MORPHY CEMETERY

The Morphy Cemetery is eight miles west of Dayton. Follow Highway No. 30 from Dayton going to the top of the mountain. Leave Highway taking the gravel road south for three miles to the Morphy Place. There are eighteen graves. Some have had markers, but have been broken down and the inscriptions are not visible. The land belongs to Miss Gladys Morphy.

Rhea County, Tennessee, Tombstone Inscriptions

RHEA COUNTY

TOMBSTONE INSCRIPTIONS
MT. SULPHUR GRAVEYARD

Follow the Dixie Highway at Dayton going eighteen miles north to Spring City. Take the Grandview road just west of Spring City going five miles on Walden's Ridge to Grandview, then go three and one half miles north of Grandview to the Roddy road. This graveyard is familiarly called Possum Trot. One hundred graves are marked with plain undated and unnamed stones.

James Oliver Daniels
Sept. 14, 1837 - Aug. 24, 1881
44 yrs.

Mary Daniels,
June 9, 1833
Oct. 19, 1882
49 yrs.

Mary Ann Lemons
May 8, 1854
May 20, 1885

Mattie B. Loy
1900 - 1935
35 yrs.

Molley E. Gibson Jolly
Mar. 26, 1871
Aug. 18, 1899
"Rest in peace."

A. J. Jolly
Apr. 30, 1830
May 13, 1903
"At rest in thee."

Mary
Wife of
W. H. Daniel
Dec. 9, 1857
Sept. 1, 1917
"At rest."

Samuel Lemons
Oct. 24, 1846
Jan. 22, 1923
77 yrs.

Tobias O. Dannel
1895 - 1932

Jessie
Son of
John and Ruthie Goss
July 18, 1903
Apr. 19, 1904
"Budded on earth
to bloom in Heaven."

Father -
J. L. Allen
Feb. 7, 1851
Oct. 20, 1926
75 yrs.

M. C.
Wife of
J. L. Allen
Jan. 29, 1852
Jan. 5, 1916
"Farewell Mother."

Ardella Malle
—
"At rest."

Mira E. Loy
Nov. 11, 1874

Rhea County, Tennessee, Tombstone Inscriptions

MT. SULPHUR GRAVEYARD

Mary L. Loy
Jan. 5, 1873
Apr. 1, 1909
36 yrs.

Tempa Tabor
Oct. 6, 1827
Apr. 21, 1912
85 yrs.

Mrs. Hettia Ray
(No dates.)

Molley Brady
July 8, 1889
Mar. 5, 1905
16 yrs.

Ann Brady
May 10, 1860
May 16, 1911

Pa Brady
Apr. 15, 1855

Ester May Garrison
Our baby
Mar. 10, 1917
Sept. 21, 1918

Bill Brady
Feb. 20, 1891
Feb. 1, 1935

RHEA COUNTY

TOMBSTONE INSCRIPTIONS
MT. TABOR GRAVEYARD

Go 18 miles north of Dayton to Spring City. Take the Grand View Highway, going about 3 miles before reaching Grandview, then take the Grassy Cove road to Grand View road, going about 3 miles west to Chas. Reed's place. Shortly thereby, you will find this little graveyard. There are about twenty unmarked graves.

Rhea County, Tennessee, Tombstone Inscriptions

RHEA COUNTY

TOMBSTONE INSCRIPTIONS
MYNATT CEMETERY

Located 6 miles northeast of Dayton and 1 mile south of Washington. On right hand side of Dixie Highway traveling north, and 3rd. District of Rhea County. This Cemetery originated during the life time of Dr. Samuel Mynatt, and was on Dr. Samuel Mynatt's property. The property now belongs to the Gideon family, and the Cemetery has become public. The Cemetery is opposite the old Mynatt home place now occupied by the Gideon family. The Cemetery has not been well kept, and is grown over with vines.

Julia F. Kelly
Feb. 4, 1824
Nov. 5, 1905
"She hath done what she could."

My husband
Jacob Kelly
Feb. 28, 1811
July 6, 1862

T. K. Crawford
Son of
J. B. & M. C. Crawford
Nov. 28, 1870
Oct. 9, 1871

Vesta K. Crawford
Nov. 4, 1874
Aug. 27, 1875

John S. Thomison
Aug. 16, 1839
Sept. 12, 1863

Zacariah (Zechabiah)
T. Thomison
June 22, 1846
Oct. 26, 1862

Virginia A.
Dau. of
R. O. & E. M. Purser
Dec. 28, 1875
Jan. 8, 1876

Margaret N. Nanny
Dau. of
Jas. T. & Orlena Nanny
April 12, 1851
July 5, 1854

Richard Waterhouse
Aug. 2, 1842
July 4, 1854

Isabella Ruth
Wife of
E. A. Lowry
Sept 27, 1862
Aug. 14, 1893
"She went about doing good."

Dr. B. K. Mynatt
March 23, 1825
Aug. 28, 1903

Mary E. Mynatt
Jan. 2, 1829
Jan. 11, 1914

S. C. Mynatt
April 10, 1935
Age.76 years.

In memory of Patrick C. Colville
who died Jan. 21, 1851
Aged 6 years, 11 months and 21 days.
(Continued)

Our Mother
Vesta Colville
Wife of W. E. Colville
March 3, 1823
April 22, 1878

Farewell - Capt. Warner E. Colville
July 25, 1876
Aged 58 yrs. 22 dys.

Rhea County, Tennessee, Tombstone Inscriptions

MYNATT CEMETERY

Mattie R.
Daughter of
W. E. & Vesta Colville
Aug. 8, 1867
Aged 5 mos. & 23 d's.

Gone to rest - Our Mother
Olivie James
Nov. 18, 1818
July 27, 1857

Our Father - John James
Nov. 16, 1812
Nov. 19, 1884

Ruth G. Ault
Feb. 13, 1836
Feb. 2, 1865

Julia F. Tucker
Feb. 14, 1869
Aged 4 mo's. & 16 D's.

Minerva M. Tucker
Wife of
G. L. Tucker
Feb. 14, 1870
Aged 25 years, 1 mo. & 24 days.

George L. Tucker
Son of
Joseph & Mary I. Tucker
April 24, 1831
Dec. 14, 1878

GILLESPIE
Mother - Hannah Gillespie
Jan. 21, 1815
July 27, 1882

In memery of
Robert N. Gillespie
Feb. 15, 1807
Aug. 18, 1865
Aged 58 years, 6 mo's. & 3 dys.

Mary A. Gillespie
Aug. 20, 1833
Sept. 6, 1839

Lilliam Gillespie
Oct. 1, 1857
Oct. 27, 1857

Martha B.
Daughter of
Dr. J. W. & N. G. Gillespie
Jan. 11, 1857
Dec. 27, 1858

George L. Gillespie
Dec. 21, 1855
Oct. 26, 1858

In memory of
James W. Gillespie
Aug. 9, 1819
Oct. 10, 1873

Emma P.
Wife of
R. N. Gillespie
Oct. 26, 1875
Aged 26 yrs, 8 mos. 24 dys.

G. E. Gillespie
Infant son of
R. N. & E. P. Gillespie
Nov. 3, 1869
Nov. 7, 1869

Nequeulla est lethi fuga - Sacred -
Samuel Frazie Esqr. who departed
this life
May 11, 1845
Aged 43 years, 2 months, and 9 days.

Elizabeth Fain Clawson
Wife of
Josiah Clawson
Born in Washington County, Tenn.
July 12, 1799
April 14, 1849

Ruth L. E.
Wife of
Samuel Frazier & daughter of
Josiah & Elizabeth Clawson
Born in Greenville, Tenn.
Aug. 26, 1808
Sept. 20, 1877
"Though once blind, she now seeth
clearly."

Rhea County, Tennessee, Tombstone Inscriptions

RHEA COUNTY

TOMBSTONE INSCRIPTIONS
NEW PORT GRAVEYARD

There are twenty two graves with rough sandstone markers. Three graves with slabs over them, each about 6 x 4 feet, and is located on the John Reed farm on White's Creek road.

Mary J. Treadway
Born Feb. 14, 1844

L. J. Treadway
Mar. 16, 1841
Nov. 4, 1909
"In my Father's house are many mansions. The Lord is my shepherd, I shall not want. He maketh me to lie down in green pastures, He leadeth me beside the still waters."

Margaret J. Garrison
Wife of
W. D. Smith
Oct. 10, 1869
Oct. 1, 1912

Clifford J.
Son of
M. J. and L. M. Keylon
July 25, 1907
Apr. 8, 1908
"Our loved one rests in slumber deep, in silent and eternal sleep."

Richard L. Garrison
Born in North Carolina
Aug. 12, 1825
Nov. 24, 1892
70 yrs.
Dead 42 yrs.
"In my Father's house are many mansions."

R. L. Garrison
Came to Rhea County while a youth where he spent the remainder of his useful life. He professed faith in Christ and joined the M. E. Church in 1894. Love to his many virtues. He served the people of Rhea Co., in the capacity of Sheriff and Trustee with honor to himself and constituents.

Juliah H. Newport
Wife of
R. L. Garrison
Nov. 18, 1844
Apr. 27, 1913

In memory of
Elder Asa Newport
Oct. 7, 1802
Dec. 15, 1876
74 yrs.
(Pastor of the Baptist Church, Hinds Valley. Ordained July, 1838, at 36 yrs. old.)

In memory of
Elizabeth, Wife of
Elder Asa Wright
Mar. 10, 1803
Oct. 4, 1877
Age 74 yrs. 6 mos. 24 dys.
"Blessed are the dead which die in the Lord."

Hannah F.
Daughter of
R. L. and J. H. Garrison
Nov. 10, 1873
Feb. 12, 1874

NEW PORT GRAVEYARD
(Continued)

James Johnson held many posts of honor and trust both in Church and State. He entered the confederate service in 1861 as a private soldier and was promoted to Quarter Master of the 26th. Tenn. Regiment with rank of Captain. Was a magistrate for 34 consecutive years.

Mary J.
First wife of
Elder James Johnson
Mar. 12, 1824
Dec. 20, 1858

Between their grandparents lies two children of Miller and Sallie J. Short
(Holy bible engraved.)
Born and died
July 1, 1860
"Budded on earth,
to bleem in Heaven."

Elder James Johnson
Born in Rhea Co., Tenn.
May 27, 1818
Mar. 29, 1895
77 yrs.
Dead 42 yrs.
He joined the Baptist Church 1831 and ordained to the full work of ministry in 1868. He contributed liberally of his means to the Church and to the necessities of the poor.
"Mark the perfect man and behold the upright, for the end of that man is peace."
Psalms 37: 37

Amy Clack
Wife of
Elder James Johnson
Feb. 20, 1829
Nov. 5, 1906
77 yrs.
(She was a devout christian and a member of the Baptist church for 56 yrs.
"Rest in peace."

Jessie Stinecipher
June 28, 1820
May 25, 1905
85 yrs.

Elizabeth
Wife of
Jesse Stinecipher
Sept. 30, 1831
Mar. 29, 1877
"Mother said follow."

Francis M. Majors
Dec. 20, 1835
Jan. 27, 1904
69 yrs.

Margaret Majors
Dec. 12, 1838
Dec. 4, 1910
72 yrs.

James M. Majors
Sept. 14, 1864
Oct. 1895
31 yrs.

William Majors
Apr. 16, 1866
Sept. 1867
1½ yrs.

Laura K.
July 28, 1874
Oct. 6, 1895
21 yrs.

NEW PORT GRAVEYARD
(Continued)

Ida McKinley
Daughter of
Harris and Sallie Peters
Sept. 29, 1897
Feb. 18, 1904
7 yrs.
"A little one from us has gone, a voice we loved is stilled, a place is vacant in our home which never can be filled."

RHEA COUNTY

TOMBSTONE INSCRIPTIONS
NORMAN FAMILY CEMETERY

The Norman family Cemetery is four miles northwest of Dayton. Follow Highway No. 27 from Dayton going to the Walnut Grove School house which is one mile north of Dayton. Leave the Highway and take gravel road west. Go one mile, take gravel road north going two miles to the Norman family Cemetery. The land belongs to Mr. Clint Norman.

RHEA COUNTY

TOMBSTONE INSCRIPTIONS
OAKMAN CEMETERY

The Oakman Cemetery is eleven miles northeast of Dayton on Highway No. 30. From Dayton go to Washington which is seven miles northeast of Dayton. Go from Washington to Clear Creek which is three miles north of Washington, going one mile east of Clear Creek to Dr. Cunningham's home. There are one hundred or more graves. No markers. Some have plain rocks. The land belongs to the Cunninghams.

RHEA COUNTY

TOMBSTONE INSCRIPTIONS
PAINE FAMILY CEMETERY

The Paine family Cemetery is six miles northwest of Dayton. Take Highway # 27 from Dayton leaving the Highway at the Walnut Grove School house which is one and a quarter mile north of Dayton. Follow the gravel road west which is called the Evensville back valley road. This Cemetery is on the Paine farm, and the land belongs to Mr. Paine. There are ten unmarked graves.

Wilford F. Weir
Sept. 4, 1888
Feb. 2, 1930

PAINE

Father - A. Paine
June 1, 1848
Aug. 10, 1911

Mother - Elizabeth N. Paine
Aug. 8, 1851
Jan. 14, 1932

Mrs. Bettie Paine
Jan. 14, 1923
Aged 70 yrs.

C. M. Paine
Feb. 8, 1875
June 24, 1910

F. Joe Paine
Jan. 19, 1872
Feb. 20, 1932

Bird Paine
Son of
R. W. and M. L. Galville
Sept. 15, 1875
Age one yr. 10 mos. 12 days.

Elvira Paine
Feb. 2, 1808
Aug. 25, 1887

Orville Paine
Feb. 27, 1800
Aug. 28, 1860

Our baby -
Mary Ella
Oct. 25, 1867
Oct. 10, 1868

C. A. Paine
Aug. 28, 1837

F. J. Paine
May 12, 1832
Oct. 9, 1893
"He trusted in Jesus."

RHEA COUNTY

TOMBSTONE INSCRIPTIONS
PARKER FAMILY GRAVEYARD

District No. 1. This graveyard is located at the back of Stinecipher's peach orchard in a strip of woodland. Leave Dayton on the Dixie Highway of Lon Foust Highway, going north to Roddy about 24 miles, turning east at 2 miles above Roddy into White's Creek road, then about one mile south of Mack Clack farm on the Toe String road. There are five graves in this plot with noticeable signs. Probably 25 graves with no visible signs.

Eli
Son of
G. C. and Tennessee Parker
Oct. 11, 1852
July 29, 1856
Age 4 yrs.

Sacred to the memory
of Wm. Parker
Apr. 30, 1855
Age 25 yrs. 1 mo. 18 dys.

Son of
Eli and Pruden Parker

Eli Parker
Sept. 12, 1791
July 12, 1856
Age 65 yrs.
(Dead 81 yrs.)

RHEA COUNTY

TOMBSTONE INSCRIPTIONS
PATRICK FAMILY CEMETERY

The Patrick family Cemetery is twelve miles northwest of Dayton. Follow Highway No. 27. From Dayton go to Evensville which is six miles north of Dayton. Leave the Highway and take the mountain road west going six miles to the Patrick Place. There are six or more unmarked graves.

E. A. Patrick
1843 - 1900

RHEA COUNTY

TOMBSTONE INSCRIPTIONS
PENDLETON GRAVEYARD

Continue on the river road one mile north of the Butler farm. At a very short turn of this road toward the river, just a few steps up in the woodland, this graveyard may be found. There are about six graves with no markers or names or dates. It was long ago abandoned.

Rhea County, Tennessee, Tombstone Inscriptions

RHEA COUNTY

TOMBSTONE INSCRIPTIONS
PETERSBURG GRAVEYARD

1st District. Take the Highway at Dayton going 18 miles to Spring City. Go one mile north of Spring City on same road, then go east by the old Barton place 1 mile. This graveyard is in a pine grove on top of hill. There are about 100 graves that are not marked, and the graveyard is not very old, consisting of colored people.

Frank Proctor
Oct. 11, 1917
Nov. 15, 1897
About 80 yrs.
"If death is eternal
life, why should
we weep?"

John Wasson
Feb. 18, 1893
75 yrs.

Hulda Wasson
Dec. 26, 1844

Mamie Gamble
Aug. 1, 1896
Mar. 14, 1899
3 yrs.

HAMMOND

Mrs. Martha Ray Hammond
Daughter of
Henry and Jane Ray
May 31, 1901
Feb. 13, 1920
Married May 19, 1919
"Darling, we miss thee."

Katie
Daughter of
Henry and Jane Ray
Feb. 27, 1890
Oct. 6, 1896
6 yrs.
"Darling, we miss thee."
(My wife top of stone.)

Nellie
Wife of
John L. Gist
Oct. 1, 1894
Feb. 8, 1920
"One who in this life
was a kind mother and
a true wife."

RHEA COUNTY

TOMBSTONE INSCRIPTIONS
PIERCE CEMETERY

The Pierce Cemetery is seven and a half miles north of Dayton. Follow Highway No. 27. From Dayton go to Evensville which is six miles north of Dayton. Go one mile north of Evensville, leaving the Highway and taking the road west. The Cemetery is one half mile from the main Highway and the land belongs to J. B. Tailors. There are one hundred and thirty five or more unmarked graves in this Cemetery, and is better taken care of than any Cemetery in Rhea County.

Elsiel Pelfrey
Feb. 10, 1900
July 6, 1902

W. H. Gentry
Jan. 22, 1918
Aug. 18, 1929

Russell

Irena
Wife of
W. M. Russell
1876 -
Oct. 14, 1921

James Gravett
Jan. 30, 1863
Oct. 20, 1907
"Gone but not forgotten."

Blanche A. Marler
Dau. of
J. & M. Marler
Sept. 23, 1904
Nov. 23, 1904

Martha M. Gambill
Wife of
H. H. Gambill
Jan. 28, 1903
Age about 80 yrs.

Easie Norman
Son of
C. & M. E. Norman
Apr. 9, 1901
July 30, 1901

In memory of
Our grandfather -
May 27, 1813
March 9, 1891

Mary Emily Harrison
Daughter of
J. H. & V. J. Harrison
Oct. 14, 1888
June 19, 1890

"Thy will be done."
Elvira Jones
Born Dec. 3, 1850

James Jones
July 2, 1850
Oct. 26, 1907
"Gone but not forgotten."

Lena Cole
Nov. 29, 1871
Apr. 11, 1890
"Her memory is blessed."

Lela Pearl Denton
Dau. of
G. M. & M. J. Denton
Sept. 12, 1890
Aug. 3, 1891
"At rest."

Maggie C. Pelfrey
Dau. of
J. W. & R. C. Pelfrey
May 16, 1882
Oct. 26, 1889

Rhea County, Tennessee, Tombstone Inscriptions

PIERCE CEMETERY
(Continued)

Caroline Pelfrey
Nov. 6, 1841
April 22, 1899
"Gone but not forgotten."

Sarah D. Hayes
Wife of
Eli Hayes
June 27, 1838
Feb. 26, 1890
"Asleep in Jesus."

Our little Robert -
Son of
R. N. & E. C. Hicks
June 8, 1889
June 13, 1891

Mary Jane Phillips
May 8, 1868
Sept. 2, 1877

Lillie Flornce Phillips
Nov. 7, 1883
Aug. 2, 1887

Rosa Dixon
Nov. 4, 1887
Jan. 6, 1889

Lula F. Crow
Dau. of
S. T. & N. E. Crow
Dec. 14, 1884
Apr. 8, 1890

Samuel Tate Crow
Nov. 25, 1934
Age 75 years, 11 months

Caleb Gravett
1826 -
Apr. 11, 1895
"We will meet again."

Father -
G. M. Denton
Nov. 28, 1863
Aug. 30, 1924

Emet Denton
Son of
J. H. & V. A. Denton
Apr. 18, 1905
Jan. 10, 1910
"He was a kind, loving son."

R. H. Denton
Son of
J. J. & L. E. Denton
Aug. 12, 1886
July 2, 1904
"At rest."

Richard Claude Denton
Son of
G. M. & M. J. Denton
Oct. 25, 1896
July 8, 1899

Our father -
Jerry Denton
Aug. 4, 1832
Jan. 30, 1898
Aged 65 yrs. 5 mos. 26 days.

Our mother -
Virginia S. Denton
Wife of
Jerry Denton
May 17, 1833
June 25, 1911

Edward D. Miller
April 3, 1901
Sept. 30, 1903

Infant daughter of
W. M. & Mary Denton
Born & died
Dec. 23, 1895

Edward Denton
June 8, 1838
Aug. 8, 1898

Nancy Denton
Apr. 6, 1842
Oct. 20, 1898

Rhea County, Tennessee, Tombstone Inscriptions

PIERCE CEMETERY
(Continued)

Della Denton
May 3, 1876
Sept. 19, 1896

Henry Denton
Sept. 26, 1871
Aug. 29, 1893

Father -
W. M. Denton
Mar. 12, 1861
Aug. 10, 1924

Thomas W. Smith
Feb. 18, 1852
Jan. 11, 1909
"He has gone
to the mansions of rest."

Lucy A. Smith
May 5, 1853
Dec. 28, 1919
"She believed and
sleeps in Jesus."

Joe S. Miller
Oct. 28, 1866
April 15, 1904

W. M. P. Darwin
Feb. 22, 1830
Nov. 4, 1894

Adelia Gillispie
Wife of
W. M. P. Darwin
July 11, 1839
Apr. 29, 1889

Clara C.
Daughter of
W. P. & Adelia Darwin
Jan. 28, 1875
June 20, 1877

Infant son of
J. T. & Laura Darwin
Feb. 19, 1896

Infant son of
J. T. & Laura Darwin
Sept. 29, 1838

Infant son of
J. T. & Laura Darwin
Oct. 11, 1891

Lillie Bithia
Dau. of
J. T. & Laura Darwin
July 28, 1889
Age 1 yr. 3 mos. 7 dys.
"Sleep on sweet babe
and take thy rest,
God called thee home
He thought it best."

Dealla Thomison
Wife of
D. R. & G. Thomison
May 10, 1864
Jan. 5, 1883

In memory of
Our mother -
Bethiah W. Darwin
Feb. 3, 1798
Apr. 27, 1873
Age 75 yrs. 2 mos. 24 dys.

In memory of
Our father -
James A. Darwin
Aug. 12, 1796
Sept. 17, 1872
Age 76 yrs. 1 mo. 5 dys.

Callie Caldwell
Daughter of
J. M. & V. Caldwell
Apr. 26, 1864
Aug. 7, 1870

Elizabeth Collins
Sept. 7, 1850
Oct. 22, 1930

Rhea County, Tennessee, Tombstone Inscriptions

PIERCE CEMETERY
(Continued)

Collins, James P.
Jan. 6, 1811
Mar. 4, 1893
"Homeward to the
 realms of peace."

Eliza M. Darwin
Wife of
Thos. Darwin
and dau. of
Henry & Rebecca Collins
Jan. 5, 1821
Aug. 5, 1882
Aged 61 yrs. 7 mos.

Thos. C. Darwin
Jan. 29, 1817
July 29, 1899
Aged 82 yrs. 6 mos.

Infant son of
W. H. & Ada Cunningham
Oct. 12, 1894
Oct. 12, 1894
"Sweetly sleeping."

Father -
Henry C. Rogers
1834 - 1880

Belindah Darwin
Feb. 9, 1828
May 12, 1901
"Faithful to trust
even unto death."

Infant Dau. of
A. C. & Eliza Darwin
July 1, 1904
July 1, 1904
"Our darling."

Ida Darwin
Wife of
J. H. Womack
May 18, 1861
Aug. 24, 1916

John Hoyle Womack
Dec. 3, 1858
Sept. 21, 1923

A. C. Darwin
Son of
T. C. & Eliza Darwin
Feb. 19, 1858
Oct. 16, 1918
"An honest man's
the noblest work of God."

Margaret Ida Womack
Sept. 27, 1920
Oct. 8, 1920
"Our loved one gone so soon."

Mary Louise Darwin
Dau. of
J. T. & Laura Darwin
Dec. 15, 1903
Nov. 23, 1906
"My grief for her will end
with death, mother."

John K. Martin
Apr. 2, 1843
Apr. 21, 1925

James T. Darwin
1854 - 1923

Isaac Travis Runyan
June 11, 1908
Jan. 28, 1910
"Asleep in Jesus."

Rivanna Runyan
Nov. 22, 1839
Dec. 23, 1918

I. L. Runyan
Dec. 27, 1834
Apr. 8, 1917
"Gone but not forgotten."

Holy Bible -
In memory of
our mother -
Jane A. Blevins
Eldest daughter of
Jas. A. & B. W. Darwin
Nov. 21, 1818
Mar. 25, 1869
Aged 50 yrs. 4 mos. 4 days.

Rhea County, Tennessee, Tombstone Inscriptions

PIERCE CEMETERY
(Continued)

Mary B. Marsh
Wife of
E. W. Marsh
And Dau. of
T. C. Darwin
Jan. 30, 1845
July 15, 1867

Susan H. Collins
Wife of
J. P. Collins
Mar. 26, 1822
July 30, 1848
"Meet me in Heaven."

Anna E.
Dau. of
J. P. Collins
APR. 29, 1861
July 28, 1866

In memory of
J. P. Collins
Eldest son of
H. C. & Mary Collins
May 3, 1845
July 25, 1861
Aged 16 yrs. 2 mos. 22 dys.

Henry Collins S. R.
Feb. 6, 1783
Oct. 28, 1848

M. A. Pierce
July 22, 1835
Dec. 25, 1893

E. D. Pierce
Feb. 24, 1835
June 13, 1913
"Gone but not forgotten."

Alnah C.
Son of
P. W. & Elida Pierce
Nov. 24, 1892
May 6, 1898

Housie
Son of
P. W. & Elida Pierce
July 19, 1895
May 16, 1898
"Sleep on sweet babe
and take thy rest,
God called thee home
He thought it best."

Maude
Dau. of
P. W. & Lide Pierce
July 23, 1892
Apr. 12, 1921
"Gone but not forgotten."

Houston

John H. Houston
Mar. 18, 1860
Aug. 28, 1924
"At rest."

E. A. Houston
Nov. 2, 1857
Feb. 26, 1914

Eliza J.
Wife of
J. M. Houston
Nov. 14, 1834
June 26, 1917
"Gone but not forgotten."

Louella Houston Runyon
Sept. 18, 1871
Dec. 24, 1898

Mary Houston
Feb. 3, 1869
May 20, 1904
"Sisters have gone
to be angels."

J. M. Houston
Oct. 18, 1832
May 13, 1907

PIERCE CEMETERY
(Continued)

Mother -
J. E. Blevins
Sept. 28, 1838
Feb. 12, 1908

Father -
J. B. Blevins
Feb. 16, 1841
Feb. 6, 1908

In memory of
James O.
Eldest son of
J. B. & J. E. Blevins
July 12, 1868
Dec. 31, 1872
Aged 4 yrs. 5 mos. 19 dys.

Infant dau. of
W. P. & Ethel Blevins
Apr. 11, 1915
"Our darling gone so soon."

S. D. Pierce
Aug. 25, 1825
Oct. 26, 1910

Eliza J. Miller
Mar. 19, 1815
Nov. 6, 1898

Louvina Stephens
Feb. 4, 1908

William Compton
Sept. 3, 1827
Dec. 22, 1893

Welthy Compton
Mar. 12, 1830
June 4, 1920

Father -
Thomas C. Collins
Sept. 2, 1858
May 7, 1918

George A. Garrison
Tennessee P. V. T.
B. A. S. E. Ho. S. P. 126
Dec. 5, 1930

RHEA COUNTY

TOMBSTONE INSCRIPTIONS
PORTER CEMETERY

The Porter Cemetery is nine miles northeast of Dayton. Follow Highway No. 27. From Dayton go to Evensville which is six miles north of Dayton, taking the Washington road north to Porter Cemetery. The land belongs to Travis. There are twenty eight unmarked graves.

Ida A. Travis
May 11, 1872
July 20, 1918
"Asleep in Jesus."

Pearl Travis
Dec. 13, 1905
Mar. 23, 1920
"Asleep in Jesus."

Albert Travis
Mar. 10, 1890
Oct. 16, 1927
"At rest in Jesus."

Henderson

Robt. F. Henderson
Oct. 23, 1839
May 13, 1900

Anna
Wife of
Robt. F. Henderson
Apr. 8, 1837
Oct. 19, 1925

Stewart
Oct. 6, 1900
Dec. 15, 1901
"At rest."

Audie Henderson
Jan. 13, 1901
Dec. 11, 1901

Hannar Dodd
Mar. 30, 1888
Apr. 29, 1912

Mrs. Sallie Mickle Hill
Jan. 13, 1928
Age 79 years.

1

RHEA COUNTY

TOMBSTONE INSCRIPTIONS
PORTER GRAVEYARD

This Cemetery is located north of Dayton on the old Stage road about 14 miles to the Add Smith farm, then ½ mile to the adjoining Porter farm. It is about 300 yds. west from the road on a little hill near a small pond, and is kept in good condition. About 43 unmarked graves.

Nerva Hill Jan. 8, 1891 Oct. 11, 1931 40 yrs.	Eliza J. Porter - Hope (?) Dec. 17, 1838 May 16, 1899
Ida May Hill May 5, 1897 Feb. 19, 1898 8 mos.	Bettie Lee Porter Feb. 14, 1926 May 14, 1927 15 mos. "Gone, our darling, but not forgotten." (About ¼ plot.)
PORTER	
E. L. P. Porter (Sand stone - High Shaft)	
John A. Porter June 24, 1833 Dec. 6, 1907	

RHEA COUNTY

TOMBSTONE INSCRIPTIONS
PORTER (JAMES) FAMILY GRAVEYARD

This graveyard is located on the James Porter farm. A beautigul lake lies near two very large pine trees. This is a childhood home of Ralph Porter, a former school teacher in Rhea County, but now is the County Court Clerk. This home is a model christian home. The head of this home has been dead for a number of years, and is a well known family, being early settlers. Take the State Highway from Dayton about 15 miles to Carp Schoolhouse, then go north about a mile to Add. Smith farm. There were no tombstone inscriptions, but the Mother of this home gave the history of the deceased from her bible.

John Henry Ward
Member of Baptist Church
Mar. 22, 1840
Apr. 5, 1901
"He was a Calvaryman
in the Civil War. 2 yrs.
in the Southern Army.
3 yrs. a home guard.

James S. Porter
Aug. 26, 1860
July 11, 1924
64 yrs.

James Roy Porter
July 24, 1898
Dec. 10, 1925
27 yrs.

Eugene C. Porter
June 8, 1914
May 7, 1917

Mother —
Lydia Knox Ward
July, 1845
Sept. 4, 1886
Age 41 yrs.

Father of
Mrs. Porter
Geo Washington Ward
(?)

Martha Ann Ward
His wife
Feb. 2, 1871
Aug. 15, 1903

Myers family also buried
in this graveyard.
(No dates.)

1

RHEA COUNTY

TOMBSTONE INSCRIPTIONS
GEN. PRICHET FAMILY GRAVEYARD

This graveyard is at High Point or Vaugh Grammar School Community. Come twelve miles north from Dayton, turn east on High Point road at Brown Spear's Farm. Go two miles east from Dixie Highway or Highway 27. At High Point or Vaughn Grammar School house, cross over the hill on same road east, there you will find about five undated and unnamed graves.

1

RHEA COUNTY

TOMBSTONE INSCRIPTIONS
RECTOR GRAVEYARD

This graveyard is now abandoned. It is located in District No. 1, on Red Mountain. Take Highway No. 27 or the Dixie Highway north from Dayton to Spring City. ½ mile north of Spring City, turn east ½ mile. There are probably twenty unmarked graves, and no markers. It is a very old graveyard.

1

RHEA COUNTY

TOMBSTONE INSCRIPTIONS
REED FAMILY GRAVEYARD

This graveyard is about ½ mile from the Hickey graveyard. Take the Dixie Highway from Dayton to Spring City, 18 miles. Travel east on State Highway, past Rhea Springs, 2 miles from Spring City, going by the old Rhea Springs water mill, turn south on State Highway 3 miles, then turn east to Hickey town. Near here on the Geo. Reed farm, you will find three graves, two without markers.

Elbert Reed	Chas. Reed
Private soldier,	Jan. 4, 1915
Tenn. Private Inf. 29	July 11, 1922
Expert Sharp Shooter	Age 7 yrs.
Dec. 15, 1904	
Aug. 25, 1934	

1

RHEA COUNTY

TOMBSTONE INSCRIPTIONS
ROBERTS AND HARRIS GRAVEYARD

District No. 1. Take the J. Lon Foust Highway at Dayton, going 18 miles north to Spring City. Then take the Grand View road, going ½ mile northwest to Shut in Gap road. Go west on the Shut in Gap road to top of Walden's Ridge. Go 4 miles back on the same road 1 mile past the home of Obed Thurman, turning to left on a logging road, then going 1 mile or more back into woodland across a creek.

J. F. Roberts May 17, 1878 July 28, 1917 "He was beloved of God and man."	Rebecca Lucinda Harris Feb. 12, 1884 Dec. 21, 1889 "Our darling."
Barnett Harris Apr. 5, 1855 Mar. 5, 1924 "An honest man, is the noblest work of God."	There are about sixty unmarked graves.
Sarah M. Harris Mar. 17, 1848 Nov. 24, 1915 "Gone, but not forgotten.	

RHEA COUNTY

TOMBSTONE INSCRIPTIONS
ROBINSON FAMILY GRAVEYARD

Dist. No. 1. Get on the Dixie or Lon Foust Highway. Go 4 miles north of Spring City, then ½ mile west of Highway on old Mart Reed Farm, now owned by widow Neal, near Mrs. Neal's home. Out by a little orchard, you will find this little graveyard. It has been long since abandoned. About 25 graves, some very old, some not marked, say 10.

ROBINSON

Brunetta Robinson
Aug. 31, 1836
June 25, 1901

Ward H. Robinson
Nov. 5, 1851
Oct. 28, 1855

James A.
Son of
John and Hanna Robinson
Apr. 20, 1846
Aug. 9, 1856

Martha E. Heiskel
Wife of
T. J. Robinson
May 4, 1855
Oct. 24, 1887

James Robinson
Jan. 27, 1805
Nov. 10, 1880
Age 75 yrs.
"Dear Husband,
we'll meet again."

Elizabeth Earnest
Wife of
James Robinson
May 10, 1810
Aug. 1, 1887
Age 77 yrs.

John Robinson
Feb. 10, 1799
July 27, 1886
Age 87 yrs.

RHEA COUNTY

TOMBSTONE INSCRIPTIONS
ROBISON CEMETERY

The Robison Cemetery is two miles and a half east of Dayton. Follow Highway No. 30 from Dayton going to the Camp Ground Hill which is one mile from Dayton. Take gravel road east just before getting to the top of the hill. Take the old road to right, going to Shaver and Robison farm. There are seven unmarked graves. The land belongs to Robison and Shaver

Rhea County, Tennessee, Tombstone Inscriptions

RHEA COUNTY

TOMBSTONE INSCRIPTIONS
RODDY GRAVEYARD

Roddy is about twenty five miles north of Dayton on the Dixie Highway in the 1st. District. Roddy graveyard is just about 300 yards north of Roddy on the east side of the Highway. A tall cedar tree stands prominent thereby. This graveyard is probably a century and a half old. Five large stone slabs over the top of graves, slabs 6 by 12 ft. Slabs are set on rock walls. One grave is fenced in by strong steel fencing. No names or dates are given.

Willie Whittenburg
June 4, 1847
Aug. 9, 1856
"Budded on earth
to bloom in heaven."
Age 9 years.
Three large concrete enclosures,
Large headstones. No names
or dated.

Children of
J. L. & M. E. Roddy

John D.
Feb. 19, 1886
Sept. 16, 1889
3 yrs.
"Gone but not forgotten."

Mary Kate Roddy
Dec. 20, 1868
May 1, 1894
"Dear children,
we miss thee,
we will soon follow thee."

Our mother -
Charlotte J. Dodson
Oct. 8, 1826
July 5, 1909
83 yrs.

Our mother -
Margaret Roddy
Wife of
James Roddy
Feb. 10, 1806
Sept. 1878
72 years.

W. T. Roddy
July 9, 1876
Dec. 3, 1915
39 years.

James L. Roddy
Aug. 21, 1837
May 18, 1916
79 years.

Thompson, John A.
Son of
Joseph & Ann Thompson
Mar. 8, 1871
July 30, 1880

Sarah
Wife of
John Dodson
Nov. 13, 1929
Sept. 19, 1861

1

RHEA COUNTY

TOMBSTONE INSCRIPTIONS
RODDY FAMILY GRAVEYARD

District No. 1. To get to this Cemetery, take the Lon Foust Highway from Dayton 18 miles to Spring City, then across Piney river, thence about 6 miles toward Rockwood untill you have reached the Roddy farm which is about ½ mile south of Roddy station, also the Roddy residence.

In memory of
James Alexander
Son of
David M. and Elizabeth B. Roddy
Mar. 19, 1853
Aug. 9, 1856
"Sleep on dear Babe
and take thy rest,
God hath called thee
He thought it best."

There are two other tall head stones, with names and dates worn off. Three with markers having no names or dates. Six or more graves in all. Two beautiful cedars at corners and an old fashioned fence around the plot.

Rhea County, Tennessee, Tombstone Inscriptions

RHEA COUNTY

TOMBSTONE INSCRIPTIONS
ROGERS CEMETERY

The Roger's Cemetery is five and one half miles northwest of Dayton, Leave Dayton on Highway on Highway # 30 northwest going five miles on Highway. After leaving the Highway, take the gravel road northeast, for about one half mile. The land belonging to Henry Rogers was given by his father years ago for this Cemetery. There are about sixty eight unmarked graves.

Sarah R. Tallmadge
Wife of
E. M. Tallmadge
Aug. 28, 1846
Jan. 10, 1903
"Rest in peace."

Emma C. Childress Headlee
Wife of
J. M. B. Headlee
July 5, 1865
March 3, 1922

Robert Earl Headlee
Sept. 3, 1891
Aug. 13, 1898

Louisa Headlee
May 31, 1853
Feb. 4, 1904

Henry B. Olinger
Jan. 30, 1884
Jan. 12, 1904

Orbell Olinger
Oct. 30, 1840
Nov. 13, 1915
"Gone to rest."

John Olinger
March 27, 1840
Jan. 26, 1916
"Gone to rest."

Margert Rogers
Oct. 1845

Mr. I. J. Oldham
Apr. 24, 1873
June 25, 1890
"At rest."

D. R. Oldham
Mar. 30, 1862
Jan. 1, 1930

L. A. Walker
May 11, 1816
Jan. 22, 1892

C. F. Pickett
May 1, 1891
Jan., 18, 1892

M. D. Pickett
Wife of
J. F. Pickett
July 24, 1853
Nov. 20, 1905

J. H. Williams
June 7, 1857
March 17, 1912

Henrietta
His wife
Nov. 25, 1836
March 24, 1914

R. L. Reed
Apr. 11, 1877
Nov. 6, 1909

W. M. B.
Son of
R. L. & M. H. Reed
Born & died
Feb. 17, 1902
"In Heaven."

BURWICK

Infant son of S. H. & Alice Burwick
Born & died Aug. 22, 1891

Rhea County, Tennessee, Tombstone Inscriptions

ROGER'S CEMETERY

Samuel H. Burwick
Jan. 18, 1868
May 21, 1901
"Beloved one farewell."

Jessie Walker
Son of
W. H. & Lizzie Walker
July 4, 1895
Oct. 15, 1896

Eddie
Son of
W. H. & Lizzie Walker
May 27, 1905
Oct. 15, 1916

James A. Reed
Son of
N. R. & Lillie Reed
Aug. 13, 1914
Sept. 26, 1920

N. R. Reed
July 15, 1879
Feb. 11, 1932
"Gone but not forgotten."

William Jessie Reed
July 18, 1903
Dec. 4, 1935
"Beloved one farewell."

Calvin Gerald
Son of
John & Melvia Reed
Sept. 16, 1935
Jan. 3, 1936
"Asleep in Jesus."
(3 unmarked graves in same lot.)

MORGAN

United Mine Workers of America
5899.
Darius Franklin Walker
Mar. 3, 1884 - Killed in the Mines
by falling slate Mar. 26, 1936
Wheelwright, Ky.
"His toils are past, his work is
done, he fought the fight,
the victory won."

R. F. Walker
Feb. 11, 1877
Feb. 22, 1901

W. M. C. Walker
Sept. 22, 1837
June 12, 1913

Alsie Jane Walker
July 13, 1849
Dec. 29, 1902

B. H. Walker
Feb. 22, 1891
Oct. 28, 1918
"Gone but not forgotten."

J. C. Curtain
Died June 19, 1928
Age 50 yrs.

Mrs. Martha Morgan
July 10, 1934
Age 81 yrs. 6 mos. 20 days.

John Morgan
Tenn. P. V. T. - 105 Engrs.
May 14, 1932

T. J. Elder
(?)

James F. Gothard
June 1, 1883
May n 27, 1901
"At rest."

Albert E. Gothard
Jan. 7, 1885
May 27, 1901
"Come unto me."

L. G. Rogers
Jan. 10, 1851
May 27, 1901
"Asleep in Jesus, blessed sleep."

J. F. Walker
Sept. 25, 1856
May 27, 1901

ROGER'S CEMETERY

J. T. Wright
Apr. 1871
May 27, 1901
"He was faithful and God has said he that endureth to the end shall be saved."

D. T. Carter
Mar. 1887
May 27, 1901

Tommy Carter
March 11, 1889
May 27, 1901

J. F. Walker
Sept. 25, 1852
May 27, 1901
Those men were all killed May 27, 1901 in the North Pole Coal Mine Explosion caused by dust. near Dayton.

RHEA COUNTY

TOMBSTONE INSCRIPTIONS
ROSE FAMILY CEMETERY

The Rose family Cemetery is eight miles west of Dayton. Follow Highway No. 30 from Dayton going one and a half miles. Leave the Highway and take old road west going six miles and a half to Rose Place. There are four unmarked graves. The land belongs to Rose.

R. C. Rose
May 1, 1836
Jan. 4, 1895

M. E. Rose
Mar. 6, 1839
Oct. 7, 1900

1

RHEA COUNTY

TOMBSTONE INSCRIPTIONS
ROSS FAMILY GRAVEYARD-RODDY SCHOOL HOUSE

Get on the Dixie Highway at Dayton, going north 18 miles to Spring City, then go five miles to Roddy, just east of Roddy Post Office. On a cross road close by the Roddy School House, you will find the Ross family graveyard.

Jack Ross
Jan. 23, 1841
July 5, 1922
Age 81

Infant son of
G. H. and M. A. Ross
Jan. 25, 1908
(Keylon plot.)

Aleen Keylon
June 4, 1920
Mar. 15, 1921

Irene Keylon
June 4, 1920
July 20, 1920

Kenneth Keylon
Jan. 17, 1916
Mar. 1, 1916

"Our Darling."
Infant daughter of
S. W. & H. Keylon
Born and died
Nov. 15, 1911

"Our Darling."
Infant daughter of
C. H. & M. A. Ross
Jan. 8, 1909

Pearl, daughter of
C. H. & M. A. Ross
Oct. 7, 1906
April 16, 1907

About 12 graves, some not marked. Graveyard in very good Condition.

1

RHEA COUNTY

TOMBSTONE INSCRIPTIONS
RUSSELL FAMILY CEMETERY

The Russell family Cemetery is five miles and a quarter south of Dayton. Follow the old Graysville Highway going to Graysville which is five miles south of Dayton. Cross the Railroad at Graysville going across the Creek. On the right is the old Russell farm. There are three unmarked graves. Mrs. Russell and two children have been buried for over eighty years. A wire fence is around the graves. The land now belongs to the Hoovers.

Rhea County, Tennessee, Tombstone Inscriptions

RHEA COUNTY

TOMBSTONE INSCRIPTIONS
SALEM CEMETERY

Located 3½ miles east of Dayton, in suburb Salem, leaving Dayton turn east at 3rd. Avenue, traveling on the old Dixie Highway until reaching the Camp Ground Hill; then follow the Double S road eastward. The Cemetery is on the left hand side of the road, and by the side of the Salem Baptist Church. Graves are grown over, and many of them have no tombstones. Located in 3rd. District of Rhea County.

J. W. Dodd
Nov. 9, 1823
March 30, 1914
"We will meet again."

Mary Dodd
March 19, 1825
Sept. 18, 1897

M. P. Huskins
July 30, 1853
Jan. 25, 1893

Robert R. Elder
Oct. 7, 1873
Jan. 29, 1898

Elder, W. A.
Oct. 1, 1848
Feb. 17, 1899
"Tis hard to break the tender cord, where love is bound the heart, 'Tis hard, so hard to speak the word, shall we forever part!"

Mary S.
Wife of
Joe Brooks
March 13, 1869
Aug. 2, 1893
"At rest."

Infant son of
B. T. & Bee Boles
Born and died
June 27, 1890

Elizabeth
Wife of
J. G. Brady
Aug. 8, 1868
April 12, 1901

J. G. Brady
May 17, 1865
Oct. 7, 1903

Lesta S. Morgan
Nov. 1, 1880
Oct. 24, 1884

F. L. Dodd
May 5, 1861
June 1, 1981
Age 20 y's. 22 d's.

Holly Ann Hardin
(?)

James W. Rice
(?)

Oley C. Cook
April 19, 1886
Feb. 11, 1890

Cordie L.
Wife of
Jas. A. Sitton
Oct 21, 1863
Dec. 14, 1890
"Weep not, she is not dead, but sleepeth."

R. M. Scroggins
Aug. 21, 1873
May 5, 1891

SALEM CEMETERY

J. T. Scroggins
Dec. 18, 1886
Nov. 20, 1915

William R.
Son of
James R. & Matilda J. Byrd
Oct. 5, 1869
Dec. 24, 1903
"Meet me on the other Shore."

G. M. Woody
Dau. of
W. R. & S. E. Woodey
Dec. 7, 1900
April 10, 1904

Claude Lee
Son of
W. R. & S. R. Woodey
Jan. 19, 1906
Feb. 5, 1910
"A little bud of love,
to bloom with God above."

RHEA COUNTY

TOMBSTONE INSCRIPTIONS
SANDELL FAMILY CEMETERY

The Sandell Family Cemetery is three miles and one half southeast of Dayton. Follow the Blythes Ferry road from Dayton to the Eva Roston farm which is three and one half miles from Dayton. There is only one grave. The land belongs to Eva Roston.

Bobbie Nell Sandell
Age 23 months.

RHEA COUNTY

TOMBSTONE INSCRIPTIONS
SANFORD FAMILY CEMETERY

The Sanford family Cemetery is twelve miles northwest of Dayton. Follow Highway No. 27. From Dayton go to Evensville which is six miles north of Dayton. Go two miles north of Evensville, leaving Highway, take the graveled road west one mile, then take road north. The land belongs to the Sanfords. There are three unmarked graves.

Shirley Sanford	Mae Sanford
1849 -	1845 -
Apr. 6, 1902	Feb. 2, 1905

RHEA COUNTY

TOMBSTONE INSCRIPTIONS
SCHOOL FIELD FAMILY GRAVEYARD

District No. 1. Take the J. Lon Foust Highway at Dayton going 18 miles north to Spring City. Then go one mile north of Spring City to Matt Landreth's farm, going ½ mile east to north west corner of his farm, and at the School Field line. There are about 6 graves in a little grove, which are not marked and is now abandoned.

REA COUNTY

TOMBSTONE INSCRIPTIONS
SHADWICK CEMETERY

The Shadwick Cemetery is fourteen miles northwest of Dayton. Follow Highway No. 27 from Dayton. Go to Evensville which is six miles north of Dayton. Leave Highway at Evensville and take the mountain road northwest. Go eight miles. There are twelve unmarked graves. The land belongs to Shadwicks.

SHADWICK

Anderson Shadwick
1843 - 1902

D. E. Shadwick
1836 - 1899

Bessie Shadwick
1845 - 1900
"Gone to rest."

Rhea County, Tennessee, Tombstone Inscriptions

RHEA COUNTY

TOMBSTONE INSCRIPTIONS
SHAVER CEMETERY

Located two miles northeast of Dayton in 3rd. District of Rhea County. Leave Dayton, following the old Dixie Highway until reaching Camp Ground Hill, Ga. up Camp Ground Hill following Double S. road. This Cemetery is located about ¼ mile off and to the left hand side of the road, on what is known as the "Old Freelen Farm" but is now the property of Lester Purser. Is not very well kept, and a few graves are without tombstones.

SHAVER

Thomas F.
Son of
Samuel & Mary Shaver
June 3, 1874
March 31, 1902

Walter E.
Son of Samuel L. & Mary C. Shaver
Sept. 2, 1885
July 20, 1912
"Though lost to sight,
to memory dear."

Cornelius Shaver
June 5, 1807
June 10, 1874

Jane H. Shaver
Dec. 22, 1812
April 28, 1863

Father - Alfred B. Kelley
March 21, 1882
June 12, 1928

Samie Dalis Kelley
Feb. 27, 1911
Dec. 15, 1918
"Christ loved him
and took him home."

J. R. Kelley
Nov. 11, 1873
July 18, 1908

Jane
Dau. of
J. Q. & E. J. Shaver
Jan. 23, 1861
Feb. 20, 1879
"Her happy soul has winged
its way to one pure bright
eternal day."

Mary Ella
Dau. of
J. Q. & E. J. Shaver
Sept. 27, 1874
Dec. 15, 1876
"Sleep on dear child
and take thy rest
in Jesus arms forever blest."

Henry Shaver
Died December, 1918
Aged 35 years.

W. A. Kelley
March 16, 1834
Dec. 9, 1904

Rhea County, Tennessee, Tombstone Inscriptions

RHEA COUNTY

TOMBSTONE INSCRIPTIONS
SHAVER CEMETERY

Located 3¾ miles east of Dayton on the hill opposite the Salem Baptist Church. On the property of H. H. Shaver, known as the "Old Shaver Place." This Cemetery is about ½ mile off, and to the right of Mud Creek road and Salem Community. It is a private family Cemetery, and is aged somewhat. It is grown over with shrubbery, but most graves have tombstones. Located in 3rd. District of Rhea County.

SHAVER

Creed Shaver
May 8, 1891
Nov. 5, 1900

Mollie Shaver
Dec. 15, 1869
April 29, 1901

Jessie Shaver
Age 59

Nancy Bolen
1824 - 1903
Age 79

T. F. Shaver
Oct. 12, 1844
March 4, 1917
"Thy life was beauty, truth and love."

Catherine Shaver
Wife of
Rev. T. F. Shaver
Jan. 11, 1853
Jan. 26, 1926

Rev. John Q. Shaver
Nov. 3, 1833
Feb. 14, 1903
"His toils are past, his work is done, he fought the fight, the victory won!"
Erected by Salem Church & friends, Missionary Baptist & member Hiwassee Association.

Cordie Shaver
Dec. 17, 1882
Oct. 2, 1917

L. G. Wade, Jr.
March 11, 1924
Age 3 days.
"From Mother's arms to the arms of Jesus."

Rosae
Wife of
G. H. Wade
Jan. 10, 1895
July 3, 1913
A lovely wife, a Mother dear lies buried here.

John M. Shaver
Nov. 18, 1872
Mar. 6, 1933

Alice A.
Wife of
W. E. Collins
Oct. 2, 1872
June 24, 1915
A lovely wife, a Mother dear, lies buried here.

Emma Parentha
Wife of
S. B. Arnold
May 9, 1864
July 20, 1914

Lillie Pearl
Wife of
U. S. Suttles
Sept. 3, 1891
July 11, 1914
"Her spirit smiles from that bright shore, and softy whispers, weep no more."

2

SHAVER

Callie Shaver
Sept. 19, 1885
May 16, 1918
"In after time we'll
meet her."

T. T. Shaver
Oct. 25, 1884
June 4, 1923
"His tdils are past,
his work is done,
he fought the fight,
the victory won."

SHAVER CEMETERY

Willis Houston
Born & died
June 19, 1909

Mrs. Bertie Burnett
Feb. 4th. --
Aged 30 yrs. 9 mos.

RHEA COUNTY

TOMBSTONE INSCRIPTIONS
SMITH CROSS ROAD CEMETERY

The Smith Cross Road Cemetery is in South Dayton near the freight station. At the time this Cemetery was started Dayton was called Smith's cross roads. There have been lots of markers in this Cemetery but they have been torn down. There is a cross tie yard in the Cemetery and there are seventy-five or more graves. The land belongs to Southern Railroad Company and D. C. & I. Company.

Rhea County, Tennessee, Tombstone Inscriptions

RHEA COUNTY

TOMBSTONE INSCRIPTIONS
Add SMITH COMMUNITY GRAVEYARD

To reach this graveyard take the old Stage road north about 15 miles to the Add Smith farm. It is just west of the road not far from Mr. Smith's home, and is covered with cedars under a wire fence. This farm and plot belong to Mr. Add Smith and heirs and is in District No. 2

Henry W. Parks
Nov. 16, 1864

Mary E. Hale
Wife of
Henry W. Parks
May 4, 1871
Sept. 27, 1926

Earl
Son of
W. H. and N. C. Parks
June 8, 1928
Feb. 11, 1929
"Our darling."

Earl
Son of
G. W. and Ackaline West
16 yrs.
May 26, 1901
May 27, 1917
"Weep not,
he is at rest."

Lela B. Byrd
Jan. 30, 1895
June 17, 1913
18 yrs.
"Stop and think when
passing by, as you are now,
so once was I. As I am now,
you soon shall be. Prepare
for death and follow me."

J. C. Kelley
Feb. 4, 1924
Dec. 8, 1925
1 yr. 8 mos.

Wm. F. Dosson
May 16, 1861
Jan. 14, 1873
12 yrs.

Thomas Lee Dosson
Oct. 9, 1865
Apr. 29, 1895
30 yrs.

Isaiah Dosson
Sept. 26, 1812
Feb. 18, 1876
64 yrs.

Virginian Ann Dosson
Sept. 17, 1859
Jan. 1861
2 yrs.

Effie Dosson
Born and died
Feb. 1856

Amanda Dosson
Jan. 23, 1852
June 14, 1873

Sarah F.
Wife of
Josiah Dosson
April 11, 1824
July 18, 1887
63 yrs.

Mary Dosson
Oct. 25, 1841
June 30, 1861
20 yrs.

Louisa Dosson
Jun 27, 1847
July 19, 1854
7 yrs.

Mother -
Jane Sutton
Jan. 14, 1854
Nov. 13, 1922
68 yrs.

ADD SMITH COMMUNITY GRAVEYARD

Wm. Luther Jones
Sept. 18, 1903
Aug. 21, 1916
13 yrs.

Calvin Datre Parks
Sept. 4, 1919
Dec. 12, 1924
5 yrs.

H. S. Smith
Feb. 29, 1863
Mar. 7, 1918
55 yrs.
"He was a kind and
affectionate husband,
a good father, and a
friend to all."

Emma Beard
Wife of
H. S. Smith
Nov. 10, 1869

Thelma Smith
Dec. 28, 1921
Oct. 12, 1929
8 yrs.
"With Christ in Heaven."

About 52 graves undated and unnamed. This Cemetery is well kept.

Rhea County, Tennessee, Tombstone Inscriptions

RHEA COUNTY

TOMBSTONE INSCRIPTIONS
SMITH AND WILKEY GRAVEYARD

District No. 2. This is the Margaret Ann Smith and J. C. Wilkey graveyard, sometimes called the Yellow Creek graveyard. Take the State Highway from Dayton about ten miles north of Dayton to the J. C. Wilkey farm. This is a community graveyard. There are about 200 graves without names or dates.

Rhoda S. Hawkins
April 6, 1858
Aug. 30, 1860
"Sweet be thy rest
loved one, 'till God
bids thee rise."

AULT

In memory of
Conrad Ault
Feb. 22, 1783
Feb. 1, 1818
Age 35 yrs.
(Solid rock vault cover.)

In memory of
Susan Ault
July 22, 1789
Dec. 9, 1859
(Solid rock cover
over grave.)

In memory of
Geo. W. Ault
Aug. 9, 1831
Mar. 1, 1862

MCCLURE

J. M. McClure
Aug. 28, 1845
Dec. 15, 1919
74 yrs.

Mary A. Gurley
Wife of
J. M. McClure
Feb. 25, 1846
"Death is the crown of life."

J. C. Garrison
Mar. 29, 1844
May 22, 1932

Nancy J. Jolly
Wife of
J. C. Garrison
Dec. 21, 1840
Jan. 3, 1908

Mother and Father -
Sallie M. Garrison
Feb. 1, 1874
July 18, 1907
(Bible engraved on top
of stone. Wilkey on bottom
of stone.)

Nellie May
Daughter of
J. C. and Sallie Wilkey
Sept. 11, 1893
June 17, 1907
Age 14.

Pearl D. Wilkey
Wife of
John McClure
Nov. 5, 1898
Aug. 7, 1922

John Actkinson
May 11, 1847
Dec. 12, 1920
63 yrs.

Isabelle Fike
Wife of
John Actkinson
July 14, 1849
Feb. 26, 1919
70 yrs.

Rhea County, Tennessee, Tombstone Inscriptions

SMITH AND WILKEY GRAVEYARD

Laura J.
Wife of
John W. Cate
Sept. 6, 1857
Jan. 23, 1906
"Asleep in Jesus."

Hilton B.
Son of
J. W. and L. J. Cate
Jan. 30, 1894
Nov. 28, 1895

FOUST

N. B. Foust
Aug. 20, 1840
Sept. 7, 1892
52 yrs.

Mary Smith
Wife of
N. B. Foust
Nov. 7, 1845
Jan. 28, 1916

Amanda J. Martin
Mar. 30, 1876
May 25, 1928

Father -
Wm. K. Day
Jan. 22, 1852
Aug. 2, 1921

Mother -
Amanda Taylor
Wife of
Wm. K. Day
July 17, 1853
Mar. 31, 1920
"Asleep in Jesus."

John Crawford
Son of
T. K. and Minnie Day
Apr. 19, 1924
July 30, 1926
"We can safely leave
our darling in trust."

PUGH

Our Father -
J. H. Pugh
May 10, 1850
May 23, 1916
66 yrs.

Our Mother -
Rebecca Pugh
Dec. 25, 1849
(Family plot in concrete walls.)

Dortha May Snider
Apr. 14, 1922
Apr. 14, 1922
"At rest."

James E.
Son of
Mr. & Mrs. G. T. Pugh
Born and died
Oct. 11, 1935

Blanche M.
Daughter of
J. S. and Celia Wright
Aug. 29, 1912
July 19, 1913
About 11 mos.

Thomas Arthur
Son of
S. M. and J. E. Wright
Jan. 28, 1906
Nov. 24, 1914

Albert J. Smith
Feb. 13, 1899
Dec. 24, 1915
16 yrs.
"His record is on high."

Father -
J. W. True
Apr. 16, 1857
Dec. 30, 1915
"Asleep in Jesus, blessed thought."

Eliza Etta
Daughter of
R. T. and E. M. Scroggins
July 12, 1913 - Sept. 16, 1913
"Budded on earth to bloom in Heaven."

Rhea County, Tennessee, Tombstone Inscriptions

SMITH AND WILKEY GRAVEYARD

Robert Taylor Scoggins
July 28, 1886
Feb. 18, 1930
44 yrs.
"At rest."

Miriam Skemills (?)
Wife of
Dave McInturff
Mar. 26, 1884
Jan. 25, 1923
"At rest."

John T. Smith
Mar. 7, 1844
May 17, 1881
37 yrs.

Margaret L.
Daughter of
J. T. and M. A. Smith
May 18, 1870
Sep. 1, 1871
14 mos.

John T. Foust
Aug. 21, 1870
Apr. 9, 1872
2 yrs.
"Gone home."

Jacob W. Foust
May 7, 1869
Aug. 10, 1869
3 mos.

Henry Wasson
July 17, 1824
Sept. 11, 1864
40 yrs.

Mary
Wife of
Solomon Henry
1824 -
July 1, 1883
59 yrs.

Charlotte Dodd
Died Oct. 8, 1866
(Mother of
J. B. Dodd and three sisters.)
59 yrs.

Thana A. Ball
Sept. 18, 1865

Sarah K. Wilson
Sept. 19, 1866

Geo. W. Armor
Jan. 21, 1843
Oct. 31, 1866
(Mason.)

C. D. Harwood
Nov. 3, 1898
Nov. 29, 1900
2 yrs.

Pinkney Collins
Dec. 25, 1818
Nov. 1883
65 yrs.

Charlotte Collins
Aug. 22, 1822
Mar. 1890
68 yrs.

Geo. C. Day
July 3, 1898
July 3, 1898

Elizabeth Day
Feb. 25, 1828
Sept. 20, 1906
78 yrs. 6 mos. 25 dys.
"Gone, but not forgotten."

F. C. Knight
Feb. 24, 1920
Feb. 29, 1920
5 dys. old.

Margaret J. Dodd
Jan. 29, 1877

SMITH AND WILKEY GRAVEYARD

Cleo M. Knight
Aug. 13, 1899
Feb. 3, 1920
21 yrs.
"At rest."

Concrete walls around two graves. No names or dates.

A. H. Vincent
Husband of
Emma Vincent
Apr. 29, 1858
Mar. 29, 1924
66 yrs.

Manda E.
Wife of
A. H. Vincent
Nov. 21, 1864
Jan. 25, 1908
44 yrs.
"In my Father's house, are many mansions."

On hill in Oak and Cedar grove in good condition.

Rhea County, Tennessee, Tombstone Inscriptions

RHEA COUNTY

TOMBSTONE INSCRIPTIONS
SMYRNA CEMETERY

Located 2½ miles northeast of Evansville, and 1 mile east of the main State Highway No. 41. The Smyrna Baptist Church is located at the foot of hill, below Cemetery. Property of Smyrna Community. Public Cemetery.

Mary Ellen Brown
Feb. 18, 1924
July 10, 1925
"Our darling Ellen, budded on earth to bloom in Heaven."

"Our Darling" Jerald Eugene
Son of
Mr. & Mrs. H. C. Wilkey
Dec. 20, 1931
Jan. 5, 1936

Eilippa Cartone
West Virginia - P. V. T. Arty
Field - 2nd. Div. Sept. 30, 1935

Manrow, A. Thompson
Son of
Mr. & Mrs. G. F. Thompson
Jan. 4, 1904
May 14, 1931
"Thy God has claimed thee as thy own."
Erected by Mrs. Mathis

Fred S. Beard
Tennessee P. V. T.
Prisoner of War -
Escort Co., 71
June 23, 1923

J. S. Miller
May 16, 1865
Sept. 14, 1928

Mrs. Sallie Marley
Sept. 11, 1934
Aged 69 Yrs. & 9 months

A. M. Marlor
73 yrs. old
Died Jan. 4, 1933

Lillin Marlor
Dec. 24, 1907
Oct. 23, 1918
"Our Darling how we miss thee."

Billie Frank
Son of Frank & Ruth Minick
Dec. 16, 1932
Jan. 16, 1934

Floyd Collins
Jan. 3, 1879
Aug. 9, 1935

Macy L.
Wife of
Eliga Pelfrey
April 24, 1888
Feb. 8, 1917

Clement G. Pelfrey
Tennessee P. V. T. 119 Inf.
30 Div.
Jan. 22, 1922

James Kermit
Son of
W. A. & Mattie Lewis
Dec. 15, 1913
Aug. 3, 1920

Father - John Stinett
Dec. 20, 1834
Aug. 28, 1911
75 yrs. & 8 Mo.

Maxine Collins
Jan. 16, 1924

James H. Raper
Son of
J. P. & M. Raper
May 23, 1904 - June 2, 1929

Rhea County, Tennessee, Tombstone Inscriptions

SMYRNA CEMETERY

Mrs. Myrtle Hidon
(?)

Mary Elizabeth Wilkey
Feb. 17, 1885
June 20, 1923

Lillie Sue Ownesby
Nov. 1, 1921
Feb. 7, 1925

Eva J. Ownesby
Wife of
B. E. Hale
Feb. 12, 1894
July 26, 1931

Annie Ownesby
Wife of
J. A. Anderson
Feb. 12, 1894
Oct. 12, 1932

Mother - L. G. Conley
June 11, 1916
Age about 60 yrs.
"At rest."

Charles William
Son of
A. L. & Rosa Hall
Nov. 13, 1917
Dec. 16, 1917
"With Christ in Heaven."
Our Baby.

Mary A. Carpenter
Wife of
W. T. Gallaher
Nov. 19, 1857
July 14, 1927

Marry Stinnett
Jan. 30, 1936
Aged 24 years, 4 months, 8 dys.

Tinnie Baker
Dau. of
A. J. Bunch
Dec. 9, 1893
Feb. 4, 1920
"We will meet again."

Mrs. Anna Bell Campbe
(?)

Mrs. Lee Bunch
Age 28 yrs.
Died May 21, 1932

Joe L. Stennett
April 14, 1934
Aged 52 years

"Come ye Blessed."
Walter T. Brown
Dec. 22, 1891
May 3, 1926

Ella D. Pauline Mize
Dec. 23, 1916
Nov. 8, 1924
"Our darling, we miss thee."

N. W. Watson
(?)

James Kenneth Swafford
Jan. 8, 1926
Nov. 24, 1926

Father - Carl C. Smith
Nov. 22, 1896
Sept. 6, 1925

W. N. Smith
(?)

Dixie
Dau. of
J. P. & G. L. Coxsey
July 23, 1912
Aug. 20, 1922

J. H. King
May 1o, 1854
Feb. 29, 1922

Lee Mathis
(?)

Lonnie L.
Son of
H. C. & R. G. Crow
Feb. 19, 1918
Apr. 28, 1918

Rhea County, Tennessee, Tombstone Inscriptions

SMYRNA CEMETERY

Ruth
Dau. of
J. H. & L. P. Thomas
Dec. 25, 1916
Dec. 29, 1917

Dewey
Son of
J. H. & L. P. Thomas
Apr. 28, 1913
Mar 22, 1923

A. P. Thomas
Sept. 15, 1860
June 20, 1917

Sergt. Wm. P. Tenesson
Co. B., U. S. A. Inf.

F. L. T. -J. M. Bramlett
Feb. 12, 1843
July 31, 1916
"Thy memories shall ever be a guiding star to Heaven."

Lilly Marler
April 24, 1925

Pola Swafford
May 16, 1912
Dec. 19, 1933

Edith Houston
June 28, 1923
June 29, 1923

Elizabeth Manis
Oct. 25, 1861
"She beleaved, and sleeps in Jesus."

E. H. Manis
Feb. 19, 1855
Sept. 5, 1927
"Death is eternal life. Why should we weep?"

Father - M. C. Bramlett
July 19, 1858
July 11, 1919

Mother - H. E. Bramlett
Aug. 19, 1863
Jan. 23, 1933
"Sweet is the sleep our father takes in Christ."

Sarah L. West
May 1, 1858
Nov. 17, 1935

Leander J. West
3 N. G. Mtd. Inf.

Robert Hurst
Aged years - 1

Rev. V. L. Hurst
May 12, 1856
Feb. 14, 1914
"Resting in peace."

Abraham J. D. Stever
Co., 1, 34 Ohio Inf.

Maggie McDonald
March 10, 1927
Aged 70 yrs.

George McDonald
Aug 25, 1893
Dec. 27, 1920

Harrie L. Jackson
March 24, 1931

Sergt. Thos. J. Pelfrey
Co., D - 5 Tenn. Inf.

George Janow
(?)

Elmer Blevins
Aug. 2, 1934

W. O. W. Walter Hurst
Mar. 19, 1891
May 11, 1920

Laura Simmons
Nov. 24, 1884
Mar. 13, 1916

SMYRNA CEMETERY

Wiley Swafford
Jan. 15, 1893
Apr. 27, 1915

Bertha Owensby
Apr. 24, 1896
July 16, 1926

Hazel V. Pelfrey
May 7, 1926
Mar. 9, 1928

Father - J. W. Conley
Sept. 26, 1927
Age about 73 yrs.

Robert Wilkey
Mar. 15, 1912
June 9, 1916

Rachel Owensby
May 25, 1856
Mar. 13, 1929

Belle Z. Gentry
Nov. 10, 1870
Dec. 13, 1923
"An agel fallen asleep."

Sarah A.
Wife of
John Jorden
Nov. 12, 1883
Jan. 29, 1930

RHEA COUNTY

TOMBSTONE INSCRIPTIONS
SNEED FAMILY CEMETERY

The Sneed family Cemetery is five miles and a half north of Dayton. Follow Highway No. 27 from Dayton. Go three miles and take the Shades Valley Road northeast going to the Sneed farm. There are three graves, two unmarked. The land belongs to Sneeds.

    Willie May Sneed
    Oct. 28, 1936
    Aged 2 months

1

RHEA COUNTY

TOMBSTONE INSCRIPTIONS
SOUTHERLAND CEMETERY

The Southerland Cemetery is ten miles northwest of Dayton. Follow Highway No. 30. From Dayton go to the top of the mountain. Leave the Highway and take the road north going four miles. The land belongs to the Morgans. There are sixteen unmarked graves.

Mary A. Southerland May, 1843 Mar. 2, 1901 "Gone but not forgotten."	Birt Southerland Jan. 1841 June 5, 1900

Rhea County, Tennessee, Tombstone Inscriptions

RHEA COUNTY

TOMBSTONE INSCRIPTIONS
SPENCE CEMETERY

The Spence Cemetery is located six miles east of Dayton. Follow Highway # 30 from Dayton, leaving the Highway at the Camp Ground Hill which is one mile from Dayton. Follow the Gillespie Bend road and turn east on Route 1. The Cemetery is on the left and the land belongs to the Colbaugh family. There are three hundred and fifty eight unmarked graves.

J. H. Hawkins
Oct. 15, 1865
Oct. 4, 1910
"Asleep in Jesus."

Andrew Euclis Haran
Feb. 19, 1899
June 23, 1906
"Our darling."

Nancy Housley
Oct. 29, 1921
Aged 81 yrs. 10 mos. 10 days.

E. P. Beck
Dec. 27, 1847
July 9, 1927

Catherine
Wife of
E. P. Beck
July 6, 1924
Aged 82 yrs.
"They are waiting for us
in the Eden land beyond
the sunset of life."

Raplh Johnson Jewell
Aged 10 years.

J. T. Houston
May 16, 1860
Sept. 28, 1912
"Gone to rest."

Homer
Son of
L. & Tennie Spence
Dec. 26, 1917
Jan. 26, 1918
"Budded on earth
to bloom in Heaven."

Roddy T. Jewell
Son of
G. W. & C. E. Jewell
July 2, 1913
Aug. 31, 1920
"Asleep in Jesus."

To my wife -
M. G.
Wife of
M. R. Carroll
Jan. 7, 1852
Dec. 19, 1909
"She was the sunshine
of our home."

Margaret A.
Wife of
Jessie Boles
Nov. 20, 1854
Jan. 11, 1924
"Gone but not forgotten."

J. H. Cochran
Jan. 18, 1855
Jan. 25, 1914

Mrs. Jane Cochran
Sept. 12, 1933
Aged 70 yrs. 7 mos. 20 dys.

Rud Boyd
May 22, 1851
Oct. 13, 1916

Texie A. Boyd
Jan. 15, 1840
Aug. 3, 1903

Bro. Boyd
June 12, 1903
July 27, 1903

Rhea County, Tennessee, Tombstone Inscriptions

SPENCE CEMETERY

J. S. Boyd
Oct. 18, 1880
Apr. 3, 1900

Perry Francis Lutz
Born in the State of
Kentucky
Feb. 8, 1866
Died in the state
of Tennessee
June 29, 1917
"An honest man's the
noblest work of God."

Meda Lutz
Oct. 8, 1912
Nov. 17, 1912
"Gone to be an angel."

T. M. Coleman
Jan. 24, 1896
Sept. 30, 1897

F. L. Coleman
Mar. 14, 1894
June 30, 1895

Mother -
Maggie E.
Wife of
T. C. Hicks
Oct. 24, 1879
Jan. 28, 1922
"Asleep in Jesus."

Isaac Bartley
Son of
J. S. & M. E. Hicks
Sept. 3, 1887
Apr. 1, 1901

W. B. Purser
May 17, 1830
May 17, 1901

M. C. Purser
Dec. 16, 1834
Mar. 13, 1904

In memory of
William Purser
Son of
James & H. E. Purser
July 2, 1898
Sept. 29, 1898

Baby of
J. W. & E. L. Purser
(?)

Scrap J. Burd
Oct. 1, 1868
Oct. 30, 1895
"At rest."

Hannah Boyd
Daughter of
Jno. & Mary Boyd
June 3, 1891
Feb. 7, 1892

Silvester
Son of
Jno. & Mary Boyd
Dec. 13, 1884
May 30, 1887

PURSER

"Come and lets go home."
In memory of
William Woodville
Son of
H. M. & A. G. Purser
May 17, 1877
Departed this life
May 13, 1888

In memory of
R. M. Purser
Son of
H. M. & A. G. Purser
Born & died
Jan. 17, 1876

S. B. Arnold
1840 -
Apr. 2, 1906

Rhea County, Tennessee, Tombstone Inscriptions

SPENCE CEMETERY

A. F. Arnold
Dec. 25, 1875
Jan. 11, 1926

Infant Daughter of
Mr. & Mrs. C. R. Housley
June 23, 1914
"Resting in the arms
of Jesus."

James W. Trotter
Son of
J. B. & J. A. Trotter
Dec. 7, 1888
June 29, 1907
"My trust is in God."

Rev. J. B. Trotter
Oct. 1, 1855
Jan. 24, 1923
"Thy life was beauty,
truth, goodness and love."

Julia A. Trotter
June 15, 1857
"She was a kind and
affectionate wife,
a fond mother and a
friend to all."
We loved them, yes
we loved them but God
loved them more and
sent his blessed angels
to bear them to yonders
peaceful shore.
Father - Mother

Naomi Lee Arnold
Oct. 28, 1925
Nov. 14, 1925
"Our darling
we miss thee."

Alverine Cochran
June 21, 1909
July 1, 1909

Infant daughter of
F. & F. M. Knight
Aug. 20, 1928
"With Christ in Heaven,
our baby."

Albert L. Knight
Mar. 8, 1889
Dec. 16, 1901

Father -
Richard Knight
May 4, 1847
Dec. 30, 1925

H. E. Knight
Feb. 26, 1848
July 31, 1899

Philadelphia Knight
Jan. 9, 1816
Nov. 20, 1892

Thomas Knight
May 27, 1816
Mar. 16, 1866

Bargey Boyd
Dec. 5, 1897
Aug. 4, 1901

J. H. Bradyy
Apr. 9, 1864
Mar. 8, 1906
"Home is not home for Papa
is not there, dark is the
room and empty his chair
sleep Papa sleep, thy toils
are o'er, sweet be thy rest
so oft needed before, oh
weary the pathway to travel
alone."

Cecil
Son of
R. L. & J. L. Moses
Feb. 2, 1913
Oct. 3, 1915
"At rest."

Virgil
Son pf
R. L. & J. L. Moses
Feb. 4, 1908
May 9, 1909
"At rest."

SPENCE CEMETERY

G. W. Kerley
Jan. 6, 1834
Feb. 23, 1913
"Asleep in Jesus."

Elizabeth C. Acree
Wife of
G. W. Kerley
Jan. 6, 1834
May 3, 1908
"Blessed are the dead
which die in the Lord."

Mattie L.
Daughter of
R. P. & S. Kerley
Dec. 13, 1903
May 2, 1908
"Budded on earth
to bloom in Heaven."

To my wife -
Julia Kennedy
May 13, 1852
Oct. 20, 1908
"At rest."

Martha E. Roddy
Wife of
J. T. Roddy
Feb. 8, 1858
Aug. 28, 1902

Sarah S. Purser
Sept. 20, 1841
Apr. 8, 1863
22 yrs. 8 mos.

John T. Roddy
Son of
W. C. & M. T. Roddy
Oct. 18, 1900
Aug. 26, 1905
"Our loved one."

At rest -
Mildred Knight
Daughter of
S. F. & P. A. Knight
Apr. 4, 1905
Feb. 25, 1915
"Our darling has gone before
to greet us on the blissful shore."

Rose Harris
Dec. 12, 1901
Sept. 19, 1917
"She was the sunshine
of our home."

Mrs. May Harris
Jan. 7, 1929

Frances Ann Morgan
Wife of
Louis Morgan
Dec. 1, 1836
Sept. 1, 1909

Octavia Melton Harris
Wife of
W. A. Harris
Aug. 25, 1870
May 28, 1918
"Faithful to her trust
even unto death."

Harold Dillard
Oct. 21, 1936
Aged 16 yrs. 4 mos. 18 days.

Mrs. Mary Patton
May 25, 1937
Aged 25 yrs. 1 mo. 15 days.

Creed E. Jewell
Sept. 16, 1892
Dec. 11, 1918

His wife -
Emma Jewell
July 6, 1894
Dec. 5, 1918
"Weep not father and Mother
for we are waiting in glory
for thee."

Violet L. Jewell
(?)

Edna A. Jewell
Oct. 10, 1896
Jan. 25, 1916
"Resting in hope of a
glorious resurrection."

Rhea County, Tennessee, Tombstone Inscriptions

SPENCE CEMETERY

Minnie Lee Bruce
Marc. 27, 1920
Dec. 29, 1923
"She's safe at home."

Miss (or Mrs.) Lora Hall
Nov. 30, 1927
Aged 42 years.

Mrs. Hattie Jewell
Age 33 years.

The light of the world -
Willie Lee Boles
July 30, 1916
Mar. 25, 1935
"Gone but not forgotten."

Charlie Boles
May 16, 1902
Nov. 2, 1918
"Asleep in Jesus,
blessed sleep."

Mother -
Elizabeth K. Mulky
June 5, 1903
Age 45 years
"Asleep in Jesus."

Viola Narris
Oct. 20, 1919
Age 24 years.

Henry Fisher
Nov. 15, 1814
May 6, 1875

Sarah Fisher
Mar. 12, 1812
Dec. 3, 1878

Mary E. Matherly
Nee Bell -
June 20, 1875
April 22, 1898

Ruhama Fisher
Wife of
T. J. Knight
Nov. 15, 1852 - May 1, 1903
"A good wife, a loving mother."

Ruhama Purser
Wife of
P. M. Purser
Jan. 7, 1820
Sept. 1858
"Faithful to her trust
even unto death."

Our Father -
P. M. Purser
Dec. 30, 1819
July 25, 1897
"Gone to a bright home
where grief cannot come."

Miller Purser
April 12, 1936
Aged 75 years, 2 mos. 14 days.

"Her record is on high"
Sarah J.
Wife of
P. M. Purser
Mar. 10, 1852
May 26, 1904

BISHOP

Sisters -
Annie Bishop
Jan. 13, 1885
Mar. 5, 1906

Lillie Bishop
Feb. 2, 1890
Aug. 15, 1891
(Buried at Goodfield Cemetery.)

Mother -
Nancy J. Bishop
Nov. 15, 1859
Sept. 23, 1932

Father -
F. M. Bishop
Mar. 28, 1859
Mar. 10, 1936

Our baby -
Bonnie May
Daughter of J. H. & Maud Bishop
Feb. 22, 1915
Apr. 8, 1915

Rhea County, Tennessee, Tombstone Inscriptions

SPENCE CEMETERY

Tennessee V. Holland
Wife of
J. F. Holland
Aug. 14, 1871
Jan. 16, 1902
Daughter of
Jas. & T. V. Prater.

J. W. Prater
Mar. 2, 1867
Nov. 4, 1935

Richard A. Prater
July 10, 1873
Mar. 19, 1874

Tennie V. Prater
Nov. 11, 1841
June 5, 1925

James Prater
April 6, 1838
June 26, 1927

W. B. Fisher
Nov. 25, 1855
Jan. 16, 1905

I. K. Brown
Oct. 23, 1842
Aug. 25, 1925
Co. D - 19 Tenn. Inf.
"Gone but not forgotten."

Sam H. Morgan
May, 1934
Aged 73 years.

Mrs. Nancy E. Massangale
Aged 86 years.

Infant of
Mr. & Mrs. Carl Revis
Died 11-4-1935

Dorthy Ann Bishop
Mar. 6, 1937
Aged 7 days.

Mrs. Molly Ansburn
April 16, 1936
Aged 55 years, 8 mos. 5 days.

RHEA COUNTY

TOMBSTONE INSCRIPTIONS
SPENCE FAMILY CEMETERY

The Spence Family Cemetery is seven miles east of Dayton. Follow Highway No. 30 from Dayton. Leave the Highway at the Camp Ground Hill which is one mile from Dayton. Follow this road to the Frazier Grammar School, taking the road leading east to the New Bethel Church. Keep the main road for one mile, take the first left hand lane. The Cemetery is one quarter of a mile from the main road. The land belongs to the Spences.

In memory of
Our father -
James Spence
Feb. 10, 1809
May 9, 1899

Savior lead me.
In memory of
our Mother
Mahala Spence
Apr. 30, 1809
June 18, 1900

In memory of
Our father -
Albion Spence
Aug. 10, 1851
Mar. 22, 1917

In memory of
Our mother -
Hattie A. Spence
May 8, 1857
Feb. 12, 1927

RHEA COUNTY

TOMBSTONE INSCRIPTIONS
SPIVEY CEMETERY

The Spivey Cemetery is eight miles southeast of Dayton. Leave Dayton on the Blythe's Ferry road. The Cemetery is at the top of hill before reaching the Ferry. The land belongs to the Spivey family. There are fifty nine unmarked graves.

W. M. Brooks
June 15, 1870
Oct. 27, 1933
"Asleep in Jesus."

Parlie Brooks
Jan. 20, 1878
Feb. 19, 1936

Mrs. Myrtle White
March 26, 1934
Aged 37 yrs. 2 mos. 25 days.

Paul Daniels
Apr. 12, 1934
Age 29 yrs.

Hellen Daniels
Aged 58 years.

R. P. Helton
--

John Fine - Father
June 23, 1861
Oct. 12, 1907
"Thy will be done."

Mrs. C. M. Davis
June 5, 1927
Aged 48 years.

Chas. Monroe Davis
Nov. 9, 1934
Aged 65 years.

Our Mother -
Louise Davis
Dec. 18, 1834
Feb. 4, 1919
"Thy trial's ended,
thy rest is won."

Charles Hutcheson
Sept. 9, 1842
Aged 35 yrs. 4 mos. 29 days.
"There is no dying there;
Blessed are the pure in haert."

Father -
S. W. Hutcheson
Jan. 17, 1834
June 1, 1886
(Mason)

Susan E.
Wife of
S. W. Hutcheson
Jan. 31, 1875
Aged 43 yrs. 7 mos. 21 days.
"Blessed are the pure in heart."

John L.
Son of
S. W. & S. E. Hutcheson
July 27, 1856
Apr. 30, 1886

Virginia Ann Carraway
April 8, 1937
Aged 7 days.

Mary C. Dickson
Wife of
A. Dickson
Oct. 15, 1858
Nov. 21, 1882
Holy Bible -

J. Clyde Spivey
Apr. 10, 1896
Aug. 3, 1934
"Rest 'till we meet again."

George W. Spivey
1844 - 1928
"Father we miss you."

Rhea County, Tennessee, Tombstone Inscriptions

SPIVEY CEMETERY

Luella G. Spivey
1876 - 1931
"She hath done what she could."

At rest -
John Luther Spivey
Nov. 15, 1893
Sept. 26, 1919
"'Till we meet again."

Our Father -
"At rest."
J. H. Storie
Feb. 16, 1838
Nov. 29, 1895 - M. D.
(Mason.)

"At rest."
We miss you Mother.
Rebecca Storie
Aug. 31, 1840
July 16, 1920

Julian Carl Daniel
Died May 2, 1936 - Infant.

Annie Lee Davis
Aug. 3, 1928
Aged 13 months.

RHEA COUNTY

TOMBSTONE INSCRIPTIONS
SPRING CITY CEMETERY

Located ½ mile south of Spring City on right hand side of road traveling south. Located in 2nd. District of Rhea County, and eighteen miles north of Dayton. This is a public Cemetery. It is well kept and almost every grave has a tombstone.

Henry W. Hart
1836 - 1919

In memory of
Nellie F. Hart
1880 - 1886
Her body rests in Leuty Cemetery.

Edward L. Tilley
Apr. 18, 1877
Mar. 28, 1920

Alice
Daughter of
Rev. & Mrs. C. G. Hines
June 7, 1914
July 5, 1919

Samuel C. Jones
Apr. 1, 1889
May 19, 1920

Husband and wife
Jones -
"God gave, He took,
He will restore."

Sarah E. Robison
Dau. of
J. R. & Matilda Byrd
Aug. 31, 1879
Nov. 20, 1921
"Her spirit smiles
from that bright shore
, and softly whispers
weep no more."

LAVENDER

D. C. Lavender
Nov. 5, 1870
Oct. 23, 1924

W. C. Lavender
Aug. 31, 1875
Mar. 3, 1918
"A tender father
and a faithful friend."

W. L.
Son of
H. A. & Hester Smith
May 30, 1893
Dec. 25, 1918
"Death is eternal life,
why should we weep?"

G. W. Jones
Mar. 1, 1856
Nov. 9, 1924

Edna B. Vaughn
Sept. 11, 1893
Feb. 18, 1920

Woodmen of the World Memorial -
William F. Hicks
May 15, 1896
April 20, 1920
"He was a loving and kind son
and affectionate brother."

Hanner
Wife of
J. P. Bollon
Mar. 6, 1857
Mar. 11, 1929
"A tender mother,
and a faithful friend."

Ella B. Ferguson
April 24, 1935
Aged 52 years, 7 days.

Rhea County, Tennessee, Tombstone Inscriptions

SPRING CITY CEMETERY

H. L. W. Ferguson
Oct. 25, 1836
Aug. 31, 1925

Texas A. Ferguson
July 18, 1850
Dec. 13, 1916

George Harvey Wasson
Jan. 14, 1935
Aged 59 years, 6 months, 26 days.

Mother - Catherine Nave
Feb. 26, 1850
Apr. 27, 1928

S. E. Paul
1857 - 1925 - Father

Albert A. Haley
Mar. 3, 1844
Feb. 28, 1894

Margaret E. Angel
Wife of
A. A. Haley
Aug. 20, 1864
Nov. 8, 1899

Robert
Son of
A. A. & M. E. Haley
(?)

Mary J.
Wife of
J. W. Angel
Sept. 2, 1841
May 22, 1916

J. W. Angel
Sept. 22, 1844
July 20, 1914
"Thy record is on high."

George W. White
June 22, 1843
Nov. 9, 1915

Elizabeth Peters
Mar. 31, 1893
Aged 72 yrs.

Margaret
Wife of
J. B. Peters
Jan. 16, 1823
Aug. 2, 1894

Mogene
Dau. of
G. C. & Laura Harris
Nov. 1, 1916
Apr. 21, 1918

Mother - Sarah L. Bailey
Wife of
W. A. Wix
Jan. 7, 1839
Feb. 11, 1918

Father - W. A. Wix
Jan. 13, 1846
Apr. 1, 1922
"A confererate Soldier."

Samantha E.
Wife of
Chas. Reed
May 17, 1844
Mar. 16, 1918

Charles Reed
May 14, 1845
Sept. 10, 1924

Husband - A. L. Long
Nov. 9, 1863
Feb. 2, 1916

William Barton
April 10, 1935
Aged 82 years, 7 months.

Charles Oscar Barton
June 9, 1890
April 4, 1911
"Meet me in Heaven."

Mother - 1860 - 1924 - Wierick

Father - 1831 - 1907 - Wierick

Green Brady
1858 - 1907

Rhea County, Tennessee, Tombstone Inscriptions

SPRING CITY CEMETERY
(CONTINUED)

Father - F. M. Marler
Mar. 10, 1844
Feb. 5, 1915

Mother - Susan Actkinson Marler
March 20, 1845
Mar. 30, 1926

Mary J.
Wife of
Daniel D. Odom
Feb. 14, 1837
Aug. 12, 1893

Daniel D. Odom
July 11, 1833
Nov. 3, 1904

Elizabeth Swan Ford
Oct. 8, 1832
May 18, 1909

Margaret Ford Evens
June 12, 1858
Feb. 6, 1914

Alvin Bishop
1893 - 1896

Frank Bishop
1891 - 1894

Father - M. A. Bishop
1848 - 1927

N. W. Wheelock
Mar. 9, 1840
July 7, 1903

Mary Permelia Wheelock
Aug 26, 1892
Mar. 2, 1895

Medore G.
Daughter of
D. S. & Mary M. Betsill
Aug. 8, 1904
May 15, 1907

John W. Barron
Feb. 17, 1891
Dec. 27, 1927

Father - F. Deluce
Apr. 24, 1857
June 6, 1925

Mrs. Minnie Lee Deluce
Sept. 6, 1936
Aged 72 years.

Margarete Posse Holloway
Aug. 30, 1936
Aged 74 years, 9 months, 15 days.

Thomas B. Holloway
Sept. 14, 1851
Oct. 1, 1915

Ruth E.
Wife of
Thos. B. Holloway
Feb. 13, 1853
May 17, 1907

Milo Holloway
Oct. 10, 1881
Sept. 25, 1908
"Fond parents weep for me here
no more, that I no more am given,
for we shall meet when life is o'er,
high up above in Heaven."

R. H. Reid
Oct. 18, 1850
May 26, 1913
"Thy loss we deeply feel."

Deltar,
Dau. of
Jack & Lillie Brady
July 20, 1913
Aug. 26, 1913

Della
Dau. of
Jack & Lillie Brady
July 20, 1913
Sept. 3, 1913

Rhea County, Tennessee, Tombstone Inscriptions

SPRING CITY CEMETERY
(Continued)

Lillie J. Hale
Sept. 26, 1899
Oct. 26, 1917

James M.
Son of
J. W. & E. E. Brady
Aug. 24, 1914
Aug. 5, 1916

Father - Francis Cash
1827-1899

Mother - Eliza West Cash
1825 - 1896

Sister - Catherine Cash
1860 - 1926

John R. Thompson
Sept. 22, 1858

His Wife
Cinnie G. Thompson
June 18, 1863
Aug 11, 1926

Sanders McClendon
Apr. 4, 1833
July 24, 1910

Tarla Ann McClendon
Feb. 8, 1840
Mar. 16, 1916

I. L. Miller
Dec. 15, 1848
Dec. 10, 1913

Nannie N.
Wife of
I. L. Miller
Oct. 12, 1872

Rufus Jones
July 25, 1875
Oct. 3, 1916 - Father

F. L. T. - John I. Holland
Apr. 3, 1858
Oct. 19, 1934
"Life's work well done,
He rests in peace."

Mary J. Ferguson
His wife
Nov. 11, 1862
Jan. 11, 1928
"She sleeps nor dreams but ever
dwells, a perfect form in perfect
rest."

William W. Renfro
1852 - 1921

Martha J. Renfro
1852 - 1915

Bertha Campbell Hilleary
Wife of
William Hilleary
Oct. 6, 1890
Feb. 20, 1926
"Absent, not dead."

Rosa Metzger Campbell
Mar. 16, 1854
Mar. 7, 1934

J. M. Campbell
Jan. 2, 1857
Aug. 19, 1912

Alfred H. Torbett
Jan. 31, 1890
Oct. 1, 1920
"Veteran of World War."

Mary A. Torbett
Nov. 25, 1860
Jan. 2, 1935

Wilcher, Torbett
Jan. 22, 1888
Feb. 12, 1925

Rhea County, Tennessee, Tombstone Inscriptions

SPRING CITY CEMETERY
(Continued)

F. L. T. James S.
Son of
J. A. & Mary A. Torbett
June 19, 1886
June 6, 1912

Frank
Son of
J. A. & Mary A. Torbett
Sept. 23, 1882
May 18, 1929

Bonnie Alice Torbett
Oct. 31, 1917
May 17, 1925

John Claglin
Mar. 1, 1812
Jan. 31, 1899

Frances M. Cartwright
1888 - 1933

Mother - Harriet N. Rhea
Wife of
Rev. L. M. Cartwright
1851 - 1929

Gertie N. Dixon
Wife of
W. B. Dixon
Jan. 31, 1856
June 5, 1897

Loretta Northup Reed
Wife of
Wm. A. G. Reed
Sept. 11, 1832
Oct. 20, 1914

Mabel E.
Wife of
Evan Moore
Jan. 5, 1870
Feb. 13, 1898

Rina Carrie
Dau. of
Evan & Mabel Moore
Dec. 18, 1893
Aug. 16, 1895

Mary Lillian
Daughter of
Evan & Ada Moore
Dec. 10, 1899
Dec. 18, 1903

Katie Bell
Dau. of
W. D. & Addy Huskins
May 15, 1891
Sept. 1, 1911

Gracie
Dau. of H. M. & M. B. Johnson
Feb. 7, 1911
May 20, 1912

Earnest L.
Son of
J. N. & Josie Mitchell
Sept. 4, 1899
Feb. 16, 1936
Private in U. S. Marine Corps.
U. S. A. Gods finger touched
him and he slept.

Father - J. N. Mitchell
Nov. 25, 1868
Nov. 27, 1912
"His record is on high."

Lillian
Dau. of
L. F. & Bertha Walker
Dec. 26, 1916
Feb. 8, 1917
"From Mother's arms,
in the arms of Jesus."

W. D. Dagley
July 26, 1872
July 23, 1907

Artie May Dagley
Sept. 22, 1891
July 23, 1907

James H.
Son of
J. W. & M. L. Simpson
Nov. 13, 1889
Nov. 21, 1889

Rhea County, Tennessee, Tombstone Inscriptions

SPRING CITY CEMETERY
(Continued)

E. J. Holloway
Feb. 2, 1841

R. W. Holloway
Aug. 15, 1824
Sept. 20, 1901

Myra Garrison
Feb. 7, 1823
June 13, 1899
Wife of
A. H. McFalls
Married
March 10, 1839

F. A. McCabe
Dec. 6, 1845
Feb. 16, 1908

Berry McCabe
Jan. 23, 1890
July 10, 1920

Little Pat
Son of
James & Julia McCabe
Dec. 1, 1893
June 27, 1894
"Sleep on little one."

Lillie May Dunlap
June 9, 1891
Feb. 7, 1914
"She was the sunshine of our home."

Doshia Ann Shelby
Feb. 1, 1889
Aug. 10, 1916
"Gone home to Jesus."

Jacob L. Dunlap
Oct. 18, 1855
Aug. 24, 1916

Nannie C.
Wife of
C. C. Kemmer
Apr. 4, 1861
Jan. 22, 1918

Rev. Wm. White
June 8, 1842
Dec. 16, 1911
Father - Loved one farewell.

Rebecca White
May 2, 1845
Jan. 20, 1912
Mother - Loved one farewell.

Mother - Mary E. King
1880 - 1923

Mary
Daughter of
D. C. & Mary E. King
Jan. 11, 1909
July 29, 1909

Susie Shelby
Aug. 11, 1935
Aged 74 years, 11 months, 9 days.

Clearcy Casey
Born 1827

Wesley Casey
Oct. 4, 1899
Aged 77 years

HOLLOWAY

Holloway, Floyd E.
May 30, 1877
Mar. 30, 1907

Mother - Leopatra Holloway
1840 - 1925

Father - Samuel H. Holloway
1837 - 1898

Callie M. Holloway
1878 - 1909

Samuel H. Holloway
Feb. 8, 1897
Mar. 31, 1898

Rhea County, Tennessee, Tombstone Inscriptions

SPRING CITY CEMETERY
(Continued)

REID

In memory of
M. V. Reid, Sr.
July 21, 1841
Mar. 4, 1907
Co. A. 62nd. Tenn. Inf.
Vaughn's Brigade C. S. A.

Savior lead me. Allice
Daughter of
M. V. & Jennie Reid
Jan. 25, 1860
Oct. 1, 1899

In memory of
Ophelia Reid
Wife of
B. S. Roberts
Nov. 19, 1884
Oct. 31, 1918

Martin V. Reid, Jr.
1871 - 1934
W. O. W.

Thos. B. Reid
1878 - 1925
Woodmen of the World, Memorial.

Mabel Shugart
Wife of
Thos. B. Reid
1879 - 1929

Florence Rose
Wife of
D. C. Kemmer
Oct. 28, 1863
Aug. 20, 1901

Edith Powel
Wife of
D. C. Kemmer
Feb. 25, 1874
Feb. 25, 1910

Richard Olney
Son of
J. M. & Leona McClark
Dec. 20, 1904
Sep. 28, 1909

Brother - Earl C. Clark
Son of
Dr. J. M. & Leona Clark
Mar. 13, 1901
Jan. 10, 1920
"None knew thee, but to love thee."

Father - Dr. J. M. Clark
Sept. 30, 1869
Apr. 9, 1922
"Kind Father of love, thou art gone to thy rest."

Father - William R. Gregory
1849 - 1919

My beloved wife - Lena M. Gregory
Wife of
Summerfield Williams
Feb. 7, 1887
Nov. 19, 1911

A. A. Millard
Feb. 12, 1847
Sept. 5, 1914

R. J. Millard
Apr. 2, 1854
Jan. 17, 1928

Myrtle Ella Wright
Wife of
Ross Brown
Jan. 14, 1895
Apr. 5, 1924
"A tender Mother gone, but not forgotten."

Herman L.
Son of
J. W. & D. S. Wright
Oct. 4, 1914
Jan. 27, 1920

W. O. W. - Memorial.
John White
Feb. 1, 1855
Jan. 6, 1918

Rhea County, Tennessee, Tombstone Inscriptions

8
SPRING CITY CEMETERY
(Continued)

Jennie Walker
Jan. 25, 1831
Mar. 27, 1911

Nettie Ray
Wife of
J. B. Mahoney
Feb. 22, 1894
Oct. 26, 1918

Mary Reid
Wife of
John Brown
May 14, --
Aged 67 yrs. 11 mos. & 23 days
"Mother."

Henry B.
Son of
J. W. & F. E. McPherson
Dec. 1, 1900
June 24, 1903

J. Walter
Son of
J. W. & F. E. McPherson
Aug. 26, 1904
Dec. 31, 1904

Pearl J. Finnell
Wife of
Thomas C. Swafford
July 29, 1907
June 21, 1935
"Live again."

Mrs. Tennie A. Benson
Aug. 29, 1936
Aged 56 years.

Samuel T.
Son of
M. R. & M. L. Waller
Oct. 12, 1900
Sept. 8, 1901

Mrs. Sarah Bell McGhee
1846 - 1927

Thomas McGhee
Aug. 16, 1924
Age 70 yrs.

W. L. Lee
Nov. 1, 1884
Jan. 30, 1919

Ruby Elnora
Dau. of Earnest & Cordie Simpson
Jan. 3, 1916
Oct. 26, 1918

Katherine
Dau. of Sam & Alice Renfro
July 7, 1917
Aug. 19, 1918
"Just when we learned to love
her most, God called her back
to Heaven."

Husband - Andrew J. Shell
Aug. 11, 1835
March 18, 1916
Co. B. 5th. Tenn. Mtd. Vol. Inf.

Martha E. McGhee
Wife of
H. Winnie
Sept. 22, 1877
Jan. 5, 1916

Miles F. McCuistion
June 12, 1872
April 1, 1927
"His toils are past, his work
is done, he fought the fight,
the victory won."

Nellie Payne
Wife of
G. W. Steinecipher
Sept. 23, 1895
Oct. 7, 1927

W. L. Gibson
1869 - 1926

Rhea County, Tennessee, Tombstone Inscriptions

SPRING CITY CEMETERY
(Continued)

James K. Peak
July 7, 1844
Nov. 8, 1928

Eliza McPherson
Feb. 1, 1859
Jan. 4, 1928

James Allen DeVaney
1870 - 19 --?

His Wife - Eureka A. Cook
1876 - 1926

Nancy Lee
Daughter of
Alvin & Nellie Tallent
1924 - 1926

Mother - Maud
Wife of
Dock Smith
May 6, 1892
Nov. 28, 1925
"Kind friends as you are
passing by, as you are now,
So once was I, as I am now
so you must be, prepare there-
fore to follow me."

Claud T. Hubbs
Apr. 21, 1924
Aug. 15, 1925
"Our darling."

Hattie Alma Dyer
Mar. 28, 1926
Apr. 30, 1927

W. O. W. Memorial
J. W. Long
Nov. 21, 1869
July 15, 1931
"He was a noble christian man."

Father - H. C. Hope
Feb. 14, 1846
Dec. 8, 1928
"Goodbye loved ones, I'm going
home, the Savior smiles and bids
me come."

Mother - Sidney J. Hope
Mar. 3, 1849
July 26, 1926
"Her sun goeth down
while it is yet day."

Junior - Son of
W. H. & Lizzie Woody
Feb. 14, 1923
Feb. 9, 1928

Husband - J. F. Dagley
Mar. 11, 1844
June 25, 1930
"It is well with my soul."

Thomas Nelson Richards
Feb. 23, 1936
Aged 82 years.

Sgt. William L. Dawson
Co. F. 28 U. S. Inf. Sp.
Am. War.

James Mosley Crawford
Oct. 13, 1933
Son of
Mr. & Mrs. J. J. Crawford
Aged 5 years, 1 day.

Mrs. James F. Gitwood
Sept. 26, 1934
Aged 79 years, 7 months, 12 days.

Mary Matilia
Wife of
Joe Harwood
June 5, 1881
May 20, 1929

Father - E. B. Phillips
1886 - 1926

Mother - E. J. Thompson
Wife of
J. T. Wright
July 22, 1855
Aug. 2, 1925
"A devoted wife and a loving
Mother."

Rhea County, Tennessee, Tombstone Inscriptions

SPRING CITY CEMETERY
(Continued)

Sarah Llewellyn - Gentry Cash
1851 - 1930

Dave Cash
April 26, 1890
Nov. 11, 1925

Infant son of
D. M. and Margaret Rhea
Feb. 18, 1902

Elizabeth Roddy
Wife of
B. F. Robinson
Died Aug. 8, 1903

Benjamin F. Robinson
Dec. 18, 1892

Mother - Mary E. Titus
Nov. 12, 1849
May 2, 1892

Father - Cyrus J. Titus
May 11, 1832
Oct. 31, 1891

Mapom Esseps
Jan. 8, 1842
Feb. 15, 1895

William J. Holloway
June 13, 1844
Nov. 7, 1897

Beulah
Daughter of
M. S. & Addie Holloway
May 2, 1884
Jan. 28, 1893

Eva Holloway
Wife of
John Heiskell
July 25, 1903

J. M. Holloway
Sept. 15, 1894
"At rest."

Richard Holloway
Feb. 23, 1833
Jan. 12, 1910

Mother - Jane Holloway
Wife of
J. A. Thomison
April 8, 1849
July 8, 1920

Father - James A. Thomison
Jan. 13, 1846
Feb. 25, 1935

Benrard
Son of
Rev. T. S. & Mollie B. Bryson
Nov. 23, 1911
July 3, 1928

Thomas Bryson
March 26, 1858
Beb. 27, 1889
"Our loved one."

In memory of
Alice, Wife of
J. H. Segrest
July 11 ••(?)
April 20, 1903
"Asleep in Jesus."

J. W. Wason
Dec. 5, 1843
Oct. 23, 1931

Susan, Wife of
J. W. Wason
May 17, 1839
Aug. 31, 1920

William A. Cate
1849 - 1920

Wife - Martha Phillips
1863 - 1926

Albert Cate
Oct. 1, 1891
June 1915

Rhea County, Tennessee, Tombstone Inscriptions

SPRING CITY CEMETERY
(Continued)

Zebar --
Oct. 16, 1891
July 18, 1894

WATERHOUSE
Franklin Waterhouse
July 20, 1823
Dec. 6, 1892

Lorenda Waterhouse
Dec. 5, 1903
Married Feb. 3, 1842

J. E. Waterhouse
April 23, 1845
1908 --

Lotta Waterhouse
Daughter of
J. E. and M. T.
Jan. 21, 1889
June 15, 1892
"Safe in arms of Jesus."

Wife of
Thomas J. Gillespie
Dec. 25, 1823
April 26, 1891

Recce Holloway
(?)

Collins,- L. T. Collins
Feb. 15, 1874
April 30, 1935

H. C. Collins
1846 - 1920

Mother - Mary Fischesser
1854 - 1921

Father - Zeno Fischesser
1844 - 1922
May 10, 1931

Baby Doris Houston
Sept. 13, 1925
May 24, 1927

Baby Grace Fischesser
Jan. 19, 1918
May 10, 1921

Elvira Thompson
Sept. 21, 1857
July 18, 1928

Father - J. M. Price
Oct. 19, 1871
Dec. 25, 1921

Flosie Thomison
Dunlap - Dec. 31, 1925

Bronce Moss
Aug. 15, 1892
Feb. 27, 1924

Thomas G. Moss
May 5, 1845
April 25, 1922

Sidney H. Gilliam
Oct. 27, 1877
Jan. 1923
"Beloved Father farewell."

Monrow W. Pope
Sept 22, 1845
Jan. 9, 1928

Rebecca, wife of
Monrow W. Pope
June 25, 1852

"At rest." - Frank Byrd
July 1902
1927

Martha Byrd
Wife of
J. R. Byrd
Dec. 24, 1848
"Here lies a kind Mother
and true wife."

John Wade
Tennessee Firman
Oct. 1933

Lennie May Wade
Oct. 28, 1900
Feb. 10, 1924
"She's at rest."

Rhea County, Tennessee, Tombstone Inscriptions

SPRING CITY CEMETERY
(Continued)

Lennie Moultin
1870 - 1932

Hattie Blair
1876 - 1920

Lona Bayless
Wife of
K. P. Blair
1845 - 1925

Kidney Powell Blair
1843 - 1928

Charles Blair
1853 -
April 1922

A. F. Devaney
1858 - 1922

Helena,
Daughter of
Jacob & Katherine Devaney
Aug. 24, 1905
Apr. 20, 1917

Father - James Wilson Snyder
Dec. 15, 1849
May 29, 1927

Mother - Elizabeth Snyder
Feb. 4, 1851
Sept. 7, 1920

Cordellia Ruffner Waller
Mar. 13, 1870
April 10, 1922

Fred Gallahon
1888 - 1922

Floyd Gallahon
1868 - 1926

H. B. Payne
July 28, 1936
Age 75 years, 4 mos. 18 days.

Mary Payne
10- 10- 1936

Sarah E.
Wife of
G. L. Dunlap
(?)

Lizzie
Wife of
John Gallahon
1868 - 1904
"Gone but not forgotten."

John Gallahon
Nov. 17, 1860
May 16, 1916
"AT peaceful rest."

Mettie Gallahon
Wife of (?) Gallahon
Dec. 16, 1912
Age 34 yrs.
"Our loss, but Heaven's gain."

Reese Watkins
1849 - 1916, - Father

Claude Watkins
1876 - 1887 - Son

Jane Watkins
1853 - 1922 - Mother

T. H. Thomison
Nov. 17, 1853
Oct. 14, 1899

Earl C.
Son of
T. A. Caldwell Thomison
July, 1894
Sept. 19, 1895

Flora, Daughter of
Walter & Flora Caldwell
1895 - 1895
5 mos., 16 days.

Rhea County, Tennessee, Tombstone Inscriptions

SPRING CITY CEMETERY
(Continued)

Walter K.
Son of
T. H. & Metta Caldwell Thomison
Feb. 9, 1887
Feb. 15, 1891

Martha Louise
Daughter of
A. N. Gawood
Oct. 9, 1876
Nov. 19, 1909

Ramond Gawood
1831 - 1903

Mallie Gawood
Wife of
J. W. Ball
April 9, 1856
Dec. 15, 1887

Levitta
Infant daughter of
J. W. & Mallie Ball
June 21, 1886
Jan. 23, 1887
"Sacred memory."

Garrett Reed
July 10, 1901
June 29, 1910

Infant son of
Pauline reed
May 17, 1925
"In this little grave,
world wild hopes here in lie."

John E. Pyatt
1838 - 1904

Barbara Pyatt
1846 - 1906

Dr. Hohn Hoyal
Age 77 yrs. 5 mos. 23 days.

Rebecca Ann
Wife of
Dr. John Hoyal
Oct. 21, 1820
Feb. 28, 1892

Virginia Hoyal
July, 1867
25 yrs.

Robert Milton
Son of
R. B. & B. Kimbrough
Died June 14, 1908

Anna Stutzman
Jan. 7, 1843
Feb. 26, 1931

Joel S. Crosby
Feb. 9, 1841
Aug. 3, 1898

T. J. Robinson
Sept. 3, 1846
March 23, 1927

George Smith
1870 - 1925

Anne Pearl Robinson
Son of
S. P. & A. P.
Oct. 25, 1884
Dec. 12, 1909

Earnest Robinson
Son of
S. P. & A. P.
Apr. 14, 1880
Sept. 5, 1908

James Lee Hoyal
1861 - 1907

In fond memory of
Bell Brady, wife of
J. F. Broyless
1870 - 1918

Emma Lee
Daughter 6f
Belle Brady
Dec. 2, 1908
Feb. 22, 1909
"From Mother's arms to
arms of Jesus."

Rhea County, Tennessee, Tombstone Inscriptions

SPRING CITY CEMETERY
(Continued)

Victoria Darwin Caldwell
1839 - 1919

M. Caldwell
May 11, 1819
Feb. 9, 1891

CUNNINGHAM
Father - P. C. M. Cunningham
Feb. 25, 1848
Jan. 31, 1917

Mother - Julia B. Cunningham
Sept. 1, 1850
May 29, 1924

Son - Luther Cunningham
1889 - 1927

James Register
April 13, 1828
July 1, 1900

Catherine Boome Register
July 17, 1835
Sept. 11, 1894
"Mother & Father."
"Take them O' death and bear away whatever thou cans't can call thy own, thy image stamped upon clay, doth give thee that but that above."

Reuben Alyworth
Nov. 11, 1820
June 12, 1905

Mary Alyworth
July 30, 1821
Apr. 2, 1908

Addie Heiskell
July 21, 1861
July 23, 1930

Luther Heiskell
1829 - 1909

His wife
Ellen Wright
1830 - 1892

Father - H. B. Heiskell
Age 73 yrs. 11 mos. & 23 days.

Mother - Rhoda Farmer
His wife
Age 50 yrs. 9 mos.

H. B. & Rhoda Heiskell
Last infant
May 2, 1871
Aug. 13, 1898

J. D. Burton, Jr.
April 9, 1917
Jan. 9, 1920

ANGEL

William N. Angel
June 7, 1867
Feb. 27, 1918

Mary A. Angel
Aug. 4, 1893
Aug. 29, 1893

Roy C. Angel
Aug. 14, 1894
Sept. 17, 1922

Roy C. Angel, Jr.
Jan. 13, 1920
Jan. 13, 1920

John Garrson
1890 - 1918
(Got killed in battle with France.)

Jessie Griffin
1846 - 1912

Monroe Griffin
1842 - 1909

SPRING CITY CEMETERY
(Continued)

Rush Brookman
Nov. 23, 1906

"At rest." - Della Felty
1869 - 1905

Mother - Ann Rogers
1834 - 1917

Emely B.
Wife of
J. H. Rogers
1870 - 1904

Ruffus Robinson
1852 - 1931

Florence Robinson
1857 - 1904

B. A. Quin
1826 - 1892

Margarite Steeles
Wife of
B. A. Quin
March 14, 1835
Mar. 5, 1917

SMITH
W. H. Smith
May 1, 1841
July 18, 1889

N. J. Smith
Jan. 1, 1846
Nov. 12, 1909

John Smith
Dec. 21, 1884
July 15, 1911
(Member of Lookout Mt. Lodge 289.)

Joseph Andy
Son of
Mat & M. J. Wett
July 7, 1884
Age 6 yrs. 5 mos. & 4 days.

Elizabeth Kiddney
1865 - 1932

Goddard --
Son of
John & Bettie McCabe
Nov. 26, 1898
Dec. 23, 1919
Age 21 yrs.

George
Son of
John & Bettie McCabe
June 17, 1887
June 17, 1914
Age 27 yrs.

Charles Henry Mills
1865 - 1914

W. F. P. Brown
April 21, 1845
May 22, 1903
"A man who was kind, patriotic and generous to all."

George Elliott
1847 - 1929

QUINN
L. M. Quinn
Sept. 4, 1867
Was killed in a wreck on the
C. N. O. and T. P. Railway,
Aug. 31, 1898 - Age 30 yrs. 11
mos., 27 days.
"Resting 'till resurrection morn."

W. M. Robert Quinn
July 1,,1875
May 4, 1930

Walter Quinn
Oct. 15, 1935
Age 58 yrs.

Jullia M. Comley
Wife of
S. B. Richards
Sept. 3, 1859
Sept. 13, 1930

Reece Richards
Mar. 17, 1906
May 15, 1906

Rhea County, Tennessee, Tombstone Inscriptions

SPRING CITY CEMETERY
(Continued)

A. M. Cates
Dec. 17, 1855
July 23, 1920

Margarette Boges
Wife of
John Alison
March 1, 1852
May 17, 1902

Jesse W. Cash
Jan. 15, 1851
Feb. 18, 1906

Hannah E. Cash
Dec. 10, 1853

Hannah Watson
1827 - 1910 - Mother.

Husband - W. A. Thomison
Nov. 8, 1857
Feb. 24, 1917

BROWN

Arthur F. Brown- Tennessee
Dec. 18, 1920

Father - C. C. Brown
Apr. 2, 1858
Dec. 26, 1920

Mother - Tennessee Crabtree
Brown
Jan. 9, 1862
Dec. 31, 1917

M. H. Galloway
Feb. 16, 1860
Nov. 13, 1906 - Father

Baby Joe
Son of
Mr. & Mrs. M. E. Brown
Oct. 9, 1903
July 25, 1906

Lanell Tallent
1924 - 1925

Garvie Mathis
Wife of
James D. Smith
1864 - 1935

Mrs. Dixie Brown
Oct. 15, 1936
Age 49 yrs. 10 mos.

Sarah Brown Kimbrough
Nov. 10, 1860
Apr. 14, 1934

Father - W. R. Johnson
Dec. 25, 1870
Mar. 14, 1928

Addie Johnson
Wife of
W. R. Johnson
Nov. 22, 1869
"In loving memory of
Father and Mother."

Nancy Jane Abbott
Sept 8, 1840
Jan. 10, 1915
And was married May 2, 1868

S. S. Abbott
Dec. 16, 1924
Age 92 yrs.
"Beloved Father Farewell."

Clarence Herbert
Son of
R. E. and I. B. Cain
April 12, 1890
Killed Sept. 28, 1911

Leona Kebnes
Wife of
George Ray
June 25, 1911
Age 19 yrs. 2 mos. 26 days.

J. L. Lewis Hartbarger
April 7, 1899
Dec. 3, 1932
"Weep not, he is not dead,
he sleepeth."

Rhea County, Tennessee, Tombstone Inscriptions

SPRING CITY CEMETERY
(Continued)

Thomas Price
Dec. 11, 1869
Nov. 2, 1913

William J. Crammer - Ky.
Died Dec. 22, 1934

George W. Smith
June 10, 1855
Han, 18, 1932

E. E. Moss
Dec. 12, 1885
Aug. 25, 1932

Mary E. Crosby
Sept. 11, 1886
Feb. 26, 1929

F. B. Ferguson
Mar. 17, 1880
May 30, 1930

Willie
His wife
July 26, 1890
April 14, 1928

Ray Greham
Dec. 16, 1934
Age 33 yrs.

"At Rest." In memory of
Eliza Broyles
Wife of
B. F. Lee
Nov. 22, 1848
Dec. 1, 1925

Alta Strathern
Feb. 11, 1890
Sept. 29, 1930

William H. Smith
Died Dec. 5, 1931

Charles
Son of
Mr. and Mrs. Earl Denton
Died Mar. 21, 1932

Perry Denton
July 28, 1936
Age 38 yrs. 7 mos.

Amanda Reed McCabe
1857 - 1931

Stephen Cawood
Oct. 15, 1936

George M. Cawood
1858 - 1927

Willie C. Dugger
1892 - 1933

Mabel Mashux
10 - 9 - 1936
Age 34 yrs.

J. C. Ketchersid
Jan. 23, 1936
Age 75 yrs.

Mettie McCorkle
Wife of
L. Hamlin Wide
Died Sept., 1931

Nettie Barton
Mar. 10, 1881
Jan 22, 1931

Robert Neal
Sep. 28, 1936
Age 15 yrs. 4 mos. 26 days.

Robert Duglas
Son of
H. G. and Nellie Meadows
Died Nov. 4, 1926

1

RHEA COUNTY

TOMBSTONE INSCRIPTIONS
SPRING CITY CEMETERY

Some names of person who have died and been buried, since the first notes and inscriptions were taken.

J. M. Wright Sept. 3, 1870 June, 1937	Mary Lee Wright Sept. 25, 1937 23 yrs. 4 mos. 2 dys
Mrs. Helen F. Pearson Mar. 19, 1848 Sept. 8, 1937 89 yrs.	Margaret Crisp Sept. 7, 1917 Sept. 12, 1937 (This yougg lady was drowned in Tenn. river at Washington Ferry. Her home was in Spring City, Tenn. (Age 20 yrs.)
Douglas D. Thompson May 6, 1867 June 28, 1937 70 yrs.	

Rhea County, Tennessee, Tombstone Inscriptions

RHEA COUNTY

TOMBSTONE INSCRIPTIONS
STEBBINS OR PRESBYTERIAN CEMETERY

Go 18 miles north from Dayton on Lon Foust Highway to Spring City, then take the Grand View road going west from Spring City. Go to top of the mountain to Grand View, taking the cross road from Grand View to Rockwood, then go south from Grassy Cove road 1 mile. This is one of the oldest graveyards at Grandview and is in District No. 1. It is owned and kept by the Presbyterian Church and is in very good condition. It is under fence and includes about 1 acre of land. Grand View was for many years a very interesting school community, sponsored and controlled by the Congregational Church. This school was the first and only High school in Rhea County for twenty five or thirty years. A great many mountain boys and girls were educated there. Other High Schools in the county have grown up and absorbed the Grand View School, now only a grammar school being maintained there. About 40 graves are marked with blank stones.

Laura A.
Wife of
C. J. Russell
Jan. 10, 1855
Jan. 26, 1916
"Gone, but not forgotten."

Prudence E. McAdoo
Mar. 30, 1848
Aug. 24, 1892
"With Christ in Heaven."

A. A. Hubbard
Apr. 19, 1882
Feb. 6, 1916

L. J.
Wife of
A. A. Hubbard
Jan. 20, 1824
Nov. 30, 1903

Edington, Mary Matilda
Sept. 18, 1840
Jan. 24, 1890
"Sleep on dear Mother
and take thy rest,
God hath called thee,
He knoweth best."

Wm. Riley Edington
Sept. 16, 1833
Jan. 18, 1890
"Asleep in Jesus,
blessed sleep from
which none ever wake
to weep."

Jessie Asbury Eddington
Jan. 1, 1868
June 24, 1890
"Gone, but not forever."

Wm. Sherman Edington
July 21, 1865
July 18, 1890
"Our home dissolved,
begins in Heaven."

Luther Riley Edginton
July 20, 1877
July 26, 1890
"Gone so soon."
13 yrs.

J. E. Edington
Mar. 18, 1863
Sept. 22, 1914
51 yrs.

Rhea County, Tennessee, Tombstone Inscriptions

STEBBINS OR PRESBYTERIAN CEMETERY

Benjamin Townsend
Dec. 2, 1838
Nov. 6, 1896

Daniel Marsh
Apr. 3, 1823
Aug. 10, 1891
78 yrs.

Wealthy Gaylord Marsh
Mar. 8, 1826
Mar. 13, 1898
72 yrs.

DEWEY

Laura Desey
Jan. 31, 1833
Jan. 2, 1898
65 yrs.

Grace Marsh Dewey
Aug. 14, 1848
Jan. 1, 1935

Woodman of the world
Memorial Stone -

Lee R. Dewey
Dec. 23, 1876
Apr. 12, 1919

Rowland Enos
1849 - 1893
44 yrs.

Rev. David M. Wilson
1818 - 1887
"A missionary of the cross."

Evalin T. Wilson
1822 - 1899 - Mother

Rev. John Silsby
1817 - 1888
71 yrs.
"Valiant for the truth."

Sarah M. Silsby
1822 - 1907
85 yrs.

Wm. C. Foster
Feb. 1, 1875
Dec. 14, 1890

Louisa Y. Foster
Jan. 30, 1848
Oct. 14, 1919
71 yrs.

James M. Foster
Feb. 12, 1842
Jan. 19, 1912
70 yrs.

Franklin, John K.
Father -
Oct. 13, 1838
Mar. 29, 1891

Meda Ruth Franklin
Aug. 5, 1890
Nov. 8, 1897
"Our Baby."

Martha -
Wife of
L. S. Foster
Dec. 2, 1858
Apr. 3, 1908

(Mary, top of stone.)
Mary Post
Jan. 24, 1905
Nov. 6, 1933
28 yrs.
"Gone from earths shadows
into Gods light."

STEBBINS

Harlang Stebbins
Sept. 3, 1838
Feb. 3, 1913

Mary Tarbox
His wife
1848 - 1921

Chas. Aaron Stebbins
Feb. 21, 1881
Sept. 3, 1882

STEBBINS OR PRESBYTERIAN CEMETERY

Evalina Starring (No dates.)	Leander Stratton Jan. 27, 1812 Nov. 30, 1899 "At rest."
Father - J. D. Wyatt Dec. 18, 1863 May 27, 1915	Beautiful scenery. Outside, 300 yds. away, one grave. Mr. Martin. No tombstone.
E. P. Searl 1835 - 1899 (Concrete wall.)	

RHEA COUNTY

TOMBSTONE INSCRIPTIONS
STEVEN'S CEMETERY

The Steven's Cemetery is eleven miles east of Dayton. Follow Highway No. 30 from Dayton going two miles. Leave Highway and take the gravel road east going to Maperl Springs School which is eight miles, then go to Charley Paul's Place, it being known as the Steven's Cemetery. The land belongs to Charley Paul.

1

RHEA COUNTY

TOMBSTONE INSCRIPTIONS
STEWART CEMETERY

The Stewart Cemetery is three miles northwest of Dayton. Go to the Walnut Grove School house which is one mile north of Dayton, take the gravel road west going one mile, take the gravel road north for one mile. The graves are on the Stewart farm. The oldest settled farm in Rhea County. There are seven graves on this farm, those of negro slaves. They were owned by the Stewarts.

1

RHEA COUNTY

TOMBSTONE INSCRIPTIONS
STUCK FAMILY CEMETERY

The Stuck family Cemetery is four miles southwest of Dayton. Follow Highway No. 30. From Dayton go one and a half mile. Leave Highway and take the gravel road south going two miles and a half to Stuck Place. There are three graves, one woman and two children buried there. The land belongs to West.

1

RHEA COUNTY

TOMBSTONE INSCRIPTIONS
SULLIVAN HILL GRAVEYARD

This graveyard is located ½ mile east of Wolf Creek Road. One negro is buried there. No names or dates are given. Go north on the old Stage Road about 15 miles. You will observe what was formerly known as the old Sullivan Hill. It is not definitely known who owns the land. In this hill you will find an indication of the above mentioned grave.

RHEA COUNTY

TOMBSTONE INSCRIPTIONS
SWAFFORD CEMETERY

The Swafford Cemetery is ten miles north of Dayton. Follow Highway No. 27. Go to Evensville which is six miles north of Dayton. Leave the Highway one mile north of Evensville traveling east on the Clear Creek road which leads to the Swafford farm. There are twenty unmarked graves. The land belongs to the Swaffords.

A. C. Swafford
Mar. 1, 1880
Jan. 30, 1926

Moses F. Moore
Feb. 17, 1833
May 28, 1894

Mary A. Moore
His wife
Mar. 22, 1837
Aug. 15, 1893
"Then spirits smiles
from that bright shore
and softly whispers
weep no more."

Rhea County, Tennessee, Tombstone Inscriptions

RHEA COUNTY

TOMBSTONE INSCRIPTIONS
SWAFFORD CEMETERY

The Swafford Cemetery is ten miles north of Dayton. From Dayton take Highway # 27 going one mile north of Evensville taking the Smyrna road east. The land is owned by J. S. Swafford and the Cemetery is just back at the back of a store owned by Mr. Swafford. There are twenty unmarked graves.

A. C. Swafford
March 1, 1880
Jan. 30, 1926

Moses F. Moore
Feb. 17, 1833
May 28, 1894

: Mary A.
: His wife
: Mar. 22, 1837
: Aug 15, 1893
: "Then spirits smile
: from that bright shore,
: and softly whispers
: weep no more."

1

RHEA COUNTY

TOMBSTONE INSCRIPTIONS
TALLENT (BILL) GRAVEYARD

This Graveyard has probably as many as six graves, and is near Bill Tallent's residence on the Toe String Road, and is also near the old home of Wallace True. No names or dates can be seen, and the graves are supposed to be very old. Go north from Dayton on the old Stage road to the old Howe water mill or the Rhea Springs mill. After passing the mill going west towards Rhea Springs, turn north on the Toe String road, going north about four miles, 1½ miles north of Friendship Church, you will find the above mentioned graves.

RHEA COUNTY

TOMBSTONE INSCRIPTIONS
TEASLEY FAMILY CEMETERY

The Teasley family Cemetery is three miles northwest of Dayton. Follow Highway No. 30 from Dayton. Go to the top of Cave Hill, take gravel road west, going to the C. T. Rudd Place where the road forks. Follow right hand road. The Cemetery is one half mile from the Rudd Place. There are three unmarked graves. The land belongs to Charley Ward.

E. A. Teasley
Born
Oct. 3, 1856

Alice A. Teasley
May 11, 1860
Oct. 11, 1913
"Gone to a better land."

1

RHEA COUNTY

TOMBSTONE INSCRIPTIONS
TELIC GRAVEYARD

Leave Dayton on Dixie Highway north 18 miles to Spring City, turning on west side road one mile to Ideal Valley, then south on Valley road and go to Rice Neal farm. This graveyard is located in District No. 2.

Uncle Tellic Neal	:	Daughter of
Wife of	:	Rice Neal -
Rice Neal	::	No dates given.

Rhea County, Tennessee, Tombstone Inscriptions

RHEA COUNTY

TOMBSTONE INSCRIPTIONS
THOMISON FAMILY GRAVEYARD

Dist. No. 1. Come up the Lon Foust Highway from Dayton 18 miles to Spring City, go 3 miles north of Spring City to the Cash farm. Here on west side of Highway in sight of Cash home, you will find the above named graveyard. This is a very old graveyard long since abandoned.

In memory of
Jane W. Thomasson
July 9, 1789
June 14, 1849
She lived about 60 yrs.
Been dead about 90 yrs.
Double slab, high headstone.
(One or two buried unknown.)

Isaac R. W. Thomasson
July 27, 1802
Jan. 10, 1815
13 yrs.
Been dead 122 yrs.
(Another large slab
and unknown grave.)

Sarah Thompson
Wife of
John Thompson
Feb. 9, 1765
Sept. 16, 1810
45 yrs.
Dead 137 yrs.

Amanda A.
Wife of
S. H. Gilliam
May 16, 1888
Aug. 11, 1908
20 yrs.
"She was a kind,
affectionate wife,
a fond Mother and
a friend to all."

Infant son of
S. H. & A. A. Gilliam
Born and died
July 10, 1908

"Our Darling"
Earnest A.
Son of
S. H. & Mattie Gilliam
Born & died Sept. 15, 1904
"Sleep on sweet babe,
and take thy rest. God called
thee, He thought it best."

Nettie J. Boles
Born Feb. 22, 1879
Married to
S. H. Gilliam
Aug. 6, 1898
Died Dec. 5, 1899
"She came to raise our hearts
to Heaven, she goes to call
us home."

Mattie M. Boles
Born Jan. 4, 1888
Married to
S. H. Gilliam
Jan. 15, 1904
Died Oct. 10, 1904
"Blessed are the pure
in heart, for they shall
see God."

In memory of
Ellis Riggs
Woodman of the World, Monument
June 9, 1868
July 27, 1919
51 yrs. old

Riggs -- "At rest."
5 yrs. old. (No name given.)

Alta, Wife of
Fred Thurman
Feb. 10, 1897 - Apr. 9, 1915
"Gone, but not forgotten."
Probably 25 or more graves unknown.

1

RHEA COUNTY

TOMBSTONE INSCRIPTIONS
THOMPSON GRAVEYARD

The land on which this Cemetery is located is owned by Milo Thompson in District No. 2. Go north from Dayton 18 miles to Spring City. Go west on Grand View pike ½ mile. Turn to left hand road, coming to Walter Shelby's home, where nearby the graveyard is located.

Geo. McDonald
Civil War Vet.
Co. H - 4th. Tenn. Cav.
(No dates.) Probably 20 unmarked graves.

1

RHEA COUNTY

TOMBSTONE INSCRIPTIONS
TODD FAMILY CEMETERY

The Todd family Cemetery is one mile and one half southeast of Dayton. Follow the Blythes Ferry Road from Dayton to the Tipton Hill. There is only one grave with no marker. The land belongs to Victor Welch.

Mrs. Todd

Rhea County, Tennessee, Tombstone Inscriptions

RHEA COUNTY

TOMBSTONE INSCRIPTIONS
TRAVIS CEMETERY

The Travis Cemetery is seven miles north of Dayton. Follow Highway No. 27 from Dayton going three miles. Leave the Highway, taking the Shades Valley Road northeast going by the Travis farm. There are twenty-eight unmarked graves in this Cemetery.

Ida A. Travis
May 11, 1872
July 20, 1918
"Asleep in Jesus."

Pearl Travis
Dec. 13, 1905
Mar. 23, 1920
"Asleep in Jesus."

Albert Travis
Mar. 10, 1890
Oct. 16, 1927
"At rest in Jesus."

At rest -
Robt. F. Henderson
Oct. 23, 1839
May 13, 1900

Anna
Wife of
Robt. F. Henderson
Apr. 8, 1837
Oct. 19, 1925

Stewart
Oct. 6, 1900
Dec. 15, 1901
"At rest."

Audie Henderson
Jan. 13, 1901
Dec. 11, 1901
"Budded on earth
to bloom in Heaven."

Hannar Dodd
Mar. 30, 1888
Apr. 29, 1912

Mrs. Sallie Mickle Hill
Jan. 13, 1928
Aged 79 yrs.

Rhea County, Tennessee, Tombstone Inscriptions

RHEA COUNTY

TOMBSTONE INSCRIPTIONS
UCHEE (COLORED) GRAVEYARD

This graveyard is on the old Gillespie lands. The colored people of this community were children and grandchildren of the old slaves. They have inherited houses and farms, given to them by the Gillsepies, their masters, and is a community of fairly good citizenship, and there is a Schoolhouse and a church. To get to this graveyard, take the old Stage road at old Wahington. To get to Washington, turn east from Dayton about 5 miles on the Washington road. From Washington, go north about 14 miles passing the old Rhea Springs Water mill, then go north for about 4 miles to the widow McCuiston farm, thence east about 3 miles to the Uchee Community. More than 50 graves unnamed and not dated.

Susie Gillespie
Jan. 13, 1935
Age 19 yrs.

Mary Gillespie
Wife of
Christever Gillespie
Aug. 14, 1880
Dec. 31, 1918
Age 38 yrs.

Christever Gillespie
Jan. 13, 1892
Nov. 11, 1913
Age 21 yrs.

Rev. T. J. Gillespie
Oct. 26, 1866
July 12, 1927

Belle S. Gillespie
Wife of
Rev. T. J. Gillespie
Sept. 20, 1863
June 1, 1907

Bessie Gillespie
Sept. 26, 1894
Apr. 17, 1912
Age 18 yrs.

Logan Gillespie
Jan. 20, 1907
May 22, 1907
4 mos.

Homer Gillespie
Feb. 11, 1899
Oct. 24, 1918
Age 19 yrs.

MOORE

Eugene Moore
May 15, 1891
Aug. 12, 1912

Willie Moore
Mar. 13, 1893
Oct. 28, 1912
"In my Father's house are many mansions."

Harry Moore,
Feb. 2, 1901
Oct. 27, 1902

Maggie and Reba Moore
May 13, 1910
July 4, 1910
(Twins, almost two months old.)

W. M. Donaldson
Feb. 2, 1879
Nov. 6, 1918
Age 39 yrs.

John Sharp
1866 - 1901
Age 35 yrs.

Manda Sharp
March 28, 1867 - 1901
"At rest."

RHEA COUNTY

TOMBSTONE INSCRIPTIONS
VAUGHN CEMETERY

The Vaughn Cemetery is ten miles northeast of Dayton. Take Highway # 30 from Dayton to Clear Creek which is eight miles northeast of Dayton and is near the Pleasant Dale school house which is two miles from the main Highway. The land belongs to Vaughns. There are twenty seven unmarked graves.

Addie Vaughn
Wife of
J. N. Vaughn
Sept. 3, 1868
May 29, 1918
"She was a kind and affectionate wife, a fond mother and a friend to all."

Robert Lee Vaughn
July 14, 1902
July 11, 1903

Father -
B. F. Vaughn
Feb. 24, 1842
June 19, 1899

Mother -
Nancy A.
Wife of
B. F. Vaughn
Sept. 29, 1843
Jan. 12, 1909
"Im my Father's mansion are many mansions."

Ollie Maning
Mar. 22, 1878
Mar. 3, 1907

Julia Barnett
Apr. 26, 1839
Dec. 11, 1915
Age 76 yrs. 7 mos. 15 days.

Malinda Waller
Sept. 13, 1834
Feb. 28, 1916
Age 81 yrs. 5 mos. 15 days.

Phillips

Jenthia Phillips
May 23, 1929
Oct. 15, 1930

RHEA COUNTY

TOMBSTONE INSCRIPTIONS
VAUGHN FAMILY GRAVEYARD

2nd. District north of Clear Creek on Clear Creek road at old Ben Vaughn Farm. Come up Dixie Highway or Highway 27 to Will Blevin's Farm. 2 miles north of Evensville, turn out east on Old Clear Creek road. Go east about 3 miles passing Smyrna Church. Also passing Clear Creek mill on left, you will come to the Ben Vaughn Farm upon a hill just west of the old home 1/4 mile. Here you will find the Vaughn Family Graveyard.

Father - Vaughn
B. F. Vaughn
Feb. 24, 1842
June 19, 1899

Mother
Wife of
B. F. Vaughn
Sept. 29, 1848
Jan. 12, 1908
Age 60 yrs.
"In my Father's house are many mansions."

Ollie Manning
Mar. 2, 1878
Mar. 3, 1907
Age 29 yrs.

Malinda A. Waller
Sept. 13, 1834
Feb. 28, 1916
Age 81 yrs. 5 mo. 15 da.

Julian Barnett
Apr. 28, 1839
Dec. 11, 1915
76 yrs. 7 mos. 15 dys.
"Fear ye not, stand still and see the salvation of of the God, which He will show to you today."

Our son,
Robert Lee Vaughn
July 14, 1902
July 11, 1903

Wife of J. N. Vaughn
Addie
Sept. 3, 1868
May 29, 1918
Age 50 yrs.
"She was a kind affetionate wife, a fond Mother and a friend to all."

Rhea County, Tennessee, Tombstone Inscriptions

RHEA COUNTY

TOMBSTONE INSCRIPTIONS
WALKER CEMETERY

The Walker Cemetery is one and a half mile south of Dayton. Follow Highway No. 27. From Dayton go one and a quarter mile south of Dayton. Leave the Highway, taking the gravel road west and crossing the Railroad. There are eleven unmarked graves. At the time the Cemetery was established, the land belonged to the Walkers. It now belongs to Abels.

WALKER

Lonnie
Son of
J. B. V. & Orlena Walker
Aug. 27, 1874
Dec. 20, 1895
"Asleep in Jesus."

Sarrah F.
Dau. of
J. B. V. & Orlena Walker
Aug. 27, 1864
Dec. 31, 1891

Orlena
Wife of
J. B. Walker
May 4, 1841
Oct. 10, 1888

J. J. Manass
Dec. 20, 1895
Age 36 yrs. 7 mos. 4 dys.
"May he rest in peace."

W. M. Pass

Tennie Morgan
Wife of
W. M. Pass
Aug. 23, 1854
July 16, 1891

Sarrah F. Sharp
Dau. of
J. P. V. & Lousia Abel
Aug. 14, 1873
Jan. 22, 1902

ABEL

Dora
Dau. of
J. E. & M. E. Abel
Dec. 13, 1899
Apr. 27, 1900

J. T. Abel
Dec. 9, 1875
Dec. 20, 1895

SHARP

Alta
Wife of
C. A. Sharp
Mar. 11, 1875
Sept. 4, 1894

Eliza Abel
Wife of
J. P. Abel
May 18, 1851
Aug. 22, 1882

Richard Thomas
Native of Ireland

Roy Ray Abel
Son of
M. R. & J. A. Abel
Nov. 12, 1879
Feb. 4, 1881

Julia
Wife of
M. W. Abel
Apr. 12, 1856
May 22, 1936

Rhea County, Tennessee, Tombstone Inscriptions

WALKER CEMETERY
(Continued)

M. W. Abel
Feb. 23, 1855
July 16, 1886

Frank Coy
Son of
M. R. & J. A. Abel
Jan. 26, 1882
July 28, 1886

M. M. Abel
Sept. 15, 1822
May 18, 1875

J. R. Abel
Sept. 20, 1816
Dec. 20, 1900

Mary A.
Dau. of
J. R. & M. M. Abel
Aug. 11, 1850
Oct. 10, 1854

William L.
Son of
J. R. & M. M. Abel
Sept. 5, 1853
Sept. 22, 1854

Holy Bible -
M. J. Martin
Dau. of
J. R. & M. M. Abel
Apr. 12, 1852
Aug. 26, 1888

R. E. Abel
Nov. 8, 1866
June 24, 1891
"Only sleeping."

Ester Abel
Mar. 15, 1826
Dec. 9, 1911

G. W. Abel
Nov. 17, 1819
Jan. 8, 1889

James M.
Son of
G. W. & E. E. Abel
Feb. 6, 1863
Feb. 17, 1878

Mary J.
Dau. of
G. W. & E. E. Abel
July 2, 1850
Aug. 18, 1852

John C.
Son of
R. K. & Grace Abel
Born & died
Jan. 9, 1918

R. K. V., Jr.
Nov. 8, 1921
Dec. 5, 1930
Sonny -

John Abel
May 22, 1855
Apr. 5, 1910

Lou D.
Wife of
John Abel
Sept. 7, 1890
Age 31 yrs. 2 dys.

Mary R. Abel
April 19, 1813
June 17, 1888

Father and Mother -
Margaret Abel
1776 -
Nov. 2, 1861

Cain Abel
1766 -
July 8, 1850

Holy Bible -
Mother - Mary A.
Wife of
R. P. Abel
Feb. 13, 1822 - Aug. 29, 1889

Rhea County, Tennessee, Tombstone Inscriptions

WALKER CEMETERY
(Continued)

R. P. Abel
Mar. 25, 1818
Jan. 1, 1864
At New Albany, Ind.
Buried there.

Ella M. Abel
Dau. of
J. J. & E. A. Abel
Feb. 29, 1864
Jan. 8, 1865

Thomas A. Abel
Son of
J. J. & E. A. Abel
June 24, 1861
Apr. 11, 1864

E. A.
Wife of
J. J. Abel
Oct. 1, 1826
Jan. 9, 1910

Bell James Thomas, M. D.
Sept. 15, 1850
Aug. 29, 1937

"Thy will be done."
Abel —
Erected in memory of
Our husband and father
J. J. Abel
Mar. 10, 1815
Feb. 10, 1902

L. M.
Wife of
J. J. Abel
May 29, 1812
July 14, 1851

M. A. Abel
Dau. of
J. J. & L. M. Abel
July 8, 1842
April 25, 1848

Catharine
Dau. of
Claude & Effie Abel
Sept. 7, 1913
Jan. 7, 1915
"Sleep on sweet babe
and take thy rest,
God called thee home,
He thought it best."

Florence Edna Abel
Wife of
William K. Tipton
1889 - 1920

Daniel Hodges
Nov. 29, 1825
Apr. 8, 1897

Jimmie Flemming
Son of
S. H. & M. J. Flemming
June 30, 1863
Oct. 27, 1863

Myra Hodges
Jan. 5, 1840
July 24, 1916

S. H. Flemming
Apr. 26, 1835
Sept. 3, 1868

Arva Zine
Wife of
L. L. Coulter
Feb. 5, 1857
Sept. 30, 1889
"Gone home."

Hettie Grace
Dau. of
F. H. & M. M. Abel
Jan. 3, 1885
Sept. 23, 1885

WALKER CEMETERY
(Continued)

Tillie Wife of G. W. Abel Apr. 17, 1870 July 27, 1898	David Greer Co. H – 4th. Mich. Cav.
Frank Abel	Gracie P. Smith Jan. 5, 1903 Aug. 21, 1904 "Our darling."
D. T. Abel Aug. 22, 1852 Mar. 23, 1886	

1

RHEA COUNTY

TOMBSTONE INSCRIPTIONS
OLD WASSOM GRAVEYARD

Take the Lon Foust Highway or Dixie Highway north from Dayton about 16 miles to the Odom farm. Cross the Railroad going west, then turn north toward Spring City, then go about 1 mile to the old Wasson farm which joins the old Hugh Furguson farm. Near the line on a west running lane, you will find the above named graveyard which is just a few yards from the old abandoned pike, and near the Cincinnati R. R.

Andrew Wassom
Oct. 28, 1821
Sept. 10, 1892
71 yrs.

Mary Jane Wassom
Apr. 27, 1834
Apr. 4, 1919
85 yrs.

Daniel Wassom
Aug. 1830
Age 50 yrs.

Jacob Wassom
Died 1830
Age 55 yrs.

Jacob L. Wassom
Jan. 26, 1856
45 yrs.

Meticia C. Wassom
Daughter of
J. L. and M. Wassom
Apr. 8, 1843
1850 -
Age 7 yrs.

44 unmarked graves.

Rhea County, Tennessee, Tombstone Inscriptions

RHEA COUNTY

TOMBSTONE INSCRIPTIONS
WATERHOUSE FAMILY CEMETERY

The Waterhouse family Cemetery is six miles northeast of Dayton. Follow Highway No. 30 from Dayton going to the Ballard farm which is five miles and a half from Dayton. Leave the Highway, take the gravel road to the left which goes through Ballard's field. The Cemetery is about a half mile from the main Highway. The land belongs to Waterhouse. There are two unmarked graves.

E. F. Waterhouse
Apr. 30, 1850
Nov. 28, 1914
"Daddy"

Harriett Caroline Sharp
Wife of
D. R. Darius Waterhouse
Feb. 27, 1827
June 1, 1904

In memory of
Darius Waterhouse
Jan. 14, 1815
Feb. 13, 1875

To the memory of
Mary Waterhouse
who departed this life
on the
28th. September, 1854
Aged 51 yr. 20 dys.

J. L. Spence
Feb. 6, 1882
June 13, 1918
"How desolate our home
bereft of thee."

In memory of
Our little daughter
H. D. Spence
Mar. 2, 1896
June 14, 1896
"Darling we miss thee."

Gladdis A.
Dau. of
W. H. & Hattie Spence
Nov. 6, 1913
Nov. 7, 1913
"Over the river my darling
is waiting for me."

In memory of
David N. Moore
Feb. 3, 1841
May 25, 1893
"Gone but not forgotten."

In memory of
Myra Ann Cash
Wife of
Capt. James A. Cash
Mar. 19, 1849
Aug. 22, 1926
"Faithful untill death."

In memory of
Capt. James A. Cash
Dec. 7, 1830
Jan. 30, 1879
"Kind husband, kind father
peace to thy dust until the
resurrection of the just."

In memory of
John, son of
Darius & Harriet C. Waterhouse
July 21, 1858
July 24, 1858

WATERHOUSE FAMILY CEMETERY
(Continued)

Vesta Ellen Waterhouse
Sept. 6, 1848
Nov. 29, 1885

Cyrus Waterhouse
Sept. 7, 1852
Mar. 3, 1925

In memory of
Our sister
Alice Waterhouse
Aug. 10, 1856
Nov. 16, 1925

Darius Waterhouse
July 12, 1935
Aged 74 years, 4 mos. 28 days.

Glenn Story
Infant dau. of
Mr. & Mrs. J. E. Story
Dec. 22, 1908
May 5, 1909
"Asleep in Jesus."

Rhea County, Tennessee, Tombstone Inscriptions

RHEA COUNTY

TOMBSTONE INSCRIPTIONS
WATERHOUSE COMMUNITY GRAVEYARD

District No. 1. A very old graveyard. This graveyard is very well kept. To find the location of this graveyard you come up from Dayton, Tenn, 18 miles to Spring City. Take the Rhea Springs road, go east 2 miles to Rhea Springs, then take Muddy Creek road, go north 1 mile to the Graesham farm. On west side of this road in a cedar grove, you will find the Waterhouse graveyard.

"Farewell."
Anna E.
Wife of
J. E. Waterhouse
Aug. 24, 1876
Age 28 yrs. 8 mos. 13 dys.

Died in peace at God's will.
Vesta Ferguson
May 27, 1870
Age 27 yrs.

Pyott, Edward
Mar. 12, 1812
June 8, 1819
Aged 7 yrs.
Dead 118 yrs.

Townsend, P.
Son of
E. and M. Pyott
Sept. 15, 1849
Jan. 2, 1885
Age 36 yrs.

Margaret Pyott
June 8, 1816
Oct. 8, 1896
Aged 90 yrs.

"At rest."

Mose Thompson
May 30, 1856
Sept. 17, 1890
Aged 34 yrs.

In memory of
Ann Eliza Waterhouse Ziegler
Wife of, W. C. Ziegler
1852 - 1873 - Lived 21 yrs.
Died in full hope of immorality.

Sacred in memory of
Prudella Waterhouse
May 29, 1861
May 6, 1879
A faithful flower of Christ
and died in the faith.

Jacob Green
Aug. 5, 1820
Aug. 6, 1894
Age 74 yrs.
He died as he lived, concrete
wall around plot.

Clyde Thompson
Apr. 4, 1880
May 30, 1909
Age 29 yrs.

Chas. C. Thompson
Dec. 19, 1889
Feb. 14, 1917
Age 26 yrs.
"Gone but not forgotten."

Ada Lee
Daughter of
J. B. & Daisy Tanksley
June 28, 1902
June 15, 1904

Newton Robbins
1842 -
Apr. 21, 1921
"Gone to rest."
"Father, we will miss you."
About 79 yrs. old.

Mary Ann
Wife of
Newton Robbins
Apr. 5, 1840
Feb. 16, 1922
Mother, we will miss you.

WATERHOUSE COMMUNITY GRAVEYARD

Eva B. Baker
Daughter of
Maggie Eddington
Aug. 28, 1895
Sept. 21, 1920
"Mother's darling, asleep in Jesus."

About 100 graves in this graveyard. Most of them not marked. Some of them very old. Situated in a beautiful grove.

1

RHEA COUNTY

TOMBSTONE INSCRIPTIONS
OLD WATERHOUSE GRAVEYARD

This Cemetery is north of Piney in the first District. Go north from Dayton 18 miles to Spring City, then go eastfrom Spring City by Ca-wood's water mibl. This graveyard is probably 200 yrs. old, and has been a neglected for a long time. Stones are torn down and graves are sunk in the ground. Most of the people buried there, are colored. Probably about fifty unknown graves.

Rhea County, Tennessee, Tombstone Inscriptions

RHEA COUNTY

TOMBSTONE INSCRIPTIONS
WEBB CEMETERY

The Webb Cemetery is eight miles north of Dayton taking Highway # 27 from Dayton to Evensville. Leave the Highway at Evensville, following the Washington road going east to White Flat on the gravel road north. The Cemetery is on the Webb farm which belongs to the Webbs. There are 152 unmarked graves.

Elwood Roberts
Co. I - 34
N. J. I. N. F.

Thomas Owensby
Aug. 17, 1813
March 14, 1910

Sneed -
Z. T. Sneed
Sept. 9, 1840
June 20, 1913

His wife -
Oct. 25, 1918
Age 84 years.

RYAN
Ida
Wife of
W. H. Ryan
May 19, 1872
Feb. 13, 1907
"At rest."

Frank Jordan
Apr. 25, 1868
Oct. 31, 1912
"Beloved one farewell."

MCMILLAN
Maud R.
Daughter of
J. W. & M. A. McMillan
Oct. 12, 1918
Oct. 16, 1918

Infant son of
J. W. & M. A. McMillan
Born & died
July 14, 1907
"Sleep on sweet babe,
and take thy rest, God called
thee home, he thought it best."

Robert Sneed
Jan. 12, 1868
Apr. 21, 1908
"At rest."

Willie Sneed
Mar. 3, 1900
Oct. 22, 1901

Walter
Son of
R. M. Sneed
Oct. 10, 1897
Jan. 17, 1917
"Gone but not forgotten."

Zennie May
Daughter of
R. & M. Sneed
May 29, 1913
Aug. 24, 1921
"Darling we miss thee."

Robert Sneed
1819 - 1891

Eady
His wife
1847 - 1910

Caldonie Sneed
Feb. 12, 1872
June 20, 1908

Lester Sneed
May 1, 1911
June 15, 1911

Frank Sneed
May 2, 1912
June 16, 1912

Mandy Cleo Sneed
March 1, 1915 - Aug. 5, 1916

Rhea County, Tennessee, Tombstone Inscriptions

WEBB CEMETERY

Ruth E. Sneed
July 2, 1915
July 8, 1921
"Our darling, we miss thee."

Roy Sneed
Born & died
June 12, 1905
"At rest."

Addie Sneed
Mar. 27, 1903
Nov. 24, 1903
"Sweetley resting."

Claud Sneed
Born & died
July 7, 1904
"Gone to a better land."

S. H. Sneed
Jan. 15, — (?)
Feb. 9, 1928
"Weep not, he is at rest."

T. J. Sneed
1853 - 1912

John Sneed
1853 - 1917
"Gone but not forgotten."

Burdett, Rev. H. B.
1855 -
May 23, 1918
(Erected by his friends.)

Thomas McBroom
Oct. 15, 1904
July 18, 1913
"At rest."

Marion Hard
Tennessee PVT 9
INF - 2 Div.
Feb. 1, 1934

In memory of
Jane Mahale Webb
May 16, 1858
May 11, 1894
(Wife of J. A. Webb.)

Mathiel
Daughter of
W. T. & N. J. Webb
Sept. 1, 1889
Nov. 19, 1893
"At rest."

Mrs. John Mize
6-28-1927
Aged 57 years.

1

RHEA COUNTY

TOMBSTONE INSCRIPTIONS
WILK'S AND THOMPSON COLORED GRAVEYARD

District No. 2. Take the State Highway from Dayton about 15 miles. Turn west at Carp School house on the old Stage road, going one mile from Carp Schoolhouse. This graveyard ½ mile south of the Franklin home, in the woodland. It is old and almost abandoned. No inscriptions. A few rough lime rocks mark some graves. There are probably about 75 graves.

Rhea County, Tennessee, Tombstone Inscriptions

RHEA COUNTY

TOMBSTONE INSCRIPTIONS
WOLF CREEK CEMETERY

Take Highway No. 27, going 18 miles north of Dayton to Spring City. Go east on Rhea Springs road two miles to Midway. Take the old Stage road from Midway, going 3 miles south passing Wolf Creek School house where nearby this Cemetery is located. This is a community graveyard. About 150 graves with plain unmarked sandstones.

FRAZIER

Pacif Y. Tinsley Gibs
Wife of
Samuel Frazier
Oct. 12, 1809
Nov. 1888
79 yrs.

Joseph C. Frazier
Sept. 23, 1834
Dec. 31, 1862
28 yrs.

William P. Frazier
Oct. 1836
Feb. 14, 1854
18 yrs.

Samuel Frazier
1800 -
May 18, 1853
53 yrs.

WALKER

Samuel Walker
Feb. 26, 1843
Mar. 6, 1910
67 yrs.

Cirene E. Wheeler
Wife of
Samuel Walker
Apr. 30, 1854
Aug. 21, 1927
63 yrs.

Sarah Bell
Daughter of
Cerena and Samuel Walker
Mar. 10, 1880 - Feb. 1884
4 yrs.

Rebecca Jane
Daughter of
Samuel and Cinna Walker
Jan. 6, 1868
Oct. 1876

WHEELER

Dr. S. J. Wheeler
Mar. 28, 1833
Sept. 14, 1901
(Mason.)

"In memory of
Dr. John M. Wheeler
Mar. 13, 1837
Jan. 29, 1879
(Mason.)

Two of his family with blank stones.

HOLLAND

Sarah S.
Wife of
T. R. Holland
Feb. 6, 1821
Oct. 25, 1895
74 yrs.

Thomas R. Holland
Jan. 7, 1806
Feb. 18, 1879
73 yrs.

Caroline Holland
Wife of
Micajah Brady
July 4, 1847
Apr. 26, 1921

Rhea County, Tennessee, Tombstone Inscriptions

WOLF CREEK CEMETERY

Hannah J. Holland
Wife of
T. H. Robertson
Sept. 1, 1849
Sept. 11, 1921
72 yrs.

E. H. Holland
May 13, 1863
Jan. 20, 1928
65 yrs.

FISHER

Henderson Fisher
Apr. 29, 1828
Jan. 15, 1899
"Asleep in Jesus."

Our Mother -
Rebecca A.
Wife of
Henderson Fisher
Apr. 29, 1827
July 9, 1895
68 yrs.
"Dear Mother,
rest in peace."

Belinda N.
Wife of
Anderson Campbell
Jan. 11, 1818
Feb. 26, 1890
72 yrs.
"Blessed are the dead
which die in the Lord."

W. R. Dagley
May 5, 1848
Jan. 28, 1920
72 yrs.
"Gone, but not forgotten."

Sarah I.
Wife of
W. R. Dagley
Jan. 2, 1862
"We will meet again."

Geo. W. Shelby
1861 -
Nov. 6, 1900
"Kind Father of love,
thou att gone to thy rest,
forever to join us the joys
of the blest."

TRENTHAM

Nancy J. Trentham
May 30, 1840
Oct. 21, 1911
"She believed and sleeps
in Jesus."

Robert M. Trentham
Sept. 18, 1855
"Earth hath no sorrows,
that Heaven cannot heal."

Mary A. Walker
Wife of
Robert M. Trentham
Dec. 16, 1857
Jan. 14, 1920
"Thy memory shall be a
guiding star to heaven."

Robert M.
Son of
R. M. and M. A. Trentham
Aug. 15, 1895
May 26, 1896
9 mos. old

Minnie D.
Daughter of
R. M. and M. A. Trentham
Nov. 11, 1890
Dec. 11, 1890
1 mo.

Double head stone -
David Walker
July 23, 1819
May 6, 1888

Rhea County, Tennessee, Tombstone Inscriptions

WOLF CREEK CEMETERY

Nancy Walker
Apr. 15, 1819
Jan. 19, 1892
"Gone, but not forgotten."

Braxton Walker
Sept. 24, 1850
Apr. 15, 1927
77 yrs.

Eliza Walker
Dec. 17, 1855
Aug. 1886
31 yrs.

Emily
Wife of
Starling Holloway
Feb. 11, 1831
Dec. 29, 1906
77 yrs.

Starling Holloway
Dec. 6, 1814
Jan. 23, 1891
77 yrs.

Archibald Berry
Co. G - 7th. Tenn.
mounted Inf.
Civil War.
Dates invisible.

Johnnie Brown
Apr. 16, 1888
May 3, 1907
19 yrs.

Chapman
Son of
J. H. and S. T. Rector
Jan. 22, 1899
July 31, 1900

Polly McClendon
Jan. 2, 1830
Feb. 22, 1914
"A true wife,
and a good Mother."
84 yrs.

J. T. Phillips
Nov. 7, 1849
"Kind Father of love,
thou hast gone to thy rest."
In my father's house are
many mansions.

Vesta J.
Wife of
J. T. Phillips
July 27, 1867
July 5, 1920
"She was the sunshine
of our home."

Cora
Daughter of
J. T. and V. T. Phillips
May 26, 1887
Jan. 16, 1905
"She was an affectionate
duaghter and a faithful
friend."

Wm. Theodore
Baby son of
Geo. and Bessie Smith
Apr. 6, 1909
Jan. 20, 1910
"From Mother's arms
to the arms of Jesus."

W. M. Lester Barger
Apr. 5, 1922
June 16, 1923

Chas. Tate Smith
Jan. 18, 1856

Delia S.
Wife of
C. T. Smith
Mar. 4, 1856
Oct. 7, 1926
"She was an affectionate Mother,
and a friend to all."

Corporal Franklin Brockdon
Co. H - 3rd. Tenn. Cav.
Civil War Veteran.

4

WOLF CREEK CEMETERY

T. P. O'Sullivan
Co F - Civil War
Veteran

BAKER

Family plot
Geraldine Baker
Jan. 9, 1930
Feb. 14, 1936
6 yrs.
"Gone to be with the angels."

1

RHEA COUNTY

TOMBSTONE INSCRIPTIONS
YOTHER CEMETERY

The Yother Cemetery is seven miles northwest of Dayton. Follow Highway No. 27 from Dayton going three miles. Leave Highway and take the gravel road west for four miles. There are nine unmarked graves. The land belongs to Pelfrey.

Yother

E. B. Yother
1843 - 1906

J. M. Yother
1859 - 1904
"Gone bu tnot forgotten."

E. P. Wiley

1

RHEA COUNTY

TOMBSTONE INSCRIPTIONS
(COLORED)

This is a colored graveyard and the name is unknown. It is located near Tenn. river on the Huff farm, and is a very old graveyard. Probably slaves of, and before Civil War times were buried there. No names or dates can be seen. To get to this graveyard, take the Dayton Pike for about 14 miles on the Pinhook Highway, then about 2 miles east on the Huff farm, it is in sight and overlooking the Tennessee river. Probably 150 graves here, some of them having short rough limestone at head of graves, and is in bad condition.

1

RHEA COUNTY

TOMBSTONE INSCRIPTIONS

The name of this Cemetery is unknown. There is only one grave, A Miss Peace, daughter of a preacher, and no dates are given. It is in Dist. No. 2 and is located on the Pentagrass farm. Go from Dayton by Washington to this farm and grave, about 14 miles on the old Stage road to the widow Fugate's farm and ½ mile back of this farm to the Pentagrass farm.

RHEA COUNTY

TOMBSTONE INSCRIPTIONS

There is only one grave, that of Floyd Kerby, a boy who drowned in Piney river probably 70 years ago. He is buried near the river, one mile below singing Bill Smith's farm. Go from Dayton about 18 miles on the State Highway to Dock Smith's water mill, then turn north on the Toe String Valley road, going about two miles to the Bill Smith farm. No dates are given.

RHEA COUNTY

TOMBSTONE INSCRIPTIONS

This graveyard is not named, and has only two graves, that of John Kelly and Jim Sims. No dates are given. It is believed that Mr. Sims was an old Steam Boat Pilot. Take the old Stage road from Dayton about 16 miles to a road turning east toward Tenn. river, going out near the Jake Ewing farm. Continue south to the Bart Ewing farm. On this farm, or near the Ewing home, these two graves may be located.

1

RHEA COUNTY

TOMBSTONE INSCRIPTIONS

This is an old abandoned graveyard and the name is unknown. It is located on the Cunningham farm, formerly known as the Lock farm. It probably consists of more colored people than white people. One white man named Morgan Harwood was drowned in the Tennessee river, reported buried in this graveyard. The number of graves could not be learned, and no one is reported to have been buried here for seventy years. The Cunningham farm is on the State Highway about 2 miles south of the Carp Schoolhouse. Take the State Highway from Dayton, going about 15 miles before reaching this farm.

1

RHEA COUNTY

TOMBSTONE INSCRIPTIONS

This graveyard consists of one grave, marked by small concrete post, and the name is Hanna Moles - No dates. Take the Lon Foust Highway 25 miles from Dayton to Roddy, going east 1 mile to top of Ridge on Bill Ross's farm.

RHEA COUNTY

TOMBSTONE INSCRIPTIONS

Four and one half miles west of Dayton, there are five unmarked graves. No one seems to know much about the people who are buried here. Leave Dayton on Highway # 30 going west about two miles from Dayton. When reaching the top of Cove Hill, leave the Highway taking the gravel road southwest traveling two miles to the West farm.

1

RHEA COUNTY

TOMBSTONE INSCRIPTIONS
FAMILY GRAVEYARDS - NAME UNKNOWN

Mr. Will Molton's farm. District No. 1. A very old graveyard. No stones standing, no dates or names given. It is about 200 yards from the Muddy Creek road on the west side. A very large wild cherry tree stands by. At Dayton you get on the Dixie Highway, come north 18 miles to Spring City, get on the Rhea Springs road, go east 2 miles, take the Muddy Creek road, go north about 3 miles to the Will Molton farm. Just above Mr. Molton's home about 300 yds. you will find the above graveyard. Probably a dozen graves. It is abandoned.

RHEA COUNTY

TOMBSTONE INSCRIPTIONS
NAME OF GRAVEYARD UNKNOWN

On Pat McCabe farm. Get on Dixie Highway at Dayton, go north 18 miles to Spring City, then take Rhea Springs road going east 1½ mile, then take Wolf Creek road 1 mile south, you will find a lonely unknown grave just east of the road. This grave is covered with a large limestone slab. It is near an old barn.

1

RHEA COUNTY

TOMBSTONE INSCRIPTIONS

(NO NAME IS GIVEN)

Three graves on the Bill Curly farm. From Dayton come up the Dixie Highway 18 miles to Spring City, then take Rhea Springs road east for 1½ mile to midway, take the Wolf Creek road for two miles, then turn east ½ mile to Bill Curly farm. Here in little clump of bushes in the open field, you will find three graves.

Mr. Profit and daughter and a little girl named Smith. No tombstones or dates.

INDEX

RHEA COUNTY

TOMBSTONE INSCRIPTIONS
INDEX

A	Page		Page
Able, Brown W.	34	Able, William	3,308
Able, Cain	2,308	Able, infant	7
Able, Catherine	309	Abernathy, Rev. Berry	159
Able, Catherine M.	1	Abernathy, J. A.	158
Able, C. W.	2	Abernathy, John Clayton	159
Able, Dora	3,307	Abernathy, Lieut. Col. J. T.	159
Able, D. T.	1,310	Abernathy, Mira	159
Able, E. A.	2,309	Abernathy, Permelia G.	158
Able, Ella M.	305	Abbott, Nancy	285
Able, Ellen M.	2	Abbott, S. S.	285
Able, Eliza	307	Acree, Elizabeth	264
Able, Ester	308	Actkinson, Isabelle Fike	251
Able, Ester E.	2	Actkinson, John	251
Able, Florence Edna	1,309	Adkins, Donea	5
Able, Frank	1,310	Adkins, T. J.	5
Able, Harry	3	Aikersons, Katie	34
Able, Hettie Grace	309	Alexander, Cyrus	171
Able, G. W.	308	Alexander, Earl	106
Able, James	2	Alexander, Edna	158
Able, James M.	308	Alexander, Harry	27
Able, J. J.	2,309	Alexander, H. M	93
Able, John	2,308	Alexander, James	232
Able, J. R.	308	Alexander, John L.	168
Able, J. T.	3,307	Alexander, Mary J.	168
Able, Julia	3,307	Alexander, R. F.	172
Able, Laura Kiker	26	Alexander, Stephen H.	168
Able, L. M.9	1	Alexander, Thomas H.	99
Able, Lou D.	2,308	Alison, Margarette Boges	285
Able, M. A.	1,309	Allen, Abner F.	79
Able, Margaret	2,308	Allen, Ann Frazier	79
Able, Mary A.	2,308	Allen, Arva A.	107
Able, Mary J.	308	Allen, Eddie Madge	65
Able, Mary R.	2,308	Allen, Elizabeth A.	107
Able, M. M.	3,308	Allen, Dr. E. M.	41
Able, M. W.	308	Allen, Emma Mildred	65
Able, R. E.	2,308	Allen, J. L.	201
Able, R. K.	2	Allen, John Gibbs	26
Able, R. K. V. Jr.	308	Allen, M. C.	201
Able, R. P.	2,309	Allen, Nancy Agnes	79
Able, Thomas A.	309	Allen, Robert	29
Able, Thomas B.	2	Allen, Sarah Peak	64
Able, Tillie	1,310	Allen, Thomas A.	64

Index

Name	Page	Name	Page
Allen, Thomas W.	79	Bacon, F. W.	169
Allen, Valentine	79	Bailey, Anna Lee	30
Allen, V. C.	41	Bailey, Roland	30
Allen, Vesta F.	29	Bailey, Sarah L.	271
Allen, Virginia Ann	79	Bailey, William C.	30
Allen William Vellentine	79	Bain, Amanda Alice	37
Alley, Cora B. Shelton	104	Baker, Chas. Warren	40
Alley, Mr. J.	69	Baker, David E.	40
Alley, Gordan	69	Baker, Eva B.	40
Attridge, Wm. Richard	26	Baker, Geraldine	324
Alyworth, Mary	283	Baker, Gertrude	58
Alyworth, Reuben	283	Baker, Ida Jane	166
Anderson, Ap	6	Baker, Margaret L.	64
Anderson, Catherine	168	Baker, Tinnie	256
Anderson, Catherine B.	7	Baker, Wayne	166
Anderson, C. E.	6	Baker, W. J.	58
Anderson Joephes	199	Ball, Levitta	282
Anderson, W. A.	168	Ball, Thana A.	253
Andrews, Mrs. Mary S. M.	93	Ballard, Chinie R. Mintie	87
Andy, Joseph	284	Ballard, Clinton	31
Angel, J. W.	271	Baldwin, Hugh W.	88
Angel, Margaret E.	271	Baldwin, Nancy H.	75
Angel, Mary J.	271	Baldwin, W. W.	75
Angel, Ray C. Jr.	283	Bales, Isabel	39
Angel, William N.	283	Bales, Laura	39
Angle, Ike	55	Bandy, May	62
Ansley, William E.	60	Banks, Alvint	58
Armor, Geo. W.	253	Banks, Viola	58
Arnold, A. F.	263	Bankston, A. J.	10
Arnold, Emma Parthena	246	Bankston James	25
Arnold, Emmitt O.	26	Barger, Arthur M.	169
Arnold, Naomi Lee	263	Barger, Bessie May	172
Arnold, S. B.	262	Barger, Ellen	172
Askin, Alice Gray	58	Barger, George Clayton	172
Ault, Conrad	251	Barger, John H.	93
Ault, Geo. W.	251	Barger, Mary M.	172
Ault, G. W.	63	Barger, Mirian Lucille	172
Ault, Margaret A.	61	Barger, M. J.	172
Ault, Mary Emily	61	Barger, Nettie	172
Ault, M. T.	63	Barger, R. B.	172
Ault, Ruth A.	61	Barger, R. H.	172
Ault, Ruth G.	205	Barger, Thomas Ray	93
Ault, Susan	251	Barger, William E.	172
Ault, Willy N.	61	Barger, William T.	165
Ausburn, Mrs. Mollie	266	Barger, W. M. Lester	322
Ayers, Charley S.	108	Barnard, Hettie	65
Ayers, Claudie	109	Barnett, Julia	305
Ayers, Eliza Jane	108	Barnett, Sarah A.	68
		Barnwell, Bertie	156
B		Barron, John W.	272
		Bartley, Isaac	262
Baber, Granville H.	92	Barton, Charles Oscar	271
Bacon, Charley	109	Barton, Delilah A.	68

Index

Name	Page	Name	Page
Barton, Edward Roy	65	Best, Hazel E.	105
Barton, Harry Edward	64	Best, H. P.	102
Barton, Nettie	286	Best, J. H.	102
Barton, T. A.	64	Best, Luther	111
Barton, William	271	Best, M. F.	111
Basket, J. E.	89	Best, Morgan B.	105
Basket, Pearl	89	Best, Ondous	105
Baskett, John E.	27	Best, Posey	11b
Baskett, M. Ora	89	Best, Tiza L.	71
Bayless, Kidney Powell	281	Betsill, Medora G.	272
Beall, Edwin	65	Bird, L. E. Star	179
Bean, Effie	149	Bishop, Alvin	272
Bean, Geo. M.	150	Bishop, Annie	265
Bean, George M.	149	Bishop, Bonnie May	265
Bean, Josie	150	Bishop, Dorthy Ann	266
Bean, Virty	175	Bishop, F. M.	265
Bean, W. M. H.	174	Bishop, Frank	272
Bean, -- Infant	150	Bishop, Lillie	265
Beard, Fred S.	255	Bishop, M. A.	272
Beard, J. H.	10	Bishop, Nancy J.	265
Beard, Pocahontus	12	Black, Annie M.	165
Beck, Catherine	261	Black, James A.	165
Beck, E. P.	261	Black, Louana Amelia	59
Bedwell, Jessie Earl	173	Black, Nellie Marie	105
Bell, C. R.	13	Black, Sylvanie	99
Bell, G. W.	13	Black, infant	105
Bell, James W.	112	Blackburn, Elmer	71
Bell, L. T.	13	Blackburn, Mary E.	71
Bell, Mary	13	Blackburn, Meridae	71
Bell, Mary A.	112	Blackburn, Ragen A.	71
Bell, Rollo Clyde	112	Blain, James H. Jr.	126
Bell, S. J.	13	Blain, Jene H.	126
Bell, S. P.	13	Blain, John R.	126
Bell, Willie T.	112	Blain, Thomas G.	126
Beene, Harold Wilber	168	Blair, Charles	281
Beene, Martha	168	Blair, Hattie	281
Beene, Martin Van Buren	168	Blankenship, Mettie	104
Bennett, Albert T.	44	Blevins, --	21
Bennett, Eulalia A.	30	Blevins, A. C.	49
Bennett, J. W.	66	Blevins, Braxton	29
Benson, Creed	174	Blevins, Elmer	257
Benson, Ed	32	Blevins, James O.	221
Benson, Margaret S.	111	Blevins, Jane A.	219
Benson, Paul	174	Blevins, J. B.	221
Benson, Mrs. Tennie A.	277	Blevins, Ladie A.	49
Benson, W. B.	32	Blevins, Mary	22
Benson, infant	55	Blevins, Mary E.	29
Benton, Selah	89	Blevins, Perry	196
Berry, Archibald	322	Blevins, Selia	196
Best, B. G.	100	Blevins, Squire	22
Best, Clay	105	Blevins, Virginia C.	49
Best, Earnest	105	Blevins, W. F.	29

Index

Name	Page	Name	Page
Boofer, H. C.	68	Brady, Green	271
Boofer, J. T.	68	Brady, Harriet	115
Boofer, Mary A.	191	Brady, James K. Polk	159
Boofer, Nellie	191	Brady, James M.	273
Bolen, Anna Lee	32	Brady, J. G.	239
Bolen, D. R.	32	Brady, J. H.	263
Bolen, J. Luther	32	Brady, John K.	15
Bolen, Nancy	246	Brady, Katy	37
Bolen, T. M.	14	Brady, Leland	159
Boles, Arch Boyd	114	Brady, Luther J.	193
Boles, Charlie	265	Brady, Mollie	202
Boles, J. H.	193	Brady, N. B.	110
Boles, Margaret A.	261	Brady, Pa	202
Boles, Muriel	113	Brady, Phoebe Ann	159
Boles, Willie Lee	265	Brady, Sarah	15
Boles, infant	239	Brady, Smith	116
Bollon, Hanner	270	Brady, S. S.	193
Bolton, Robert N.	176	Brady, Vivian Wanita	159
Bolton, Sidney A.	176	Brady, Walter	115
Bower, Albert S.	173	Brady, Will	115
Bower, F. M.	92	Brady, infant	193
Bower, Francis	173	Bramlett, H. E.	257
Bower, Virginia Rains	92	Bramlett, J. M.	257
Bowmen, Isaac	174	Bramlett, M. C.	257
Bowman, Jennie	174	Brandon, Anna	149
Bowman, W. D.	174	Brandon, Dorthy T.	38
Boyd --	261	Brandon, Judith Ann	150
Boyd, Ada	104	Brandon, J. W.	51
Boyd, Bargey	263	Brandon, Rachel E.	150
Boyd, E. H.	27	Brandon, S. J.	34
Boyd, Eula	27	Brandon, U. T.	51
Boyd, Hannah	262	Brandshaw, Stephen R.	85
Boyd, J. S.	262	Brickey, Emma L.	170
Boyd, Kate	41	Breeding, Byram	20
Boyd, Lester	38	Breeding, Jane	20
Boyd, Louise	41	Breeding, John B.	20
Boyd, Margaret	41	Breeding, Nancy E.	20
Boyd, Mary C.	27	Breeding, Sarah Ann	20
Boyd, Reed	261	Breeding, Stephen	20
Boyd, Silvester	262	Breeding, Wm. J.	20
Boyd, Texie A.	261	Breedlove, Ellen Maud	40
Bradshaw, Mary A.	43	Brewer, Dixie	42
Brady, Amanda	158	Brewer, Rev. G. W.	42
Brady, Ann	202	Brewer, Martha	30
Brady, Bill	202	Brewer, Mary J.	42
Brady, D. B.	36	Brewer, Mildred	30
Brady, Della	272	Brewer, Nannie	30
Brady, Deltar	272	Brewer, T. J.	30
Brady, Elizabeth	239	Bridgman, Eddie Lee	62
Brady, Emma Lee	282	Bridgman, Sarah F.	62
Brady, Ethel May	110	Bridgman, infant	63
Brady, Farley	15	Bridgeman, F. L.	63
Brady, Fred W.	110	Bridgeman, L. C.	29

Index

Name	Page	Name	Page
Britt, infant	168	Broyles, Maryl	52
Brock, J. H.	179	Broyles, Nellie	66
Brockdon, Corp. Franklin	327	Broyles, Nile M.	88
Brookman, Rush	283	Broyles, Oscar	52
Brooks, H. L.	36	Broyles, S. D.	59
Brooks, James M.	40	Broyles, W. T.	61
Brooks, Kary Emma	40	Broyles, infant	156
Brooks, Mary S.	239	Broyles, Bell Brady	282
Brooks, Parlie	268	Bruce, Minnie Lee	285
Brooks, T. O.	36	Brumagin, A.	40
Brooks, Wallace R.	44	Brumagin, Sarah E.	40
Brooks, W. M.	268	Bryant, John A.	26
Bronce, Moss	280	Bryson, Sarah A.	155
Brown, Amanda M.	114	Bryson, Thomas	279
Brown, Arthur F.	285	Buck, Charlotte	56
Brown, Bertha C.	68	Bunch, Mrs. Lee	256
Brown, Bessie	116	Burd, Scrap J.	262
Brown, Bessie L.	116	Burdett, A. A.	190
Brown, C. C.	285	Burdett, Rev. H. B.	318
Brown, Mrs. Dixie	285	Burdett, Margaret	131
Brown, D. J.	22	Burdett, Rebecca	190
Brown, E. H.	68	Burdett, T. H.	131
Brown, Eugene Franklin	116	Burka, Joan	36
Brown, Dr. G. R.	127	Burkett, L. Tennie	38
Brown, I. K.	266	Burkhalt, Abigail	66
Brown, James R.	175	Burkhalter, I. D.	41
Brown, Jane	139	Burnett, Mrs. Bertie	247
Brown, J. H.	22	Burnett, Clara Mae	167
Brown, J. L.	22	Burnett, Cynthia E.	111
Brown, Joe	285	Burnett, Elijah	14
Brown, Johnnie	322	Burnett, Lula Grace	111
Brown, Margaret Lee	116	Burnett, Teddie	111
Brown, Marie	116	Burnett, W. F.	198
Brown, Mary Ann	36	Burns, Maggie	53
Brown, Mary Ellen	255	Burrell, Martha L.	102
Brown, Maudie L.	116	Burton, J. D. Jr.	283
Brown, Riley S.	22	Burwick, Samuel	152
Brown, Sophronia J.	50	Burwick, Samuel H.	234
Brown, Tennessee Crabtree	285	Burwick, W. A.	72
Brown, Walter T.	256	Burwick, infant	152-233
Brown, W. F. P.	284	Buttram, Alice	43
Broyles, A. C.	59	Buttram, Asbury	44
Broyles, Addison M.	88	Buttram, James C.	69
Broyles, Alfred	59	Buttram, James G.	45
Broyles, Amanda	15	Buttram, Lucy E.	44
Broyles, Chas. Edward	35	Buttram, Martha Alice	69
Broyles, Ella	66	Buttram, Orton J.	45
Broyles, Danial	156	Buttram, Raymond	43
Broyles, Delilah C.	59	Buttram, Synthia	69
Broyles, Eleanor C.	88	Buttram, infant	34
Broyles, Eliza	286	Byrd, A. J.	195
Broyles, Flora	59	Byrd, Frank	280
Broyles, Mary Elizabeth	60	Byrd, George Dibrel	195

Index

	Page		Page
Byrd, Isaac	194	Cash, Capt. James A.	312
Byrd, Lela B.	249	Cash, James I.	97
Byrd, Martha	280	Cash, Jesse W.	285
Byrd, Nancy	195	Cash, Lucinda S.	122
Byrd, William	--	Cash, Myra Ann	312
		Cash, Sarah Ann	97,122
C		Cash, Sarah Llewellen Gentry	279
		Cash, Wm. W.	122
Cain, Clarence Herbert	285	Cate, Albert	279
Caldwell, Callie	218	Cate, Rev. Gay Catherine Wasson	161
Caldwell, Flora	281	Cate, Hilton B.	252
Caldwell, M.	283	Cate, Laura J.	252
Caldwell, Victoria Darwin	283	Cate, William A.	279
Calwell, James C.	165	Cates, A. M.	285
Campbell, Mrs. Anna Bell	256	Caudle, Evelyn	38
Campbell, Belinda N.	321	Cawood, --	179
Campbell, Joe	196	Cawood, George M.	286
Campbell, J. M.	273	Cawood, Stephen	286
Campbell, Rosa Metzer	273	Chambers, Arminda	67
Campbell, William	196	Chambers, Clyde	68
Canady, Mrs. Sidney	195	Chambers, Harry	64
Cantrell, Lorinda J.	123	Chambers, Rev. Homer	134
Capps, C. M.	164	Chambers, Kitty Elizabeth	65
Capps, F. M.	164	Chambers, Lizzie	64
Caraway, W. R.	67	Chambers, Rita Irene	68
Card, Milo M.	175	Chambers, Rosa	64
Carlock, Laura May	167	Chatman, G. L.	95
Carney, Alfred	193	Chattin, F. D.	49
Carney, Mary Magdaline	193	Chattin, John Cook	86
Carney, James C.	193	Chattin, Mary E.	86
Carney, James P.	41	Chattin, Susan	86
Carney, Lucy Tatitia	193	Chauncey, Helen Elizabeth	28
Carney, Margaret A.	58	Childress, Ellen	102
Carpenter, Mary A.	256	Clack, Amy	207
Carraway, Virginia Ann	268	Clack, John S.	87
Carroll, M. G.	261	Clack, Margaret	87,88
Carter, D. T.	152	Clack, Missouri	87
Carter, Tommy	152,235	Clack, Philo T.	87
Carter, T. M.	33	Clack, Sabria C.	114
Cartone, Elippa	255	Clack, Sterlina G.	88
Cartwright, E. D.	67	Clack, Wm. M.	87
Cartwright, Frances M.	274	Clack, Wm. R.	114
Casey, Clearcy	275	Claglin, John	274
Casey, Westley	275	Clark, --	75
Cash, Ann	97	Clark, Celia R.	75
Cash, Ann B.	97	Clark, Earl C.	276
Cash, Catherine	273	Clark, Emma	41
Cash, Dave	279	Clark, James H.	194
Cash, Eliza West	273	Clark, Dr. J. M.	276
Cash, Francis	273	Clark, Leander W.	113
Cash, Hannah E.	285	Clark, Maggie	53
Cash, Hannah J.	97	Clark, Rachel	40

Index

Name	Page	Name	Page
Clark, Rena	46	Collins, Susan H.	220
Clark, Sarah	113	Collins, Thomas C.	221
Clark, William	41	Colville, Ella Ann	34
Clark, Wm. H.	75	Colville, Mattie R.	205
Clawson, Elizabeth Fain	205	Colville, Patrick C.	204
Clifton, Nancy F.	21	Colville, Vesta	204
Clingan, Beulah	101	Colville, Warner E.	204
Clingan, Billy R.	103	Colville, Young	48
Clinging, R. T.	103	Comley, Jullia M.	284
Clonce, Effie May	171	Compton, Welthy	221
Clonce, John W.	92	Compton, William	221
Coates, Vance	53	Condra, Susan G.	91
Cobb, Julia A.	158	Conner, Thomas	37
Cochran, Alverine	263	Conner, Violet	37
Cochran, Mrs. Jane	261	Conley, J. W.	258
Cofer, Arthur H.	42	Conley, L. G.	256
Cofer, Mrs. Ida	53	Coppinger, R. L.	166
Cook, Ada	34	Corvin, Crockett	118
Cook, Charlotte	57	Corvin, O. P.	70
Cook, Eureka A.	278	Coulter, Arvazine	1,309
Cook, Oley C.	239	Coulter, C. C.	1
Cook, Dr. Robert F.	57	Coulter, Charles L.	92
Cole, Dora Lucile	54	Coulter, Frankie	171
Cole, Lena	216	Coulter, Julia A.	170
Coleman, Emma E.	26	Coulter, Lewis Owen	92
Coleman, F. L.	262	Coulter, L. L.	1
Coleman, Lucy	40	Coulter, Maurice	92
Coleman, T. M.	262	Coulter, Robert J.	92
Coleman, W. C.	40	Coulter, T. B.	171
Coleman, W. M.	40	Coulter, Thomas	171
Collier, John	174	Coulter, Ula	1
Collier, Mrs. Lizzie	174	Cox, Charles	196
Collins, Albert H.	180	Cox, Dallas	23
Collins, Alice A.	246	Cox, E. S.	118
Collins, Anna E.	220	Cox, Frank	308
Collins, Callie	180	Cox, Nellie L.	174
Collins, Charlotte	253	Cox, Rebecca	196
Collins, Dellie May	198	Coxey, Imogene	196
Collins, E.	30	Coxey, John	78
Collins, Elizabeth	218	Coxsey, Dixie	256
Collins, Edward L.	194	Coy, Frank	3
Collins, Floyd	255	Cozart, Mary J.	91
Collins, H. C.	280	Craighead, Mary	44
Collins, Henry	220	Crawford, Harry	43
Collins, James P.	219	Crawford, Mrs. C. P.	40
Collins, John	181	Crawford, Henry A.	43
Collins, J. P.	220	Crawford, James Mosley	278
Collins, L. T.	280	Crawford, James R.	29
Collins, Maxine	255	Crawford, James T.	35
Collins, Nancy J.	90	Crawford, John R.	43
Collins, Pinkney	253	Crawford, Martha	73
Collins, Ramon H.	180	Crawford, Mary A.	29

Index

Name	Page	Name	Page
Crawford, Mary C.	29	Daniels, Ellen E.	51
Crawford, M. Josephine	73	Danieks, Hellen	268
Crawford, T. K.	204	Daniels, James Oliver	201
Crawford, Vesta K.	204	Daniels, L. A.	51
Crammer, William J.	286	Daniels, Mary Jane	201
Creaba, Jessie	38	Daniels, Paul	268
Crisp, Margaret	287	Dannels, Tobias O.	201
Crosby, Mary E.	286	Dart, Joseph E.	169
Crosby, Joel S.	282	Darwin, A. C.	219
Crosby, Louella	86	Darwin, Belindah	219
Cross, Sarah M.	92	Darwin, Bethia W.	218
Crow, Elizabeth	22	Darwin, Clara C.	218
Crow, Lonnie L.	256	Darwin, Eliza M.	219
Crow, Lula F.	217	Darwin, Frederick, Wayne	31
Crow, Robt. N.	22	Darwin, Ida	219
Crow, Samuel Tate	217	Darwin, Jack B.	32
Cunningham, Catherine	115	Darwin, James A.	218
Cunningham, Catherine A.	54	Darwin, James T.	219
Cunningham, James	115	Darwin, Mrs. J. W.	35
Cunningham, Julia B.	283	Darwin, Lillie Bithia	218
Cunningham, Laura	115	Darwin, Mary Louise	219
Cunningham, Luther	283	Darwin, Thomas A.	32
Cunningham, P.	54	Darwin, Thos. C.	219
Cunningham, P. C. M.	283	Darwin, W. M. P.	218
Cunningham, infant	219	Darwin, infants	218, 219
Cunningham, D. W.	195	Daugherty, Dellie	100
Cunningham, Elvina	195	Daugherty, Mary Ann	103
Cunningham, Elvira	195	Daugherty, Willie Mae	100
Cunningham, Eva Ann	36	Davenport, John A.	83
Cunnyngham, F. L.	56	Davenport, Johnse	83
Cunnyngham, George Tucker	32	Davenport, Lucy	122
Cunnyngham, Larry	37	Davenport, Thomas	83
Cunnyngham, Lorinda Jane	195	Davis, Annie Lee	269
Cunnyngham, Mattie T.	195	Davis, Cecil	9
Cunnyngham, N. W.	84	Davis, Chas. Monroe	268
Cunnyngham, T. N. L.	196	Davis, Mrs. C. M.	268
Cunnyngham, W. H.	195	Davis, Condon	160
Cunnyngham, infant	195	Davis, Exa B.	169
Curtain, J. C.	152, 234	Davis, Gaynell	170
		Davis, Girtrude C.	104
D		Davis, Hassell Eugene	94
		Davis, John F.	160
Dagley, Amanda	156	Davis, Louise	268
Dagley, Artie May	274	Davis, Mamie	25
Dagley, J. F.	278	Davis, Nancy	18
Dagley, Sarah I.	321	Davis, R. A.	102
Dagley, W. D.	274	Davis, R. M.	33
Dagley, W. R.	321	Davis, Samuel Jeremiah	160
Dagman, P. F.	164	Davis, Walter	103
Daniel, J. L.	60	Dawson, Sgt. William L.	278
Daniel, Julian Carl	269	Day, Elizabeth	253
Daniel, Mary	201	Day, Geo. C.	253

Index

Name	Page	Name	Page
Day, Geo. C.	253	Dillard, Harold	264
Day, John Crawford	252	Dillard, Hershel	72
Day, Wm. K.	252	Dillard, Mrs. Mary	100
DeBlieux, O'Lena Keen	100	Dillard, W. J.	100
DeBlieux, Paul Lewis?	109	Dismong, Susan M.	191
Defender, Anna May	191	Dixon, Gertie N.	274
Degraw, Anna M.	94	Dixon, Rosa	217
Deluce, F.	272	Dobbs, A. H.	197
Deluce, Minnie Lee	272	Dobbs, Lorenda	197
Dennis, Isham	175	Dodd, Abbie May	110
Dennis, Johnie	173	Dodd, Artie Lenia	110
Dennis, infant	173	Dodd, Bibl	102
Denton, Charles	286	Dodd, Carl	42
Denton, Della	218	Dodd, Charlotte	253
Denton, Edward	217	Dodson, Charlotte J.	231
Denton, Emet	217	Dodd, Cynthia Jane	91
Denton, G. M.	217	Dodd, Ella	110
Denton, Grover	165	Dodd, F. L.	239
Denton, Henry	218	Dodd, Hannar	222
Denton, Jerry	217	Dodd, Jessie	42
Denton, J. R.	99	Dodd, J. W.	239
Denton, Lela Pearl	216	Dodd, Margaret J.	253
Denton, Lois Callie	68	Dodd, Margie	32
Denton, Maggie	48	Dodd, Mary	239
Denton, Mary M.	109	Dodd, Rettie	42
Denton, Nancy	217	Dodd, Roy	110
Denton, Perry	286	Dodd, Mrs. Sarah	103
Denton, P. H.	217	Dodd, Thelbert	92
Denton, Richard Claude	217	Dodd, Thomas Lee	110
Denton, Virginia S.	217	Dodd, Warren	197
Denton, W. M.	218	Dodd, Winford	197
Denton, infant	217	Dodd, infant	197
Devaney, A. F.	281	Dodson, Sarah	231
Devaney, Albert	78	Doffey, Margaret Louise	53
Devaney, Alma	78	Doll, Frederick	53
Devaney, Helena	281	Donaldson, W. M.	304
Devaney, James Allen	278	Donam, J.	13
Devaney, John H.	78	Dorsett, S. M.	56
Devaney, Mary J.	78	Dortch, Anna Hickman	93
Devaney, Sarah C.	78	Dorton, Canzada	122
Devaney, Weltha A.	90	Doss, Sallie	174
Devault, Mary J.	80	Dosson, Alice M.	53
Dewey, Grace Marsh	289	Dosson, Amanda	249
Dewey, Laura	289	Dosson, Isaiah	249
Dewey, Lee R.	289	Dosson, J. F.	31
Dickey, Ruth	27	Dosson, Louisa	249
Dickson, Alex	32	Dosson, Mary	249
Dickson, James Lee	39	Dosson, Sarah F.	249
Dickson, L. C.	50	Dosson, Sarah Hutcheson	53
Dickson, Mary C.	268	Dosson, Thomas Lee	249
Dickson, Winnie Hazel	39	Dosson, Virginia Ann	249
Dier, Eddie L.	78	Dosson, Wm. F.	249
Dillard, Earl	72	Dott, J.	193

Index

Name	Page
Douglass, Nancy Margaret	50
Douglass, William F.	132
Doughty, Florence	132
Dowlen, Norman B.	91
Drake, Sherman	179
Dudley, C. G.	179
Dugan, J. T.	169
Duggan, Tressie	175
Dugger, Willie C.	286
Dunlap, Jacob	275
Dunlap, Lillie May	275
Dunlap, Sarah E.	281
Dunn, Albert Stice	118
Dunn, Martha	118
Dunn, Paul	197
Dyer, Adda Mae	52
Dyer, Hattie Alma	278
Dyer, Sarrah	68

E

Name	Page
Earhart, Wm. O.	48
Earle, Florence	159
Early, Rev. A. P.	82
Early, Hannah Minerva	82
Eastland, Henry L.	114
East, Iva G.	193
Eddington, Jessie Asbury	288
Edington, J. E.	288
Edington, Luther Riley	288
Edington, Mary Matilda	288
Edington, Wm. Riley	288
Edington, Wm. Sherman	288
Edwards, Anna Mary	83
Edwards, Harrison	83
Edwards, Haskell	167
Edwards, J. B.	167
Edwards, John Robson	76
Edwards, Mack	83
Edwards, Malcom	167
Edwards, Robt. G.	167
Elder, Mary Crayton	44
Elder, Robert R.	239
Elder, T. J.	234
Elder, W. A.	239
Elder, W. Jerome	100
Eldridge, Albert	97
Eldridge, Harriet E.	97
Eldridge, Isabelle	49
Eldridge, Lucy P.	97
Elexander, William H.	168
Elliott, George	284

Name	Page
Ellis, G. Jane	43
Ellis, Sidney L.	32
Ellis, W. S.	43
Elsea, Mrs. Sudie	94
England, E. A.	43
England, James P.	35
England, Lula M.	35
England, P. M.	33
England, Mrs. P. M.	33
English, Susie E.	105
Enos, Rowland	289
Ervin, John H. J.	109
Ervin, Provy	109
Essens, Mapom	279
Essex, L. P	191
Evans, A. J.	136
Evans, Ed	83
Evans, Lucinda C.	122
Evans, --	136
Evens, James G.	84
Evens, J. E.	84
Evens, H. H.	84
Evens, Joseph C.	84
Evens, H. H.	84
Evens, Margaret Ford	272
Evens, Robert Floyd	84
Evens, Sarah J.	84
Evens, T. H.	84
Evens, Winnie D.	84
Everett, Hazel Pearl	166
Everett, Ray B.	173
Evins, Dewey Essie	171
Ewers, J. E.	40
Ewers, Martha M.	40
Ewing, A. C.	115
Ewing, E. B.	31
Ewing, Jacob E.	86
Ewing, James P.	86
Ewing, Julia	31
Ewing, Mary Lou	31
Ewing, Sarah Fine	115

F

Name	Page
Fann, Synthia	53
Farley, J. T.	95
Felty, Delia	283
Fergson, J. W.	96
Ferguson, Ella B.	270
Ferguson, F. B.	286
Ferguson, Floyd Marie	190
Ferguson, H. L. W.	271

Index

Name	Page	Name	Page
Ferguson, Hortie	78	Foust, Lettie W.	180
Ferguson, James	78	Foust, Manda May	98
Ferguson, John H.	66	Foust, Margaret L.	56
Ferguson, L. C.	190	Foust, Margaret McPherson	98
Ferguson, Margaret A.	78	Foust, Mary	63
Ferguson, Mary E.	190	Foust, Mary Smith	252
Ferguson, Mary J.	273	Foust, Nancy A.	106
Ferguson, Samuel B.	190	Foust, N. B.	252
Ferguson, Sarah B.	190	Foust, Philip	106
Ferguson, Texas A.	271	Foust, Philip T.	106
Ferguson, Vesta	314	Foust, P. L.	34
Ferguson, Willie	286	Foust, Rebecca	181
Ferguson, --	74	Foust, Rufus M.	181
Field, Claudie M.	173	Foust Sarah	106
Fillers, Cora H.	155	Foust, Sarah J.	181
Finch, Mattie J.	164	Foust, Susan	108
Fine, John	268	Foust, Susannah	108
Fischesser, Grace	280	Foust, Timothy	181
Fischesser, Mary	280	Foust, Wm. M.	98
Fischesser, Zeno	280	Foust, Wm. P.	181
Fisher, Abbie A.	35	Foust, Wm. T.	181
Fisher, Francis A.	30	Foust, --	181
Fisher, Henderson	321	Fout, Capt. John W.	63
Fisher, Henry	265	Fox, Alice B.	169
Fisher, Rebecca A.	321	Fox, Harry	170
Fisher, Ruhama	265	Fox, Henry T.	169
Fisher, Sarah	265	Fox, Mary	170
Fisher, W. B.	266	Fox, Mildred Swearingen	92
Fleming, James T.	61	Fox, S. Rosa	169
Fleming, Jimmie	1,309	Fraley, Haver	23
Fleming, Samuel H.	61	Fraley, Mary Etta	23
Fleming, S. H.	1,309	Franklin, B. C.	157
Ford, Elizabeth Swan	277	Franklin, John	114
Foster, James M.	289	Franklin, John K.	289
Foster, John R.	169	Franklin, Joseph W.	93
Foster, Icie	162	Franklin Miss Lucy A. L.	58
Foster, Louisa Y.	289	Franklin, Lydia A.	158
Foster, Martha	289	Franklin, Rebecca L.	193
Foster, Wm. C.	289	Franklin, Salena E.	39
Foust, Andrew J.	181	Franklin, Meda Ruth	289
Foust, Deborah R.	98	Frazier, Abner W.	42
Foust, Docie E.	97	Frazier, Barbara	79
Foust, Dora E.	171	Frazier, Beriah	79
Foust, Eddie Lee	157	Frazier, Joseph C.	320
Foust, Emma	157	Frazier, Josephine	31
Foust, Geo. W.	157	Frazier, M. Louisa	79
Foust, Jacob	108	Frazier, Dr. Nicholass	82
Foust, Jacob W.	253	Frazier, N. P.	39
Foust, James	181	Frazier, Pacif Y. Tinsley	320
Foust, James E.	157	Frazier, Ruth L. E.	205
Foust, John S.	35	Frazier, Samuel	31,320
Foust, John T.	97,253	Frazier, Samuel Esq.	205

Index

	Page		Page
Frazier, William	320	Gentry, W. H.	216
Frields, Malcolm	166	Gerald, Calvin	234
Fugate, Aska Ann	89	Gibson, Bertie Lilian	62
Fugate, Edith	88	Gibson, Catherine	59
Fugate, F. S.	89	Gibson, Earnest	122
Fugate, Lewis	89	Gibson, E. S.	59
Fugate, Raymon	180	Gibson, G. C.	122
Fugate, S. A.	180	Gibson, Geo. W.	62
		Gibson, Henry C.	59
G		Gibson, Henry M.	101
		Gibson, Jacob	122
Gad, J. D.	171	Gibson, Jane	122
Gad, Walter	171	Gibson, Mary A.	59,116
Gadd, John B.	172	Gibson, Mary Ann	122
Gadd, Lizzie	172	Gibson, Ollie Theodore	123
Gallagher, Cassie C.	53	Gibson, Rosa Lee	53
Gallagher, Catherine	54	Gibson, Roy E.	62
Gallagher, J. C.	54	Gibson, W. L.	277
Gallagher, Mary	54	Gilbert, Henry	9
Gallahon, Floyd	281	Gill, Alvin	118
Gallahon, Fred	281	Gill, John	118
Gallahon, John	281	Gill, Sarah H.	118
Gallahon, Lizzie	281	Gillespie, Anna	126
Gallahon, Mattie	281	Gillespie, Bell S.	304
Galville, Bird Paine	211	Gillespie, Bessie	304
Galloway, M. H.	285	Gillespie, Charles Gibbs	46
Gamble, Mamie	215	Gillespie, Christever	304
Gamble, Martha M.	216	Gillespie, Elizabeth C.	29
Gannaway, Edmund Norville	45	Gillespie, Emma P.	205
Gannaway, Mary J.	45	Gillespie, G. E.	205
Gannaway, Mary P.	156	Gillespie, Geo.	126
Gannaway, Terza Jane	78	Gillespie, George L.	205
Garrison, Bertha Jane	112	Gillespie, Geo. Samuel	155
Garrison, Eliza	189	Gillespie, G. W.	37
Garrison, Ester May	202	Gillespie, Hannah	205
Garrison, Eugene	112	Gillespie, Homer	304
Garrison, George A.	221	Gillespie, Dr. James R.	46
Garrison, Geo. W.	112	Gillespie, James W.	205
Garrison, Hannah F.	206	Gillespie, Lillian	205
Garrison, J. C.	251	Gillespie, Lillie W.	32
Garrison, John	283	Gillespie, Logan	304
Garrison, John W.	112	Gillespie, Martha B.	205
Garrison, Margaret J.	206	Gillespie, Mary	46,81,304
Garrison, Myra	275	Gillespie, Mary A.	205
Garrison, Richard L.	206	Gillespie, Robert N.	32,205
Garrison, Sallie M.	251	Gillespie, Susie	304
Gass, Co. W. T.	120	Gillespie, Thomas J.	29,126,280
Gawood, Mallie	282	Gillespie, Rev. T. J.	304
Gawood, Raymond	282	Gillespie, Whitney	35
Gemoa, Alice	74	Gillespie, Wm. N.	126
Gennoe, William	38	Gillet, Amanda A.	300
Gentry, Bell Z.	258	Gillet, Andrew D.	9
Gentry, S. D.	71	Gillet, Anna S.	9

Index

	Page		Page
Gilliam, J. D.	128	Green, Mammie L.	173
Gilliam, Nathaniel M.	127	Green, Mary C.	176
Gilliam, S. A.	128	Green, R. M.	170
Gilliam, Sallie	127	Green, T. K.	107
Gilliam, Sewell A.	127	Green, David	310
Gilliam, Sidney H.	280	Greer, Dora S.	60
Gilliam, infant	300	Greer, Jennie	64
Gillispie, Adelia	218	Greer, Moses	60
Gist, Nellie	215	Greer, Myrtle	60
Gitwood, Mrs. James F.	278	Greer, Orpha	60
Gitwood, J. R. C.	40	Greer, Smith	60
Givens, Rebecca L.	163	Gregory, James	179
Gladman, Arzona	114	Gregory, Lena M.	276
Gladman, Wm.	114	Gregory, William R.	276
Glispie, A.	164	Griffin, Jessie	283
Godby, Sabilla Taylor	137	Griffin, Monroe	283
Godby, Thomas	137	Grimsley, James Monroe	176
Godsey, Mary J.	31	Grimsley, Nannie J.	176
Godsey, Myrtle Campbell	31	Grinsley, Sarah Rebecca	176
Godsey, Stephen Scott	51	Gross, Anderson Jackson	25
Godsey, W. C.	31	Gross, Dayton	30
Goodrich, G. W.	47	Gross, Harriet M.	25
Goodrich, T. W.	47	Bruze, Lula B.	91
Gornany, Geo.	52	Gurley, Mary A.	251
Goss, Jessie	201	Gurlliam, Caroline	66
Gothard, Albert E.	151,234	Gurlliam, John D.	66
Gothard, Dump	72	Gurlliam, Rees	66
Gothard, James F.	151,234	Gurlliam, Roger	66
Gothard, Kenneth Lee	103		
Gothard, Thomas	103	**H**	
Gothard, Lieut. W. B.	72		
Graham, Arnold B.	191	Haga, Dorman E.	166
Graham, Leslie	104	Haggard, Andrew Jr.	46
Graham, Ray	286	Haggard, A. P.	46
Graham, Robert E.	191	Haines, Martha	39
Graham, Windle P.	191	Hale, Barb	106
Gravett, Caleb	217	Hale, Bednego	50
Gravett, James	216	Hale, Elizabeth	88
Gravett, Katie A.	29	Hale, Geo.	88
Gray, George	102	Hale, Rev. J. H.	60
Gray, James M.	170	Hale, Lillie J.	273
Gray, John S.	170	Hale, Mary E.	249
Gray, Rachel A.	102	Hale, Willie	99
Gray, Sarah A.	170	Haley, Albert A.	271
Greceory, Lucinda	167	Haley, Robert	271
Green, Edith May	106	Hall, Bell	194
Green, Emma P.	174,177	Hall, C. A. Eld.	166
Green, Emmet P.	176	Hall, Charles William	256
Green, Mrs. Gladys	102	Hall, F.	130
Green, Jacob	314	Hall, Flora M.	92
Green, J. B.	171	Hall, James M.	92
Green, Lida E.	171	Hall, John M.	33

Index

Name	Page	Name	Page
Hall, John R.	194	Hart, Henry W.	270
Hall, Lester	130	Hart, Nellie F.	270
Hall, Miss (or Mrs.) Lora	265	Hartbarger, J. L. Lewis	285
Hall, Lydia Daniels	75	Hartbarger, Rufus	71
Hall, Margarett	193	Harwood, B. F.	10
Hall, Mary	130	Harwood, C. D.	253
Hall, Mrs. Minnie	130	Harwood, Claborn	89
Hall, Mollie Mary Clift	173	Harwood, John D.	89
Hall, Nancy J.	169	Harwood, J. Z. Tack	10
Hall, Nancy Jane	84	Harwood, Mary M.	88
Hall, Roy	130	Harwood, Mary Matilda	278
Hall, Sally	130	Harwood, Sol	88
Hall, infant	193	Hase, Litten	21
Hallock, W. S.	142	Hatfield, M. E.	32
Hambrick, Lillie	164	Hatfield, W. A.	169
Hamby, Bulah	32	Hatfield, Mrs. W. B.	93
Hamilton, H. K.	104	Hatfield, infant	169
Hamilton, James Loyd	68	Haughey, Mara G.	55
Hamilton, J. M.	104	Hawkins, Rhoda S.	251
Hamilton, Margaret	68	Hawkins, --	102
Hammond, Mrs. Martha Ray	215	Hawkins, Amanda	37
Hampton, Joe	52	Hawkins, Eliza J.	109
Haran, Andrew Euclis	261	Hawkins, H. H.	104
Harbeck, Mary Susan Gennoe	39	Hewkins, J. E.	102
Harbeck, Sheldon	40	Hawkins, J. H.	261
Hard, Marion	318	Hawkins, John W.	88
Hardin, Aubry	61	Hawkins, Joseph Albert	37
Hardin, James Wm.	181	Hawkins, Martha	88
Hardin, Jane Elizabeth	181	Haworth, Laban	50
Hardin, John	181	Haworth, Mary M.	50
Hardin, John S.	61	Haws, J.	84
Hardin, Polly Ann	239	Hayes, Estey May	168
Harmon, Andrew	113	Hayes, Harold	55
Harmon, (father & mother)	113	Hayes, Sarah D.	217
Harmon, Rebecca L.	113	Head, Hugh Andrew	110
Harmon, Sina A.	113	Head, Willie	28
Harris, Barnett	228	Headlee, Emma C. Childress	153,233
Harris, Emaline	109	Headlee, Louisa	233
Harris, James	47	Headlee, Robert Earl	233
Harris, Mrs. May	264	Headler, Louisa	153
Harris, Mogene	271	Headler, Robert Earl	153
Harris, Octavia Melton	264	Hebbred, Cyrus	167
Harris, Rebecca Lucinda	228	Hedgecoth, L. J.	193
Harris, Rose	264	Hefner, Marvin	26
Harris, Samuel	41	Hefner, M. J.	26
Harris, Sarah M.	228	Heiskell, Addie	283
Harris, Sarrah Adline	47	Heiskell, H. B.	283
Harris, Tennie F.	41	Heiskell, Luther	283
Harris, Thos. J.	41	Heiskell, Martha E.	229
Harrison, J. William	35	Heiskell, Nellie J.	33
Harrison, Mary Emily	216	Heiskell, Pope	161
Harrison, Mattie	35	Heiskell, Rhoda Farmer	283

Index

Name	Page	Name	Page
Heiskell, infant	283	Hilton, Irva	135
Helton, Dan'l.	58	Hindes, R. D.	136
Helton, Edith	32	Hindes, S. L.	136
Helton, Margarete	171	Hindman, D. H.	47
Helton, R. P.	268	Hinds, F. E.	136
Helton, S. H.	173	Hinds, Myrtle Lee	142
Henderson, Anna	222, 303	Hines, Alice	270
Henderson, Audie	222	Hixon, S. Ann	31
Henderson, Clyde	104	Hoback, Frances Louise	53
Henderson, Mary Ann	72	Hobbs, Elizabeth J.	166
Henderson, Riller	93	Hodges, Danieb	1, 309
Henderson, Robt. F.	222, 303	Hodges, Myra	309
Henderson, Susan F.	40	Hodges, Myra J.	1
Henderson, Thad	72	Hoge, Alda May	102
Henderson, W. M.	72	Hoge, Dick L.	101
Hendricks, Emma Louise	26	Hoge, J. H.	111
Henry, Anderson Bryan	108	Hoge, Myrtle M.	111
Henry, Julia T.	108	Hoge, S. G. T. J. W.	175
Henry, Mary	253	Holden, Robert A.	110
Henry, Oliver	196	Holden, Walter F.	110
Henry, Rachel F.	196	Holland, Adolphia G.	63
Henry, Ruey A.	69	Holland, Caroline	320
Henry, Solomon	196	Holland, E. H.	321
Henry, W. R.	196	Holland, E. M.	137
Henry, infant	196	Holland, Hannah J.	321
Hensley, Eliza J.	175	Holland, James F.	63
Hensley, Nammie C.	27	Holland, John I.	273
Hensley, W. M.	42	Holland, M. A.	137
Hensley, infant	42	Holland, Nahoma	63
Hickey, Froston D.	132	Holland, Oscar A.	62
Hickey, Kendall	132	Holland, Sarah S.	320
Hickman, James L.	93	Holland, Tennessee V.	266
Hickman, W. H.	176	Holland, Thomas R.	320
Hicks, Joseph	139	Holland, infant	105
Hicks, M. B.	42	Holloway, Beulah	279
Hicks, Robert	217	Holloway, Callie M.	275
Hicks, Susan J.	139	Holloway, Emily	322
Hicks, T. C.	262	Holloway, Eva	322
Hicks, William F.	270	Holloway, Floyd E.	275
Hidon, Mrs. Myrtle	256	Holloway, Jane	279
Higby, Nelson F.	74	Holloway, J. M.	279
Higdon, Roselee	52	Holloway, Leopatra	275
Hildebrand, Mildred L.	92	Holloway, Margarete Posse	272
Hill, Ida May	223	Holloway, Milo	272
Hill, Mattie E.	180	Holloway, Reece	280
Hill, Mildred	34	Holloway, Richard	279
Hill, Nerva	223	Holloway, R. W.	275
Hill, Mrs. Sallie Mickle	222	Holloway, Samuel H.	275
Hilleary, Bertha Campbell	273	Holloway, Starling	322
Hilleary, Henry C.	75	Holloway, Thomas B.	272
Hilleary, Mary Thompson	75	Holloway, Ruth E.	272
Hilleary, Orin	75	Holloway, William J.	279
Hilton, A. J.	135	Holm, Nora R.	166

Index

Name	Page	Name	Page
Holman, Annie	52	Hoyal, Rebecca Ann	282
Holman, Erna	52	Hoyal, Virginia	282
Holman, G. F.	55	Hoyl, Clinton D.	106
Holman, Pauline	52	Hubbard, A. A.	288
Holman, Robert L.	55	Hubbard, L. J.	288
Holmes, Mrs. Caroline	101	Hubbs, Claud T.	278
Holmes, Thomas	101	Hubbs, Bethel	101
Holmes, Will M.	100	Hudson, David G.	54
Holt, McDavid	164	Hudson, J.	29
Holt, Robert	63	Hudson, John W.	40
Holt, Sarah E.	94	Hudson, Leroy	10
Holt, W. M. R.	94	Hudson, Nancy Ann	65
Hood, Henry Clay	80	Hudson, Sarah Jane	54
Hood, Rosa Ann	80	Hughes, Mrs. Anna	101
Hope, H. C.	278	Hughes, A. W.	105
Hope, Sidney J.	278	Hughes, Burford	63
Horton, Ella Zora	49	Hughes, Ellen	176
Horton, Marian H.	191	Hughes, Etta Mae	101
Horton, Wm. E.	74	Hughes, George	101
Hosfore, George L.	55	Hughes, Hazel	100
Houser, S. L.	151	Hughes, J. H.	100
Housley, Nancy	261	Hughes, Pearl	100
Housley, infant	263	Hughes, Thomas	100
Houston, Doris	280	Hughes, Willie	106
Houston, E. A.	220	Hughes, infant	101
Houston, Edith	257	Humphrey, Daisy	10
Houston, Eliza J.	220	Humphrey, Capt. Morris	10
Houston, J. M.	220	Humphrey, Sarah C.	9
Houston, John H.	220	Hunter, Mrs. Elvira	103
Houston, J. T.	261	Hunter, J. L.	100
Houston, Margaret	197	Hurst, Granville	141
Houston, Mary	220	Hurst, Mary Elizabeth	141
Houston, Willis	247	Hurst, Robert	257
How, Hester	155	Hurst, V. L.	257
Howard, Alice	45	Hurst, Walter	257
Howard, Ella	45	Huskins, Katie Bell	274
Howard, Hemil J.	47	Huskins, M. P.	239
Howard, Jas. A.	45	Hutcheson, Charles	268
Howard, John	47	Hutcheson, John L.	268
Howard, John M.	47	Hutcheson, Mary	29
Howard, John P.	47	Hutcheson, S. W.	268
Howard, R. T.	38	Hutcheson, Susan E.	268
Howard, Rev. R. T.	58	Hutchins, Sarah M.	7
Howard, W. A.	45	Hutchins, W. W.	48
Howard, Wylie R.	31		
Howell, Susan Elmira	59	**I**	
Howerton, Elizabeth A.	139		
Howerton, Grief	139	Ingle, Ella	142
Howerton, Jane	139	Ingle, E. M.	142
Howerton, Micajah	139	Ingle, Jessie J.	142
Hoyal, James Lee	282	Ingle, J. W.	34
Hoyal, Dr. John	282	Ingle, M. A.	142
		Ingle, Stella	142

Index

Name	Page
Ingram, Edward	93
Irland, B. W.	143
Irland, J. E.	143
Irland, Martha A.	143
Ivester, J. A.	105

J

Name	Page
Jackson, E. A.	145
Jackson, Harris L.	257
Jackson, James H.	194
Jackson, Mrs. J. H.	194
Jackson, Meda	106
Jacobs, S. M.	93
James, Mrs. Chas. W.	71
James, John	205
James, Olive	205
James, George	257
Janow, S. L.	51
Jargas, Fred	144
Jeffres, Della	100
Jenkins, N. E.	145
Jenks, Ena A.	93
Jennings, Emma	41
Jennings, John C.	41
Jewell, Creed T.	264
Jewell, Dixie C.	118
Jewell, Edna A.	264
Jewell, Emma	264
Jewell, Floyd	46
Jewell, Francis	35
Jewell, Mrs. Hattie	265
Jewell, J. H.	101
Jewell, Louisa F.	46
Jewell, Ralph Johnson	261
Jewell, Roddy T.	261
Jewell, S. E.	35
Jewell, Violet L.	264
Hewett, Charles	74
Jewett, John Freeman	74
Jewett, Mary Nutting	74
Johns, Cora Lee	109
Johns, Richard Arthur	106
Johnson, Addie	285
Johnson, Armintha	49
Johnson, Asa	61
Johnson, Mrs. Effie	152
Johnson, Ettie	61
Johnson, Fred D.	49
Johnson, Gertrude	49
Johnson, Gracie	274
Johnson, Howard	55
Johnson, Ida	60
Johnson, Isaac	52
Johnson, James	207
Johnson, Martha G.	49
Johnson, Martha Irene	49
Johnson, Mary J.	207
Johnson, Melia	61
Johnson, Nancy	48
Johnson, Nancy E.	9b
Johnson, Susan Catherine	61
Johnson, Virgil G.	38
Johnson, Wm. A.	61
Johnson, Wm. R.	285
Jolly, A. J.	201
Jolly, Martha	100
Jolly, Molly E. Gibson	201
Jolly, Nancy J.	251
Jones, A. P.	95
Jones, Cecil Clay	67
Jones, Elvira	216
Jones, Gay	155
Jones, G. W.	270
Jones, James	216
Jones, J. N.	31
Jones, Lucy	53
Jones, Maggie	155
Jones, Paul Gross	25
Jones, Rufus	273
Jones, Samuel C.	270
Jones, Warren K.	55
Jones, Wm. Luther	250
Jordan, Frank N.	314
Jordan, James N.	7
Jordan, Susan	173
Jorden, Della	177
Jorden, Pearl	177
Jorden, Sarah A.	258
Jorden, Will	165
Jorden, infants	177
Jordon, Mrs. Bell	170
Julian, Pauline	80

K

Name	Page
Kate, Bonnie	162
Kaylor, Melba Rose	99
Keedy, Rachel E.	168
Keith, Alice Beatrice Light	91

L

Name	Page
Lacewell, infant	171

Index

	Page		Page
Lambert, Maud	99	Locke, Robert	163
Landreth, L. V.	166	Locke, Sabella T.	195
Lane, Mandy C.	109	Locke, Thomas M.	162
Lane, Thomas E.	109	Locke, T. J.	163
Lane, Thomas M.	100	Loden, Laura	21
Lane, William H.	100, 109	Lodermilk, Malinda	60
Larmer, E. S.	64	Logan, Nancy	55
Larry, Azariah	83	Long, A. L.	271
Lavender, D. C.	270	Long, Archibald	178
Lavender, W. C.	270	Long, Cyrene Emily	113
Lawson, Annie	154	Long, J. W.	278
Lawson, Dave L.	154	Long, Margaret J.	179
Lea, Thomas J.	93	Long, Mary	178
Ledford, Allice	107	Long, N. H.	178
Ledford, Bettie Bell	107	Long, Z. T.	178
Lee, Dixie	38	Lord, Maude	55
Lee, Ira	7	Love, Jas. K.	107
Lee, W. L.	277	Love, William S.	32
Lemons, Mary Ann	201	Lovelace, W. A.	53
Lemons, Samuel	201	Lowe, Jane	182
Lenty —	157	Lowe, Mary	180
Lenty, Virginia A.	157	Lowe, S. W.	182
Leonard, Joseph H.	29	Lowry, Della	101
Leuty, Floyd	48	Lowry, Isabella Ruth	204
Lewallan, M. M.	100	Lowry, James Ernest	93
Lewallan, M. W.	100	Lowry, Margaret	103
Lewis, C. G.	33	Lowry, Rhoda K.	52
Lewis, H. W.	67	Lowry, Robert Emmett	43
Lewis, Julia	173	Loy, Mary L.	202
Lewis, R. R.	67	Loy, Mattie B.	201
Lewis, Sam M.	170	Loy, Mira E.	201
Lewis, Sarah C.	107	Loyd, Roland	64
Lillard, Minnie	62	Lutz, Meda	262
Lillard, Robert	108	Lutz, Perry Francis	262
Lillard, Robbie	108	Lyon, Olive	156
Lillard, Will	62	Lytle, Cora	83
Lilliard, Zoa E.	108	Lytle, Sarah	83
Locke, Adaline	162		
Locke, Adeline	162, 163	**M**	
Locke, Addison	162		
Locke, Alfred	194	Mack, George	10
Locke, D. J.	162	Mack, Gladys	10
Locke, Judge Franklin	195	Mack, Hellen	10
Locke, James H.	163	Mackinney, Stewart	110
Locke, Jocie	195	Madaris, Charles S.	51
Locke, John	162	Mahaffy, Susan L.	88
Locke, Leah A.	162	Mahoney, Mattie Roy	277
Locke, Minerva	162	Magill, Johnnie	64
Locke, Nancy	163	Majors, Freddie	104
Locke, Nancy Harris	162	Majors, James M.	207
Locke, Newton	195	Majors, Laura K.	207
Locke, Pink	162	Majors, Margaret	207
Locke, Pliny	163	Majors, Susan L.	104

Index

Name	Page	Name	Page
Majors, William	207	Meadows, Early Estil	159
Malle, Ardella	201	Meadows, Robert Duglas	286
Malone, Dorthy	38	Mealer, Bessie	41
Manass, J. J.	3,307	Mealer, B. F.	42
Maning, Ollie	305	Mealer, Martha	42
Manis, E. H.	257	Mealer, Robert B.	41
Manis, Elizabeth	257	Melton, Frances L.	54
Manning, Ethel	113	Melton, James Leon	54
Manning, J. S.	113	Meredith, J.	74
Mansfield, Jennie	7	Meredith, Wm. C.	74
Marler, Blanche	103	Merrill, J. J.	106
Marler, Blanche A.	216	Messer, Op Lenam	167
Marler, Clyde Leonard	33	Millard, A. A.	276
Marler, F. M.	272	Millard, C. W.	69
Marler, Hazel Ruth	33	Millard, Mattie	69
Marler, Kattie	173	Millard, R. J.	276
Marler, Lilly	257	Miller, Aimee	28
Marler, Nick	10	Miller, Austin Gibson	47
Marler, Susan Actkinson	272	Miller, Bettie J.	55
Marler, W. V.	164	Miller, Edward D.	217
Marley, Mrs. Sallie	255	Miller, Elbert S.	191
Marlin, T. E.	144	Miller, Eliza J.	221
Marlor, A. M.	255	Miller, F. J.	55
Marlor, Lillin	255	Miller, George Alfred	37
Marney, J. C.	48	Miller, Guy	28
Marrs, Aaron	127	Miller, Harriet C.	67
Marrs, Delila	127	Miller, I. L.	273
Marrs, Lucinda	127	Miller, Jane	78
Marrs, Nancy Ann	127	Miller, Joe S.	218
Marsh, Alfred	186	Miller, John S.	10
Marsh, Daniel	289	Miller, John T.	28
Marsh, Rev. E. W.	186	Miller, J. S.	255
Marsh, Gravener	186	Miller, Katharine	28
Marsh, G. S.	186	Miller, Mollie D.	190
Marsh, J. L.	186	Miller, Nannie N.	273
Marsh, Mary B.	220	Miller, Robert	21
Marsh, Orinda	186	Miller, Roscoe	28
Marsh, Wealthy Gaylord	289	Miller, Sophronia C.	10
Marshall, G. M.	189	Miller, Violet	180
Martin, --	176	Miller, Virginia T.	36
Martin, Amanda J.	252	Milbican, Claudie	45
Martin, Harry D.	105	Millican, Elizabeth	55
Martin, I. A.	171	Mills, Charles Henry	284
Martin, John K.	219	Minick, Billie Frank	255
Martin, M. J.	3,308	Minton, Franklin	72
Martin, Tate	64	Minton, Robert	165
Massengale, Mrs. Nancy E.	266	Mitchell, --	92
Mashux, Mabel	286	Mitchell, Carrie Louella	189
Mason, Nancy C.	102	Mitchell, Chas.	127
Matherly, Mary E.	265	Mitchell, Chas. W.	190
Mathis, Lee	256	Mitchell, Chester	39
Mathis, Willie J.	99	Mitchell, David Matison	189
Matthews, Claud	49	Mitchell, Earnest K.	274

Index

Name	Page	Name	Page
Mitchell, Emma	190	Morgan, Arlow	72
Mitchell, Everett	37	Morgan, Byron V.	8
Mitchell, Francina	127	Morgan, Calvin	111
Mitchell, J. C.	37	Morgan, Cory W.	72
Mitchell, J. N.	274	Morgan, Darius Franklin	15
Mitchell, John H.	190	Morgan, Delia P.	28
Mitchell, Lue	170	Morgan, Elias H.	106
Mitchell, Minnie	189	Morgan, E. T.	34
Mitchell, Sara A.	190	Morgan, Frances Ann	264
Mitchell, Vesta Ella	112	Morgan, Helen	103
Mitchell, Vestie Stelie	170	Morgan, Henegar	35
Mitchell, W. G.	190	Morgan, Henry N.	106
Mize, Ella D. Pauline	256	Morgan, I. W.	176
Mize, Ellen	27	Morgan, James E.	176
Mize, Mrs. John	318	Morgan, Dr. J. C.	48
Moench, Theodore	44	Morgan, Jessie Mildred	8
Monroe, A. J.	192	Morgan, Joe Lufoy	45
Montgomery, Cyntha	197	Morgan, John	152,234
Montgomery, David	150	Morgan, John Daniel	44
Montgomery, Elizabeth	196	Morgan, J. Mariah	103
Montgomery, James	196	Morgan, John P.	29
Montgomery, J. H.	197	Morgan, Leslie A.	38
Montgomery, Lizzie	150	Morgan, Lesta S.	239
Montgomery, Martha Lou	197	Morgan, Lula C.	50
Montgomery, R. A.	197	Morgan, Mrs. Martha	152,234
Montgomery, R. C.	197	Morgan, Martha Jane	107
Moon, Ruth C.	42	Morgan, Mary E.	79
Moore, A. B.	80	Morgan, Matilda	50
Moore, Abner	80	Morgan, P. C.	111
Moore, Ainsworth B.	79	Morgan, Pearl Irene	28
Moore, A. J.	199	Morgan, R. D.	107
Moore, Mrs. Amanda	60	Morgan, Sallie	28
Moore, B. Franklin	25	Morgan, Sallie A.	37
Moore, C. T.	199	Morgan, Sam H.	266
Moore, David N.	312	Morgan, Sarah L.	111
Moore, Dora R.	60	Morgan, Susan C.	50
Moore, Eugene	304	Morgan, Tennie	3,307
Moore, Harry	304	Morgan, Thersey	71
Moore, Mabel E.	274	Morgan, Thomas A.	79
Moore, Maggie	304	Morgan, Tomeasy J.	106
Moore, Mary F.	295	Morgan, T. W.	101
Moore, Moses F.	295	Morgan, W. F.	62
Moore, Reba	304	Morgan, W. H.	39
Moore, Rebecca	80	Morgan, Wm. Gideon	107
Moore, Rinna Carrie	274	Morgan, infants	28,44
Moore, Walter	60	Morrison, Catherine	43
Moore, Warren G.	60	Morrison, F. M.	43
Moore, Willie	304	Morrison, J. G.	37
Moore, infant	25,48	Morton, John	101
Morgan, Albert A.	107	Moseley, Betty	7
Morgan, Albert W.	110	Moses, Cecil	263
Morgan, Alice	72	Moses, Virgil	263
Morgan, Amanda P.	28	Moss, E. E.	286

Index

Name	Page	Name	Page
Moss, John G.	180	McClure, J. M.	251
Moss, Lillie May	116	McCorkle, Mettie	286
Moss, Thomas G.	280	McCuiston, Dolly	115
Moulton, Lannie	281	McCuiston, (Father & Mother)	115
Mowry, Chasie E.	9	McCuiston, Miles F.	277
Mowry, Minnie	9	McCully, Eugene	178
Mowry, Nancy E.	9	McCully, Lillian Cleo	178
Mowry, Polly	9	McCully, Verna	178
Moyer, Martha J.	164	McCully, infant	178
Moyers, C. H.	164	McDaniels, Catherine	149
Moyers, P. D.	164	McDonald, Beulah	44
Moyers, Sam	164	McDonald, B. F.	36
Mulkey, Minnie	25	McDonald, Bryan R.	46
Mulky, Elizabeth	265	McDonald, Caroline	43
Murphey, Sarah	37	McDonald, C. F. Jr.	36
Myers, George F.	173	McDonald, Mrs. Dora E.	92
Myers, J. C.	172	McDonald, Mrs. E. A.	108
Myers, L.	105	McDonald, Ellen	43
Myers, Noah	9	McDonald, Geo.	48
Myers, Mrs. S. E.	9	McDonald, George	257
Mynatt, Dr. B. K.	204	McDonald, Harriet C.	47
Mynatt, Mary E.	204	McDonald, John	44
Mynatt, S. C.	204	McDonald, Ida	81
		McDonald, Jonis	110
Mc		McDonald, Lewis F.	46
		McDonald, Lilly	47
McAdoo, Prudence E.	288	McDonald, Lou E.	45
McArthur, Jonnie	55	McDonald, Louisa J.	44
McBride, Martha N. J.	173	McDonald, Maggie	257
McBroom, Thomas	318	McDonald, Mary J.	47
McCabe, Amanda Reed	286	McDonald, M. G.	36, 44
McCabe, Berry	275	McDonald, Nancy	47
McCabe, Ethel	26	McDonald, Orpha Jane	46
McCabe, F. A.	275	McDonald, Roland Foster	46
McCabe, George	284	McDonald, S. W.	30
McCabe, Gettie	178	McDonald, Virginia E.	45
McCabe, Goddard	284	McDonald, Wm.	47
McCabe, Nick A.	26	McDonald, infant	46, 47
McCabe, Pat	275	McDowell, Jacob	97
McCabe, Willie F.	27	McDowell, W. R.	69
McCaleb, Andrew	188	McElwee, C. L.	116
McCaleb, Archie	188	McElwee, John R.	116
McCaleb, Nancy J.	188	McElwee, Mattie	116
McClandon, Mrs. Savana	118	McElwee, Moss	116
McClark, Richard Olney	276	McFalls, Edith	83
McClendon, Bessie	189	McGhee, Marcus Walker	38
McClendon, Bettie J.	189	McGhee, Martha E.	277
McClendon, Edenia	106	McGhee, Mrs. Sarah Bell	277
McClendon, Louisa	142	McGhee, Thomas	279
McClendon, Polly	322	McGhee, Walter	99
McClendon, Sanders	273	McGill, Addie	165
McClendon, Tarla Ann	273	McGill, Maggie	173

Index

Name	Page	Name	Page
McJunkins, Gertie	53	Neal, Louis A.	103
McJunkins, James	56	Neal, M. F.	191
McJunkins, Willie E.	102	Neal, Robert	286
McMary, J. N.	144	Neal, Sarah G.	103
McMillan, Hetty An	69	Neal, Susan T.	158
McMillan, Joseph	190	Neal, Telic	299
McMillan, Robert S.	107	Neal, Rev. Wm. Wiley	158
McMillan, infant	314	Neal, --	299
McMillen, Bessiee	107	Nelson, Robert	49
McMillen, Elizabeth	105	Newell, Jimmy	25
McMillen, George W.	107	Newman, Austel M.	114
McMillen, Irvin Arthur	105	Newman, Carder M.	114
McMillen, Susan	167	Newman, Henry C.	105
McMillen, Z. L.	107	Newman, Maggie	102
McMurry, Ida C.	175	Newman, Rachel	49
McNeal, Nellie	115	Newport, Elder Asa	206
McNelis, Grace	54	Newport, Juliah H.	206
McNett, Eliza E.	93	Nicholas, --	56
McNutt, Timothy M.	113	Nichols, Elsa	170
McKenzie, Jennings	28	Nichols, J. L	165
McKenzie, infants	32, 63	Nichols, M. W.	165
McKinley, John F.	62	Nicholson, L. G.	39
McPheeter, Lieut. Alf. D.	68	Norman, Easie	215
McPheeters, Azza A.	68	Norton, Grace G.	28
McPheeters, Walter R.	68	Northrop, Mrs. Bessie	168
McPherson, --	157	Nowlen, Ethel T.	174
McPherson, Eliza	278		
McPherson, Elizabeth J.	186	**O**	
McPherson, Elizabeth S.	188		
McPherson, Henry B.	277	Odom, Daniel D.	272
McPherson, James D.	157	Odom, Mary J.	272
McPherson, Juliett Ann	157	Oldham, D. R.	233
McPherson, J. Walter	277	Oldham, I. J.	233
McPherson, Thomas H.	157	Oldham, Mrs. I. J.	153
McPherson, infants	188	Olinger, Arbell	151
		Olinger, Emmeratter	10
N		Olinger, Henry B.	151, 233
		Olinger, James	151
Nail, Harold C.	167	Olinger, John	151, 233
Nail, I. R.	169	Olinger, infant	10
Nail, Lola Edna	175	Oliver, Robert	194
Nail, infant	167	Orbell, Olinger	233
Nanny, Margaret N.	204	Organ, Phebe	54
Narris, Viola	265	Organ, Walter J.	55
Nash, Bennie	111	O'Sullivan, T. P.	322
Nash, Effie	111	Ottinger, Fred	174
Nash, James	111	Ottinger, J. C.	166
Nash, Johnnie	111	Owen, Homer	39
Nash, John W.	111	Owens, Sam J.	197
Nash, W. H.	111	Owensby, Eva J.	256
Nave, Catherine	271	Owensby, Bertha	258
Neal, H. T.	67	Owensby, Lillie Sue	256

Index

Name	Page
Ownesby, Rachel	258
Ownesby, Thomas	314
Ownesby, Annie	256

P

Name	Page
Paine, A.	211
Paine, Mrs. Bettie	211
Paine, C. A.	211
Paine, C. M.	211
Paine, Elizabeth N.	211
Paine, Elvira	211
Paine, F. J.	211
Paine, F. Joe	211
Paine, Mary Ella	211
Paine, Orville	211
Painter, Pairlee	168
Painter, Thomas	168
Palmer, S. R.	74
Parham, Eunice	34
Parham, Jesse	122
Parham, J. F.	39
Parham, Martha C.	122
Parker, --	212
Parker, Eli	212
Parker, Wm.?	212
Parkhurst, Mary Jane	176
Parks, Calvin Datre	250
Parks, Earl	249
Parks, Henry W.	249
Parks, Maggie C.	155
Parks, Nancy	150
Pass, E. K.	178
Pass, W. M.	307
Paton, Walter James	48
Patten, Eva	29
Patton, Carrie	30
Patton, Eliza J.	89
Patton, Mrs. Mary	264
Patrick, E. A.	213
Paul, A. D.	20
Paul, Cynthia	20
Paul, Lillie	197
Paul, Rebecca	113
Paul, S. E.	271
Paul, infant	197
Payne, H. B.	281
Payne, Mary	281
Peace, Kathryn	167
Peak, James	278
Pearman, Henry	195
Pearson, Ella T. Brady	159
Pearson, Georgia T.	159
Pearson, Mrs. Helen F.	287
Pearson, Mahala	156
Peavyhouse, m Hugh L.	25
Pelfrey, Caroline	217
Pelfrey, Clement G.	255
Pelfrey, Elsiel	216
Pelfrey, Hazel V.	258
Pelfrey, Macy L.	255
Pelfrey, Maggie C.	216
Pelfrey, Ovie	131
Pelfrey, Sergt. Thos. J.	257
Perkinson, Joel	155
Perkinson, Nancy J.	155
Perry, J. C.	194
Peters, Elizabeth	271
Peters, Ida McKinley	208
Peters, Margaret	271
Petty, Jennie	53
Phillips, Carter	104
Phillips, Cora	322
Phillips, E. B.	278
Phillips, Flora	169
Phillips, Jenthia	305
Phillips, J. T.	322
Phillips, Lelia M.	105
Phillips, Lena	104
Phillips, Lillie Flornce	217
Phillips, Martha	279
Phillips, Mary Jane	217
Phillips, Odist	105
Phillips, Robert C.	104
Phillips, Vesta J.	322
Phillips, Wanda Jean	93
Phipps, Harry W.	191
Pickard, Effie N.	7
Pickard, Francis Marion	8
Pickard, Grace M.	8
Pickett, Bernice	7
Pickett, C. E.	152
Pickett, C. F.	233
Pickett, M. D.	152, 233
Pickett, Thelma	10
Pickle, B. M.	52
Pierce, Alanah C.	220
Pierce, E. D.	220
Pierce, Housie	220
Pierce, M. A.	220
Pierce, Maude	220
Pierce, S. E. Lindsley	91
Pierce, S. D.	221
Pierce, infant	197

Index

	Page		Page
		Pugh, James E. P. 252	
Pierott, Francis A.	55	Pugh, J. H.	252
Pitts, Oatious R.	9	Pugh, Rebecca	252
Pitts, Robert	9	Pugh, Sarah	162
Ploughaus, Mrs. Johanna	26	Purser, Elizabeth	40
Poague, Robert N.	26	Purser, F. Mogene	108
Poague, Victor B.	26	Purser, Frank	108
Poe, Mary E.	27	Purser, Grady	108
Poe, William H.	27	Purser, Mary J.	100
Pogue, Arvin	27	Purser, May	108
Pogue, Carl	102	Purser, M. C.	262
Pogue, J. G.	103	Purser, Miller	265
Pogue, Joe	103	Purser, P. M.	265
Pogue, infant	27	Purser, R. D.	108
Pope, Monrow W.	280	Purser, R. M.	262
Pope, Rebecca	280	Purser, Robert Morgan	108
Porter, Betie Lee	223	Purser, Ruhama	265
Porter, Eliza J.	223	Purser, Ruth	32
Porter, E. L. P.	223	Purser, Ruth Agnes	50
Porter, Eugene C.	224	Purser, Sarah J.	265
Porter, James Roy	224	Purser, Sarah S.	264
Porter, James S.	224	Purser, Virginia A.	204
Porter, John A.	223	Purser, Wanneta	40
Post, Mary	289	Purser, W. B.	262
Potter, Mrs. Martha	104	Purser, William	262
Potter, Sam	104	Purser, William Woodville	262
Potter, Silas	104	Purser, W. T.	46
Pottett, (or Pattett) L. L.	166	Purser, infants	100, 262
Pottett, M. E. Fousts	166	Pyatt, Barbara	282
Powel, Edith	276	Pyatt, John E.	282
Powell, Eugene	37	Pyott, Edward	314
Powell, Ida	105	Pyott, Margaret	314
Powers, Mary A.	165		
Powers, S. D.	165	Q	
Prater, James	266		
Prater, J. W.	266	Queen, Nancy	165
Prater, Richard A.	266	Quick, S. S.	74
Prater, Tennie V.	266	Quilliam, Robert Laurence	35
Presly, G. W.	111	Quin, B. A.	284
Presnell, Della Jeffres	100	Quinn, Walter	284
Pressnell, John C.	100	Quinn, W. M.	284
Preston, Jennie	71		
Preston, Wed	60	R	
Prestwood, Mrs. N. G.	179		
Price, J. M.	280	Raper, James H.	255
Price, Lydia K.	196	Rawlings, Philip T.	37
Price, Mary	115	Ray, Condon	132
Price, Mrs. Media	91	Ray, Mrs. Hettia	202
Price, O. S.	115	Ray, Katie	215
Price, Thomas	286	Ray, Leona Kebnes	285
Prickett, G. A. (C A Pritchett)	139	Rector, Chapman	322
Pritchet, J. D.	25	Redgely, W. H.	26
Proctor, Frank	215	Reed, Calvin Gerald	151
Proctor, George William	81	Reed, Charles H.	61

Index

Name	Page	Name	Page
Reed, Chas.	227, 271	Riddle, Pearl	54
Reed, Doyle F.	34	Rideout, Arthur	93
Reed, Elbert	227	Rideout, J. L.	164
Reed, Elizabeth	7	Riggins, John H.	88
Reed, Garrett	282	Riggs, Jessie M.	87
Reed, James A.	151, 234	Riggs, Oscar F.	87
Reed, Margaret T.	35	Rigsby, Edith E.	9
Reed, Loretta Northup	274	Rigsby, W. D.	7
Reed, Nathan D.	61	Riley, J. L.	168
Reed, N. D.	35	Ritchey, Carl Clayton	165
Reed, N. R.	151, 234	Ritchey, D. L.	8
Reed, R. L.	152, 233	Ritchey, Frances L.	165
Reed, Samantha E.	271	Ritchey, Sarepta	8
Reed, William Jessie	151, 234	Rivers, Mary	180
Reed, Wm. H.	152	Rivers, Robert	180
Reed, W. M. B.	233	Roberson, J. C.	115
Reed, infants	61, 282	Roberson, Mary	115
Reel, Barbara Ellen	92	Roberts, Elwood	314
Register, Catherine Boom	283	Roberts, J. F.	228
Register, James	283	Roberts, Lucy	118
Reid, Alice	276	Roberts, infant	27
Reid, Martin V. Jr.	276	Robertson, Chas. H.	64
Reid, Mary	277	Robertson, Harvey	156
Reid, M. V. Sr.	276	Robeson, James	37
Reid, Ophelia	276	Robeson, Lorea	37
Reid, R. H.	272	Robbins, Newton	314
Reid, Thos. B.	276	Robins, Mary Ann	314
Renfro, Katherine	277	Robinson, Anne Pearl	282
Renfro, Martha J.	273	Robinson, Benjamin F.	279
Renfro, William W.	273	Robinson, Brunetta	229
Revis, James	101	Robinson, Chas. Rice	34
Revis, Lee E.	102	Robinson, David F.	97
Revis, infant	101, 266	Robinson, Earnest	282
Reynolds, Royal R.	43	Robinson, Elizabeth Earnest	229
Reynolds, Solomon	55	Robinson, Eula May	34
Rhea, Harriet N.	274	Robinson, Florence	284
Rhea, Lucy	110	Robinson, James	229
Rhea, Maggie	52	Robinson, James A.	229
Rhea, infant	279	Robinson, John	229
Ribble, Elizabeth A.	98	Robinson, Mary	162
Rice, James W.	239	Robinson, Ruffus	284
Richards, Reece	284	Robinson, Samuel	162
Richards, Thomas Nelson	278	Robinson, Sarah E.	270
Richardson, Helena A.	91	Robinson, T. H.	155
Riddle, Guy	81	Robinson, T. J.	282
Riddle, James R.	107	Robinson, Ward H.	229
Riddle, Jashua I.	175	Rockhalt, Melven	26
Riddle, Jessie D.	55	Rockholt, W. H.	26
Riddle, John S.	55	Rockholt, Elsia	195
Riddle, Martha	175	Roddy, Elizabeth	279
Riddle, Mary O.	175	Roddy, James L.	231
Riddle, Sgt. M. S.	107	Roddy, John	31

Index

Name	Page	Name	Page
Roddy, John D.	231	Ross, Pearl	237
Roddy, John T.	264	Ross, infant	237
Roddy, Margaret	231	Roy, James	106
Roddy, Martha E.	264	Roy, Ray	3
Roddy, Mary Kate	231	Rudd, Elijah L.	108
Roddy, Rosana	15	Rudd, Eliza C.	108
Roddy, Sarah Bailey	31	Rudd, J. L.	194
Roddy, Willie	52	Rudd, Mary	23
Roddy, W. T.	231	Rudd, Mattie A.	6
Rodgers, Dorothy	39	Rudd, Sarah	108
Rodgers, Leland N.	29	Ruffles, Ada M.	66
Rodgers, W. H.	29	Runyan, I. L.	219
Rodgers, infant	29	Runyan, Isaac Travis	219
Rogers, Ann	284	Runyon, Louella Houston	220
Rogers, Emely B.	284	Runyon, Rivanna	219
Rogers, Emily Godson	172	Russell, A. G.	89
Rogers, Emma E.	65	Russell, Irena	216
Rogers, F. R.	63	Russell, J. H.	89
Rogers, Henry C.	219	Russell, John W.	166
Rogers, John H.	63	Russell, Laura A.	288
Rogers, John P.	172	Ryan, Ida	314
Rogers, L. G.	153, 234		
Rogers, Maggie	172	**S**	
Rogers, Margaret	233		
Rogers, Mary E. Loyd	63	Sanborn, Laura Lee	34
Rogers, Mary J.	172	Sanborn, Martha Eliza	35
Rogers, Oscar	152	Sandell, Bobbie Nell	241
Rogers, Rebecca	172	Sanford, Mae	242
Rogers, Ruby	51	Sanford, Shirley	242
Rogers, Sarah A.	176	Saul, (Father)	158
Rogers, Susan	172	Saul, (Mother)	158
Rogers, T. L.	39	Sawyer, J. E.	46
Rose, Albert	174	Sawyer, Mary E.	46
Rose, Amanda	158	Saxton, Corp'l. Robt. T.	119
Rose, Arthur	106	Scarbrough, Earl H.	38
Rose, Cecil	59	Scarbrough, Oza K.	38
Rose, Charlie W.	60	Scarbrough, S. C.	38
Rose, Creed	174	Scarbrough, Wm.	38
Rose, Florence	276	Schatzel, Juliet	91
Rose, Jessie A.	165	Schild, Alfred	50
Rose, J. H.	174	Schild, Harold M.	39
Rose, Joseph	174	Schild, Martha	50
Rose, J. W.	174	Schild, Morgan	39
Rose, Lenora Ferguson	93	Schild, Tennie	39
Rose, M. E.	236	Schild, infant	50
Rose, N. J.	158	Schill, Harry T.	102
Rose, O. E. A.	174	Schill, Mary	100
Rose, R. C.	236	Schill, Pete	102
Rose, Wm. F.	158	Scroggins, Eliza Etta	252
Rose, Wm. Lee	158	Scroggins, J. T.	240
Ross, Charlie	50	Scroggins, Mary A.	37
Ross, H. C.	60	Scroggins, R. M.	239
Ross, Jack	237	Scroggins, Robert Taylor	253

Index

Name	Page	Name	Page
Searl, E. P.	290	Shelton, Tennie	81
Segrest, Alice	279	Sherlin, Frances R.	37
Sexton, Ellen	119	Sherman, Robert M.	30
Sexton, Frank	100	Sherman, Rosa D.	30
Sexton, Lillian L.	105	Sherman, Walter R.	30
Sexton, Martha E.	119	Shidler, Rachel	27
Sexton, Nancy Jane	118	Shipley, Eva Gean	36
Shadden, Miss	178	Shirley, Rufus B.	156
Shadden, Charley	195	Short, infant	207
Shadden, Frank	195	Shugart, Mabel	276
Shadden, Martha	178	Silsby, Rev. John	289
Shadwick, Anderson	244	Silsby, Sarah	289
Shadwick, Bessie	244	Simmons, Laura	257
Shadwick, D. E.	244	Simpson, James H.	274
Shadwick, Very Anis	72	Simpson, Ruby Elnora	277
Shankle, Julia Ann	50	Sitton, Cordie L.	239
Shankle, Rachel N.	32	Skemills, Miriam	253
Shannon, Wm. M.	64	Slawson, Sewell	33
Sharp, Alta	3,307	Small, C. F.	44
Sharp, Eliza	3	Small, G. M.	44
Sharp, Freddie T.	110	Small, Mrs. M. J.	91
Sharp, Harriett Caroline	312	Small, M. S.	91
Sharp, John	304	Small, Oley	44
Sharp, Lena	81	Smedley, Carl H.	119
Sharp, Manda	304	Smedley, Chas. W. King	119
Sharp, Sarah F.	3	Smedley, Mamie B.	119
Sharp, Sarrah F.	307	Smith, Albert J.	252
Sharpe, George	171	Smith, Alexander	21
Shaver, Callie	247	Smith, Amos L.	65
Shaver, Catherine	246	Smith, Mrs. Ann Bailey	31
Shaver, Cordie	246	Smith, Bell	50
Shaver, Corneilus	24,245	Smith, B. F.	21
Shaver, Creed	246	Smith, Carl C.	256
Shaver, Henry	245	Smith, Chas. Tate	322
Shaver, Jane	24,245	Smith, Chroshie	99
Shaver, Jane H.	245	Smith, Colman	112
Shaver, Jessie	246	Smith, Delia	99,322
Shaver, John M.	246	Smith, Dock	99,278
Shaver, John Q.	246	Smith, Elizabeth	105
Shaver, Mary Ella	24,245	Smith, Emma Beard	250
Shaver, Mollie	246	Smith, Esther	58
Shaver, T. F.	246	Smith, Frederick	21
Shaver, Thomas F.	24,245	Smith, Frederick P.	9
Shaver, T. T.	247	Smith, Garvie Mathis	285
Shaver, Walter E.	24,245	Smith, George	282
Shelby, Doshia Ann	275	Smith, George W.	286
Shelby, Geo. W.	321	Smith, Gracie P.	4,310
Shelby, Susie	275	Smith, H. H.	167
Shell, Andrew J.	277	Smith, Hope	167
Shelton, Cordie	40	Smith, H. S.	250
Shelton, J. F.	40	Smith, Jack	116
Shelton, Mary J.	176	Smith, J. N.	23
Shelton, Nail A.	176	Smith, John	284

Index

Name	Page	Name	Page
Smith, John T.	253	Sneed, Zennie May	317
Smith, Juanita	52	Sneed, Z. T.	314
Smith, Keever	58	Snider, Charlie E.	26
Smith, Kelly R.	35	Snider, Dortha May	252
Smith, Kelly R.	35	Snoden, Thomas	54
Smith, Laura E.	8	Snow, Rev. James H.	7
Smith, Leander	179	Snow, infant	8
Smith, Mr. Lee	131	Snyder, Elizabeth	281
Smith, Lou A.	105	Snyder, James Wilson	281
Smith, Lou P.	109	Southerland, Birt	260
Smith, Lucy A.	218	Southerland, Mary A.	260
Smith, Manda	33	Sparks, Dima	164
Smith, Margaret	112	Sparks, Mildred Marie	10
Smith, Margaret L.	253	Sparks, Nellie M.	165
Smith, Martha	21, 58	Sparks, Ralph	164
Smith, Mary A.	21	Sparks, Ruth E.	165
Smith, M. R.	23	Sparks, W. M.	164
Smith, Nancy W.	65	Spears, Bessie	120
Smith, Nellie Mae	178	Spears, Jacob A.	120
Smith, N. J.	284	Spence, Albion	267
Smith, Perry	99	Spence, Gladdis A.	312
Smith, Polly Ann (Mrs.)	26	Spence, Hattie A.	267
Smith, Sarah C.	90	Spence, H. D.	312
Smith, Thelma	250	Spence, Homer	261
Smith, Thomas A.	104	Spence, John S.	64
Smith, Thomas W.	218	Spence, James	267
Smith, T. N.	23	Spence, James L.	312
Smith, T. R. G.	167	Spence, Mahala	267
Smith, Weldon O.	176	Spence, Martha J.	63
Smith, W. H.	284	Spiney, George W.	268
Smith, William H.	286	Spiney, J. Clyde	268
Smith, W. L.	270	Spiney, John Luther	269
Smith, W. M.	168	Spiney, Luella G.	269
Smith, Wm. Theodore	322	Stanfer, Addie	52
Sneed, Addie	318	Stanfield, G. W.	62
Sneed, Caldonie	317	Stanfield, John F.	62
Sneed, Clarence R.	26	Stanfield, Nancy Lee	62
Sneed, Claud	318	Stanfill, Gracie E.	25
Sneed, Cran A.	22	Stansbury, Clifford G.	34
Sneed, Eady	317	Stansbury, Johnnie Herbert	62
Sneed, Frank	317	Stansbury, Mattie C.	62
Sneed, J. B.	111	Stargel, Jessie F.	56
Sneed, John	318	Starns, William D.	118
Sneed, Lester	317	Starns, infant	118
Sneed, Mandy Cleo	317	Stebbins, Chas. Aaron	289
Sneed, Robert	314	Stebbins, Harlang	289
Sneed, Roy	318	Steele, Mary T.	173
Sneed, Ruth E.	318	Steele, William A.	173
Sneed, S. H.	318	Steeles, Margarite	284
Sneed, T. J.	318	Steelman, Coy	102
Sneed, Walter	317	Steincipher, Nellie Payne	277
Sneed, Willie	317	Stennett, Joe L.	256

Index

Name	Page	Name	Page
Stephens, Caroline	55	Tanksley, Ada Lee	314
Stephens, Ike	55	Tarbox, Mary	289
Stephens, Louvina	221	Taylor, Amanda	252
Stever, Abraham J. D.	257	Taylor, H. H.	29
Steward, E. L. D. T. M.	166	Taylor, Tillie	29
Stewart, --	63, 222	Taylor, W. H.	91
Stewart, Robt. B.	8	Teasley, Alica A.	298
Stinecipher, A. J.	115	Teasley, E. A.	298
Stinecipher, Amanda J.	115	Templeton, Adda	48
Stinecipher, Jessie	207	Templeton, Beckie J.	48
Stinett, John	255	Templeton, J. G.	48
Stinnett, Marry	256	Templeton, J. H.	49
Stookie, Lizzie	179	Templeton, J. L.	49
Storie, Glenn	312	Templeton, Mary	48, 49
Storie, G. W.	61	Templeton, N.	49
Storie, J. H.	269	Templeton, Sarah	48, 49
Storie, Rebecca	269	Templeton, W. A.	48
Stout, Carl	29	Tenesson, Sergt. Wm. P.	257
Stranahan Mary A.	60	Tennor, William	26
Strathern, Altha	286	Thomas, A. P.	257
Stratton, Leander	290	Thomas, Bell James	309
Stuart, C. L. B. L.	10	Thomas, Bert	21
Sturdevant, Charles E.	91	Thomas, Dewey	257
Stutzman, Anna	282	Thomas, Donna Sue	94
Sullivan, Minnie M.	169	Thomas, Flora	21
Sullivan, Samantha J.	71	Thomas, George	21
Suttles, Lillie Pearl	246	Thomas, James	27
Sutton, Jane	249	Thomas, Maggie E.	156
Swafford, A. C.	295	Thomas, N. F.	21
Swafford, Agnes Genevia	118	Thomas, R. E.	21
Swafford, James Kenneth	256	Thomas, Richard Z.	307
Swafford, Pearl J. Finnell	277	Thomas, Ruth	257
Swafford, Pola	257	Thomas, Samuel A.	59
Swafford, Wiley	258	Thomas, Thelma	26
Swicegood, C. L. ?	174	Thomasson, Isaac R. W.	300
Swicegood, Harry T.	102	Thomasson, Jane W.	300
Swicegood, Roy M.	175	Thomison, Ada R.	64
Sykes, Edd F.	7	Thomison Callie L.	64
Sykes, L. S.	7	Thomison, Dealla	218
		Thomison, Earl C.	281
T		Thomison, Felix V.	44
		Thomison, Flosie	280
Taber, Tempa	202	Thomison, Fred W.	45
Tallent, Edward F.	65	Thomison, James A.	279
Tallent, Garrett	112	Thomison, John S.	204
Tallent, Lanell	285	Thomison, Lena R.	44
Tallent, Margaret	65	Thomison, Mary Mae	41
Tallent, Nancy	112	Thomison, Nannie Clair	45
Tallent, Nancy Lee	278	Thomison, Sarah Virginia	34
Tallent, Robert F.	65	Thomison, T. H.	281
Tallent, Wallace Gaines	25	Thomison, T. Zacariah (Zechabiah)	204
Tallmadge, Sarah R.	151, 233		

Index

Name	Page
Thomison, W. A.	285
Thomison, Walter B.	64
Thomison, Walter K.	285
Thompson, Cinnie G.	273
Thompson, Chas. C.	314
Thompson, Clide	314
Thompson, Delila June	97
Thompson, Francis	156
Thompson, John	156
Thompson, John A.	231
Thompson, John F.	149
Thompson, John R.	273
Thompson, Levy B.	190
Thompson, Manrow A.	255
Thompson, Margaret	20
Thompson, Mary	84
Thompson, Mose	314
Thompson, Samuel W.	84
Thompson, Sarah	300
Thompson, Wm. A.	156
Thornburg, James U.	36
Thornburg, Louise	36
Thornburg, William A.	36
Thorpe, Oliver	91
Thurman, Charlie Frank	109
Thurman, W.	35
Tilley, Edward L.	270
Tingley, Gaylord N.	48
Titus, Cyrus J.	279
Todd, Mrs.	302
Tolle, John James	9
Tolle, Nettie Pleasant	9
Tolle, Philip Samuel	9
Torbett, Alfred H.	273
Torbett, Bonnie Alice	274
Torbett, F. L. T. James S.	274
Torbett, Frank	274
Torbett, Mary A.	273
Torbett, Marye	186
Torbett, Thos. F.	186
Townsend, Benjamin	289
Townsend, P.	314
Townsend, Sarah	54
Travis, Albert	222, 303
Travis, B. B.	22
Travis, Garbie Lelia	99
Travis, Ida	303
Travis, Ida A.	222
Travis, Joseph	22
Travis, Joseph H.	103
Travis, Laura Bell	22
Travis, Levina	22
Travis, Lucinda	22
Travis, Nany	103
Travis, Neal M.	103
Travis, Pearl	303
Travis, Thos. C.	103
Treadway, L. J.	206
Treadway, Mary J.	206
Tredway, Wilma Sue	178
Trentham, Minnie D.	321
Trentham, Nancy J.	321
Trentham, Robert M.	321
Trotter, James W.	263
Trotter, Rev. J. B.	263
Trotter, Julia A.	263
Troutman, Lola Bell	103
True, J. W.	252
Tucker, George L.	205
Tucker, H. Minerva	56
Tucker, Julia F.	205
Tucker, Minerva M.	205
Turner, Oleva	118
Turner, Robt.	118
Turner, Steve Edward	118
Typton, Nancy J.	104

U

Name	Page
Umbarger, Velma Lillian	106
Underwood, Hiley	196
Underwood, J. W.	196

V

Name	Page
Vance, Della	35
Vaughn, Addie	305
Vaughn, Amos S.	38
Vaughn, Benjamin	67
Vaughn, B. F.	305
Vaughn, Edna B.	270
Vaughn, Nancy A.	305
Vaughn, Robert Lee	305
VanVoorheis, Sherman	92
VanVoorhis, Elizabeth	91
VanVoorhis, Ida A.	92
VanVoorhis, Jimmie O.	92
VanVoorhis, Lawrence D.	92
Vilas, Lucy Blanch	46
Viles, S. P.	46
Vincent, A. H.	254
Vincent, Maude E.	254
Vineyard, Martha Elizabeth	86
Vreeland, (or Veerland) George S.	177
Vreeland, Jennie	167

Index

	Page		Page
Vreeland, Lula H.	167	Wallingford, J. G.	40
		Wampler, Mrs. W. H.	118
W		Ward, Charles F.	9
		Ward, Geo. Washington	224
Wade, Cranvil H.	181	Ward, John Henry	224
Wade, Ellen	169	Ward, Lydia Knox	224
Wade, John	280	Ward, Martha Ann	224
Wade, Lennie May	280	Washburn, Claudie	101
Wade, L. G. Jr.	246	Washburn, Elizabeth	101
Wade, Roscoe	246	Wason, J. W.	279
Waldorf, Rev. Joseph	65	Wason, Susan	279
Walker, Mrs.	189	Wasson, Ada P.	161
Walker, Alsie Jane	152,234	Wasson, Andrew	311
Walker, Annie V.	25	Wasson, Blanche Louise	160
Walker, B. H.	152,234	Wasson, Catherine Hood Gay	160
Walker, Braxton	322	Wasson, Chapman	160
Walker, C. A.	152,233	Wasson, Daniel	311
Walker, C. F.	152	Wasson, Eugene Clayton	160
Walker, Darius Franklin	234	Wasson, George Harvey	271
Walker, Eddie	152,234	Wasson, Henry	253
Walker, Eliza	322	Wasson, Hulda	215
Walker, George	23	Wasson, Jacob	311
Walker, G. T.	59	Wasson, Jacob L.	311
Walker, Hannah	23	Wasson, Dr. J. C.	161
Walker, Jennie	277	Wasson, John	215
Walker, Jennie Alice	28,277	Wasson, Luella	160
Walker, Jessie	152,234	Wasson, Martha M.	161
Walker, J. F.	152,234,235	Wasson, Mary Jane	311
Walker, Capt. J. P.	59	Wasson, Meticia C.	311
Walker, Lannie	3	Wasson, infants	159,160
Walker, Lillian	274	Waterhouse, Alice	312
Walker, Lonnie	307	Waterhouse, Anna E.	314
Walker, Lula	23	Waterhouse, Cyrus	312
Walker, Margaret A.	185	Waterhouse, Darius	312
Walker, Mary A.	321	Waterhouse, E. F.	312
Walker, Nancy	322	Waterhouse, Franklin	280
Walker, Nola	101	Waterhouse, John	312
Walker, Orlena	4,307	Waterhouse, Mary	312
Walker, Rebecca Jane	320	Waterhouse, Lorenda	280
Walker, R. F.	152,234	Waterhouse, Lotta	280
Walker, Rollie	165	Waterhouse, Prudella	314
Walker, Roy	23	Waterhouse, Richard	204
Walker, Samuel	94,320	Waterhouse, Vesta Ellen	312
Walker, Sarah F.	4	Waterhouse, infant	48
Walker, Sarah Bell	320	Watkins, Claude	281
Walker, Sarrah F.	307	Watkins, Jane	281
Walker, W. M. C.	234	Watkins, Reese	281
Walker, W. M. G.	152	Watson, Della Barton	68
Walker, infants	60,165	Watson, Hannah	285
Waller, Cordellia Ruffner	281	Watson, Joseph S.	38
Waller, Malinda	305	Watson, Mamie	68
Waller, Samuel T.	277	Watson, N. W.	256

Index

Name	Page	Name	Page
Watson Vivian	47	Whittenberg, Willie	231
Watt, J. D.	290	Wiener, Della	104
Watts, Horace	52	Wier, T. B.	35
Weaver, Alice J.	28	Wierick, --	271
Weaver, Martin C.	28	Wiggins, Amanda	189
Weaver, Mary F.	56	Wiggins, Dessie	181
Webb, Jane Mahale	318	Wiggins, James	194
Webb, Mathiel	318	Wiggins, W. M.	194
Webster, Rachel E. Hobbs	166	Wilcher, Torbett	273
Weir, Martha Matilda Conner	36	Wilcox, Mary E.	75
Weir, Wilford F.	211	Wiley, E. P.	324
Welch, Fletcher	36	Willard, Francis	166
Welch, Roy	167	Wilkey, Abner	197
West, Carrie	139	Wilkey, Andy	101
West, Earl	249	Wilkey, Bertha	36
West, Isaac	69	Wilkey, Campbell	194
West, Leander J.	257	Wilkey, Christopher C.	194
West, Mary	69	Wilkey, Creed	100
West, Sarah L.	257	Wilkey, Cynthia	197
Whaley, Abner Witt	109	Wilkey, Floyd Edgar	194
Whaley, Emma Jean	32	Wilkey, Hugh	197
Whaley, J. E.	79	Wilkey, James	36
Whaley, John S.	110	Wilkey, Jerald Eugene	255
Whaley, Lou	109	Wilkey, Lizzie	37
Wheeler, Catherine C.	49	Wilkey, Lucindie	194
Wheeler, Cirene	320	Wilkey, Malinda Jane	23
Wheeler, Della	38	Wilkey, Margaret	23
Wheeler, Elwin M.	175	Wilkey, Marion ?	194
Wheeler, John H.	38	Wilkey, Mary Elizabeth	256
Wheeler, Dr. John M.	320	Wilkey, Nancy C.	100
Wheeler, Jow	39	Wilkey, Nellie May	251
Wheeler, R. Alice	175	Wilkey, Pearl D.	251
Wheeler, Robt. C.	58	Wilkey, Rebecca	196
Wheeler, Rommie F.	58	Wilkey, Robert	258
Wheeler, Dr. S. J.	320	Wilkey, Samuel	197
Wheeler, Dr. W. E.	48	Wilkey, S. E. V.	197
Wheeler, William L.	175	Wilkey, S. L.	196
Wheelock, Mary Permelia	272	Williams, Bessie	52
Wheelock, N. W.	272	Williams, Flora ?	81
White, Ada	162	Williams, Genevieve	42
White, Eliza	87	Williams, Henrietta	151, 233
White, George W.	271	Williams, Jennie L.	63
White, John	276	Williams, J. H.	151, 233
White, J. P.	87	Williams, Maud	42
White, Lynn	91	Williams, Tom	52
White, Rebecca	275	Williams, Walter O.	42
White, Mrs. Myrtle	268	Williams, William Bailey	42
White, Rev. Wm.	275	Williamson, Edwin E.	31
Whitlock, Parentha	43	Williamson, Eva	48
Whitlock, Lieut. Wm.	43	Williamson, J. W.	48
Whittenberg, M. J.	149	Williamson, Katie	53
Whittenberg, Nathan	149	Williamson, Tillman G.	31

Index

Name	Page
Williamson, infant	31
Wilmont, Della	162
Wilson, Aubrey C.	35
Wilson, Charley	89
Wilson, C. R.	109
Wilson, David	89
Wilson, Delora	85
Wilson, Ellen	109
Wilson, Evalin T.	289
Wilson, Geo. Thomas	114
Wilson, Isabella	87
Wilson, Isabella G.	87
Wilson, James A.	53
Wilson, Dr. J. F.	8
Wilson, John	93
Wilson, L. N.	65
Wilson, Mable	72
Wilson, Morgan	103
Wilson, Ray M.	72
Wilson, Sallie	114
Wilson, Sarah K.?	253
Wilson, William L.	72
Wilson, Dr. W. M.	114
Winters, Elizabeth	71
Wise, Robert	36
Wix, W. A.	271
Wolfe, R.	8
Wolfe, Vesta	8
Womack, John Hayle	219
Womack, Margaret Ida	219
Wooddy, William	49
Woodey, Claude Lee	240
Woodie, Sarah Elizabeth	22
Woodruff, Simeon	74
Woody, G. M.	240
Woody, Grace	171
Woody, Harold J.	33
Woody, Hugh	22
Woody, J. R.	33
Woody, Ruth	33
Woody, Junior	278
Woody, Sarah	22
Woody, Walter	33
Woody, William R.	33
Wright, Bertha A.	9
Wright, Blanche M.	252
Wright, Burke	114
Wright, E. C.	156
Wright, Edward	113
Wright, Elizabeth	206
Wright, Ella G.	90
Wright, Ellen	283
Wright, Herman L.	276
Wright, J. M.	156,286
Wright, J. T.	151,235
Wright, Mary Lee	287
Wright, Myrtle Ella	276
Wright, Thomas Arthur	252
Wyatt, Martha Jane	32
Wyatt, Nancy J.	35
Wyrick, A. J.	78
Wyrick, Eliza J.	105
Wyrick, Mallie Davis	103
Wyrick, Nancy	20
Wyrick, Pearl	193

Y

Name	Page
Yates, Henegar	33
Yates, J. N.	31
Yates, Minnie	25
Yather, L. P.	101
Yong, H.	68
Yongs, Louis Miner	170
Yongs, Stephen	170
Yother, E. B.	324
Yother, J. M.	324
Young, Charley C.	53
Young, Gracie Maud	53

Z

Name	Page
Zebar, --	280
Zeigler, Ann Eliza Waterhouse	314